M000279632

RADIO FREE AFGHANISTAN

RADIO FREE AFGHANISTAN

A Twenty-Year Odyssey for an
Independent Voice in Kabul

SAAD MOHSENI
WITH JENNA KRAJESKI

HARPER
An Imprint of HarperCollins*Publishers*

RADIO FREE AFGHANISTAN. Copyright © 2024 by Saad Mohseni. All rights reserved. Printed in the United States of America. No part of this book may be used or reproduced in any manner whatsoever without written permission except in the case of brief quotations embodied in critical articles and reviews. For information, address HarperCollins Publishers, 195 Broadway, New York, NY 10007.

HarperCollins books may be purchased for educational, business, or sales promotional use. For information, please email the Special Markets Department at SPsales@harpercollins.com.

FIRST EDITION

Library of Congress Cataloging-in-Publication Data
Names: Mohseni, Saad, 1966– author.
Title: Radio free Afghanistan: a twenty-year odyssey for an independent voice in Kabul / Saad Mohseni.
Description: First edition. | New York: Harper, [2024]
Identifiers: LCCN 2024013135 | ISBN 9780063299801 (hardcover) | ISBN 9780063299818 (trade paperback) | ISBN 9780063299825 (ebook)
Subjects: LCSH: Mohseni, Saad, 1966– | Mass media—Afghanistan. | Mass media—Censorship—Afghanistan. | Afghanistan—Politics and government—2021–
Classification: LCC P92.A3 M64 2024 | DDC 384.5406/5581—dc23/eng/20240621
LC record available at https://lccn.loc.gov/2024013135

24 25 26 27 28 LBC 5 4 3 2 1

For my parents, Safia and Yassin Mohseni, who encouraged us to be passionate and curious; for my children, who, at times, had to share their father with Afghanistan; and to our fallen colleagues at Moby, whose memory inspires us to keep working.

CONTENTS

PART I

CHAPTER 1

TALIBAN RAID

KABUL, 2022

When the Taliban official arrived at the Kabul offices of Moby, the media company I founded with my siblings over twenty years ago, Khpolwak Sapai, our head of news, expected him to be angry. Sapai was prepared to be yelled at, told to cancel or to censor a television show, to pull a news story, to apologize on air, even to be detained. If possible, he was ready to negotiate. Interactions like this had become commonplace since the Taliban had taken over six months earlier in August 2021, in the wake of the American withdrawal, and we did what we needed to do, not just to survive but to coexist.

The Taliban were the government now. If we expected there to remain an Afghan media operating within Afghanistan, and not to be reduced to screaming from the margins in DC or London, we had to learn to adapt. The Taliban themselves understood, or claimed to understand, the importance of having a free Afghan media. Months after the fraught early days after the fall of Kabul, when people clung desperately to planes taking off at the airport and thousands of others crowded the gates to get inside, things had appeared to calm down. But, in the midst of that relative calm, the new government had begun to put more pressure on the Afghan media, and one of my Taliban contacts had called me. "You're not going to leave, are you?" he asked, worried that, from abroad, I was strategizing how to close down our Kabul offices.

"Not if I can help it," I had said. But I was thinking, *That's kind of up to you, isn't it?*

Sapai is a legendary figure in Afghanistan with a commanding presence tempered only slightly by a preference for authorial brown suit jackets and wire-framed glasses. When Kabul fell, he was in his midsixties and had been working as a journalist in the country for nearly two decades. He was determined and decorated; he had contacts in the Taliban, and he knew how to talk to them, most helpfully to their spokesperson, Zabihullah Mujahid. Like most of the Taliban, he was Pashtun himself. Over the last four tumultuous decades of his life he had never felt compelled to leave Afghanistan, his beloved country, home to his children. Unlike most of the hundreds of staffers and guests who had come through Moby over those two decades—those who had lived for a generation as refugees in Pakistan, rich Afghans who had been educated in the West, international consultants, actors and journalists and DJs and countless on-air guests—Sapai wasn't scared of the Taliban. He knew that beneath the cloak of extremism they were Afghans, and he wanted to understand them. A good journalist, Sapai thought, doesn't see anyone as an enemy or as a friend while they're working. "You only become a human being again with likes and dislikes after you close the story," he would tell our staff.

It had been Sapai who ultimately made the call to run the story that had so angered the Taliban official in the first place, bringing him to our offices to conduct a raid. The decision hadn't come easily—Sapai might have been more comfortable than his colleagues talking to the Taliban spokesperson, but he wasn't naïve about what the organization was capable of—yet he felt he had no choice. After six months in charge, during which they worked to cement their power over the Afghans who remained in the country, Taliban officials had begun asserting their authority over our offices, summoning Moby employees or dropping by the offices almost daily. Abdul Nafay Khaleeq, a young man who was the head of Moby's legal department, had been detained twice and in secret, without any warning given to his colleagues or his family. Like Sapai, Nafay was more comfortable around the Taliban than the average Kabul resident; although he had lived most of his early life as a refugee and student in Pakistan, his roots were in Kandahar, also the Taliban's birthplace and where its leadership was based. It was Nafay who had been one of our main on-the-ground negotiators with the Taliban in the months after their assumption of power in August 2021, visiting judges and ministries, fielding text messages and phone calls, trying to argue against the rules and demands made regarding the programming on our radio and TV stations, which grew harsher with each passing day.

Kabul had fallen so quickly. In the aftermath, our company stayed afloat hour by hour. Moby survived the first few days by helping staffers who wanted to leave—in the end, the majority of our on-air staff—fill out the paperwork necessary to show they were at particular risk because of their role in the media. Sapai had to replace the staffers who were fleeing daily, train the new ones, and keep the programs going. He had made the call to air footage of the panicked crowds around the airport, to make the story the human toll of the withdrawal. When one of his high-ranking Taliban contacts asked to come on air at TOLO to, he said, reassure the public that this government will be different from the Taliban of the 1990s, Sapai allowed it, assigning a female journalist to do the interview, viewers relishing the official's obvious discomfort. "Saad," Sapai promised me. "I won't let the screens go dark."

Every day, we adjusted to the new reality, sometimes by trying to anticipate what decisions the Taliban might make next. Our music programs on both TV and radio were the first to go—no surprise there; playing and listening to music had been banned under the first Taliban regime. Then we canceled all the programs where men and women appeared together, including on radio shows that had been on air for nearly the entire twenty years. We accepted that our employees would now have to pass through Taliban security when they came to work; the same group who, in 2016, had declared TOLOnews an "important tool of warfare of America and the crusaders" and a legitimate target, were now our best defense against other lethal threats like the Islamic State–Khorasan (IS-KP), the local branch of ISIS. All female employees made sure that their heads were scrupulously covered and, after a Taliban edict in May 2022, their mouths and noses too, although we staged a protest requiring male presenters and guests, including Taliban officials, to wear black surgical masks on air. "It's hard to talk, isn't it?" one of our journalists asked a Taliban minister during an interview.

We stopped using the term "Taliban" to refer to the new government and instead started referring to them as representatives of the "Islamic Emirate." We put up curtains in our offices to separate the seating areas for men and women and, after women were banned from appearing in them, canceled many of our entertainment shows—singing competitions, some foreign dramas, locally produced mixed-gender comedy and talk shows—which we knew Taliban leadership would find irredeemably offensive. Because morale in the office, and in the country, was so low—not only had President Ashraf Ghani and the ruling elite fled, but so had authors, writers, academics, doctors, schoolteachers, and, of course, media personnel—we wrote PSAs intended to promote national unity in a time of crisis. "They're part of this country," we sighed. "Let's send a message of peace."

When Kabul fell, I was by coincidence abroad. I avoided being consumed by dread by consenting to almost every interview request that came my way; there were hundreds. "There's no government, there's no one else, no one understands what's going on," my friend Tom Freston, the cofounder of MTV and former CEO of Viacom and a Moby board member, told me. "You need to talk to them." Meanwhile, I implored the pragmatists I knew within my own contacts in the Taliban to make their objections to the hard-liners known.

When we could, we have rebelled. In April 2022, an Islamic scholar delivered a Ramadan sermon on TOLO TV wearing a suit and tie, going against the Taliban's preference for traditional dress. While we separated male and female hosts, we tried to give them equal speaking time on air. Sometimes, that meant that, while men appeared on camera, women read the promotional material off-screen. We worked on the studio classroom where we planned to film educational shows for children, now mostly girls banned from going to school beyond sixth grade. We hired more and more women, in Kabul and in the provinces, until in some departments they outnumbered the men on staff. We booked a female Islamic scholar, educated at Egypt's Al-Azhar University, to appear on a segment of our popular Ramadan talk show. (Afterward, a Taliban contact called one of my colleagues to say, just between them, that he had been "impressed" by her knowledge of Islam.)

But no matter what we did, and no matter how many times the pragmatists assured me we would be able to continue to operate in Kabul, the Taliban seemed to harden its stance against media independence and what role it might play in people's lives. Within three months, despite much negotiation and resistance, nearly half of Afghanistan's media outlets shut down. Each day delivered a heated phone call, a threat, more questions. At our Moby offices in Kabul, we scrambled to balance our mission with the reality of the new government, continuing to run our reporting but looking over our shoulder, wondering what the next day would look like. Our news remained robust, but our entertainment suffered; since November, all remaining media companies had been grappling with a Taliban directive that we drastically cull our entertainment offerings. Still, we managed. As with so many of the changes under the Taliban, new rules were often laid out slowly, enforced sporadically, intentionally misinterpreted, or rebelled against with the hope that the overwhelmed government might lose interest. The shape of the new government, thrust upon the country so suddenly, was sinking in slowly. And so when one morning, a few months after they had taken power, a Taliban representative called Nafay and told him, "Your television shows do not comply with our cultural values. You have to cancel them all, now," it took many anxious weeks to understand what, exactly, he meant.

Foreign shows—Indian and Turkish soap operas, mainly—had been a mainstay of our programming since Moby's television station, TOLO, was launched. Without resources to make original Afghan serials, we purchased content from abroad, and Afghans had received these dubbed soap operas with an almost instant and obsessive love, which now, with so little available to distract from the reality of a second Taliban era, had only grown stronger. Asking for the sudden disappearance of these shows was, as Sapai said to me, like asking us to suddenly turn off the water to a thirsty village. "They are basically telling us to shut ourselves down," he said.

Without knowing what to do, and thinking perhaps the new edict was more the grievance of one man than the new policy of the entire organization, we ignored him. We weren't going to start digging our own grave just because one guy from the ministry told us to, and we weren't the only media company to push back. For a few weeks, soap operas, foreign dramas, and comedies were broadcast into Afghan homes as though nothing had changed, and although every time the phone rang in our offices we were sure it would be the Taliban official, nothing happened and no one complained. But we were foolish to think a rebellion, even one via soap opera, would sail under the Taliban radar, and soon enough Nafay, along with representatives from all the remaining media companies, were ordered to attend a meeting at the General Directorate of Intelligence for a scolding. Once there, we continued to push back, a more or less united front against an unreasonable request. "Getting rid of all the foreign content is impossible," one of the media heads complained in the meeting. "There's just not enough Afghan content."

"Why not broadcast some nice scenery?" GDI officials suggested, echoing what their colleagues at the Ministry of Information and Culture and the Ministry for the Propagation of Virtue and the Prevention of Vice had been telling the Afghan media since September 2021. "You can send people to villages and take some nice videos," the officials said. "Play those instead."

"They have no idea how the media works, or what the audience wants," Nafay complained to me. "They suggested airing recitations of the Koran. We're supposed to do that for sixteen hours a day?" The government channel had been airing such footage, but only, Nafay assumed, because they were at a loss for how else to fill the airwaves. No Afghan was really sitting down to watch hours of water flowing over rocks in some remote part of Afghanistan, no matter how beautiful that part of the country might be.

Among the GDI officials at the meeting was Jawad Sargar, a young Talib whom Nafay had dealt with more than once and thought of as relatively sensible and open-minded. Sargar was well educated and spoke fluent English, following contemporary religious scholars from Egypt, and once or twice, during Nafay's many visits to the ministry during those months, the two had joked together. Prior to 2021, Sargar had a job delivering newspapers around Kabul, including to the Moby offices, but since the withdrawal he had risen quickly through the ranks. As negotiations stalled, and the media heads resoundingly rejected the idea of replacing popular soap operas with footage of village life, he took the lead at the meeting.

"By tomorrow you need to have cleaned up the shows or replaced them with something else," Sargar told the room. It was very important, he stressed, that we not air any program that featured a woman who was not wearing a hijab. As always, the most important part seemed to be about women.

It was five in the evening, though, when the meeting was dismissed, too late to reasonably change or censor that night's lineup, and so we went to bed again hoping that our small rebellion would fly under the radar but waking up with the sneaking suspicion that it would not. "You have one more day," Sargar told Nafay over the phone, annoyance creeping into his voice. "That's it."

Now a little shaken, but still feeling we were in the right to push back, we reached out to ministry officials who might be less zealous than those in intelligence at enforcing the rules. Nafay appealed directly to officials he knew at the culture ministry and the vice and virtue ministry, who were more open to negotiation. Sargar's directive, that we cease airing shows that went against Islamic values or Afghan culture, was too subjective, he said. If we didn't know what the red line was, how could we avoid crossing it? One of our most popular Turkish soap operas at the time was based in the early Ottoman era, and the actresses were exquisitely but chastely dressed. (Built around a flattering, nostalgic depiction of Muslim warrior-leaders, it was also a favorite of the Turkish president Erdoğan.) Nafay invited an official from the vice and virtue ministry to visit our editing room, where he could approve of the changes our editors were making to certain scenes. In place of our Indian shows, where Hinduism and other elements of Indian culture were on display, we added in a few more bombastic hours of *Kuruluş: Osman*.

But the few other remaining media companies didn't make as

many changes as we did. Maybe they weren't as organized, or didn't have as much expertise or as many resources to snap into action quickly, or they didn't take the government as seriously. Perhaps it was a protest, which they were willing to take further than we were. Whatever the reason, they continued to broadcast as usual, with the same images that had gotten them into trouble before, and sure enough a few weeks later Nafay and the other media heads were called back to the Taliban offices, where the mood in the room let Nafay know this would not be another round table on the beauty of rural Afghanistan.

The meeting started late, "by design," Nafay told me. "To intimidate us." Taking his position at the front of the room of men—at least none of the companies had thought it an appropriate provocation to send a woman representative—the young official now felt personally insulted. Sargar began by rebuking them. "We support the media continuing to operate in Afghanistan," he insisted. "But it has to be within the limitations and boundaries set by the government."

When that didn't work, he tried explaining why, now that they were in charge, the Taliban were obligated to carry out their vision for the country. "The people who sacrificed their lives for our cause, their families are looking to us now," he told them. "Their families say, our sons died to bring this kind of law to Afghanistan and when you don't implement it, you are betraying us."

Finally, seeing that he was getting nowhere, Sargar lost what remained of his patience. "If you don't do this," he threatened, "then don't blame us for what happens next."

What might happen exactly, he did not say. "Will they come to our offices? Will they shut us down? Will they take us from our homes and detain us?" Nafay asked me over the phone, and I had to admit that I didn't know. It could be all of that, I thought. It could be worse. It could be nothing; it was often nothing.

Not for the first time since the American withdrawal, we had no idea what to expect. And so, without any other ideas and not wanting to abruptly abandon the Afghans who watched our soaps for comfort, we defied the Taliban yet again. That evening, we aired three hours of the epic retelling of the founding of the Ottoman Empire. "Surely it is compliant enough," we all agreed, Sapai and Nafay in the Kabul office, my brother Jahid and me on Zoom from outside the country. "The women are covered. Islam is triumphant. There is no valid way the officials can argue in good faith that it goes against their values." But the next day, Nafay was detained.

This time, after waiting in Sargar's office for hours without any information, our head of legal knew he would be kept overnight. Nafay was blindfolded and taken into a room both so intimidating and in such disrepair that he thought it must have been used for interrogation by the previous governments. A table fitted with a metal loop for securing handcuffs sat in the middle surrounded by a couple of rickety chairs, a fluorescent overhead light blinking on and off. "I don't know whether it was broken, or meant to be that way," he told me. It felt too much like something out of a movie. Either way, the light hurt his eyes.

Security searched through Nafay's phone; he assumed they were looking for incriminating text messages or emails. When he asked to use the bathroom, he was blindfolded again and escorted roughly down the hall, told to hurry. Otherwise, though, he was treated mostly with indifference. Every once in a while, an official would come in and ask him, "Do you have anything you want to say?" and Nafay would shake his head. "It didn't matter what I said at that point," he told me later. "They were going to keep me overnight no matter what." His holding cell was cold and uncomfortable; he heard screams from other parts of the building and assumed it must be other detainees. But he told me he stayed calm. Mainly, he worried about his family, who didn't know where he was and who would, understandably, imagine the worst.

"My life was transformed by the terrible things that forced my family to leave Afghanistan in the first place," he told me later, when I asked about his mental state. "I studied Islam really intensely after that." Growing up, Nafay had read the Koran and Islamic scholars, and he was familiar with many different varieties of Islamic thought. His devotion and religious education, he told me, gave him courage during his family's moves and now, through all the upheaval in Afghanistan. "Islam changed me, Saad," he said. I needn't worry about him, he insisted.

In the morning, Nafay said his prayers, ate breakfast, and spent a few hours reading the Koran, which the guards had delivered to his room the night before along with a prayer mat. Around 2:30 that afternoon, after nearly twenty-four hours in detention, Nafay was blindfolded again, and his wrists bound. He was taken to a car and, he thinks, driven around in circles for a while to confuse him, although he sensed that he had never been very far from our office, where he was deposited. At the Moby gate, Sargar, who had been in the car with Nafay, told him to call Naim Sarwari, Moby's managing director. "What should I say to him?" Nafay asked. He sensed Sargar was irritated by his calmness.

"Tell him to promise that the company will do what we say from now on," Sargar replied. "Tell him there are three conditions. One, you cannot air any television dramas. Two, you cannot air any foreign content at all, of any type. And three, you will not tell anyone why you stopped airing these shows, or what has happened over the past few days." Sarwari would have to send someone to the entrance to sign a form pledging to observe those terms or come himself.

Nafay made the phone call. He quickly explained that he was safe; we had been waiting, anxious, to hear from him. To Sarwari he explained the Taliban's first two conditions. "No foreign content at all," he said, the official watching him. "Not even the Turkish show." Then he called Sapai. "No one can find out about my detention," he said. "Or the reasons we've taken the shows off the air, or who we met at the GDI." Sarwari sent the head of security, who signed and stamped Sargar's pledge. Once the Taliban official was satisfied, Nafay got out of the car.

"I now understand that the Taliban expects you not only to do what they say but to do it quietly," Sapai told me after getting off the phone with Nafay. His voice was strained; as a journalist he felt obligated to report on what had happened, but he worried about the consequences. "What should we do?" he asked.

I was too far away to make the call, knowing it would be the staff on the ground who were at risk. "It's not fair for me to say," I said. "What do you think?"

"I think if we let them do this in secret," Sapai replied, "then one day we'll wake up and there will be no more Moby."

Sapai wrote the copy himself for the anchor to read on that evening's news.

SEEING HIM LEADING the raid later that evening, Nafay wondered how he had ever considered Sargar to be sensible, even funny. Now, storming through the Moby gates, the young Taliban official was trailed by a handful of his armed guards, his car left haphazardly on the street, the young official too furious even to close the doors. Sapai had gone home. Whatever reaction he had expected from the Taliban to TOLO's story about the ministry's new edict on foreign programming, he hadn't been prepared for the degree of anger.

In early spring, Kabul air is crisp and clean, the city glowing with new plants. Our compound, a repurposed residential block full of bright green lawns and lovingly pruned delphinium bushes, wild roses growing over archways, and flowering plum trees—surrounded, as most things are in Kabul, with blast walls and armed guards—is also at its most beautiful in spring. When Taliban fighters had first set foot behind our gates in August 2021, they had seemed at first a little stunned, then curious. They asked to look in the studios, to meet presenters, to see inside the offices, like schoolkids on a field trip. Sargar himself, for the first time passing easily by the front gate where he had once left his stacks of newspapers, seemed keen to explore this previously off-limits place. It was the lack of animosity on display in those days that had been unnerving, Sapai had told me.

But that day, there was no curiosity, and certainly no admiration. Sargar walked quickly, pushed along by his fury at having been, in his mind, personally defied and embarrassed by the evening news segment. Sitting around the long wooden table in Sapai's office, a tranquil space that the head of news had filled with potted green plants and flowers, Sargar told the Moby team what he really thought about Afghan media.

"You are lucky," one staffer remembers him saying, "that we are giving you a chance to talk to us at all."

For two decades, the Taliban's plan for how to deal with media companies like Moby had been violence, he said. There had been no fewer than fifteen proposed attacks against us, he told the team, and he didn't know how we had avoided greater bloodshed; in twenty years, there had been only one successful targeted attack against us, in 2016, when a suicide bomber in a car exploded himself beside a bus carrying three dozen Moby staffers, killing seven of them. "The only reason you are still alive is because we were told to spare Afghans who stayed in the country," Sargar said. Taliban's leadership, in an effort to foster stability after the withdrawal, had declared general amnesty for all Afghans. In a press conference, Mujahid, their spokesperson, had addressed the private media specifically, saying we would be permitted to continue working as long as journalists "did not work against national values." As vague as the wording had been, we had in fact been allowed to function. Now, confronted with some of those independent journalists, the young official whined the amnesty was "unfortunate."

Sargar began presenting, in alarming detail, evidence of Moby's disobedience over the previous few months, producing tweets and Facebook posts; stills from television shows; instances when a woman's headscarf slipped past her hairline. He recited headlines that depicted the Taliban in a negative light, that crossed the red lines that seemed to be reset daily, or that he said undermined the Taliban's ability to rule the country. Here was a story about IS-KP in Afghanistan, while the Taliban was trying to project an image of peace; here was a story that was about resistance fighters in the north; here was a woman reporting on a bustling street. "What Afghan with a sound mind and sound faith would want to see his wife or sister like this?" he shouted to the room.

One of our employees raised his hand. "I would watch it," he said. "I have no issue with that."

This sent Sargar over the edge. Angrily, he gestured to one of his armed security guards who brought over three pairs of handcuffs. "You are not real Afghans," he said. "You are all just leftovers of the occupation."

Nafay was summoned to the office and again arrested. This time, they made him wait blindfolded, standing in a room where he could hear every voice around him, every footstep over his head, and the ones thundering down the hall. Not wanting to anger the officials further, he stayed upright as long as he could and kept his eyes closed under his blindfold. Bahram Aman, the young presenter who had delivered the story on the nightly news, had also been arrested. He'd be held for twenty-four hours, slapped by his interrogators, he later told us, but nothing too bad.

Sapai was at home when Sarwari called him to say that Taliban officials were at the office. "They are not happy with the story,"

Sarwari said. "They are looking for you." Sapai was put into the back of a government car and told he would be taken to the same interrogation office as Nafay. His first thought was he wished he had been able to explain to his wife what was happening, that Moby had crossed a Taliban line and there had been a raid. In the moment he hadn't wanted to worry her.

Sapai braced himself for questioning. But while the car inched slowly down the street, I had been reaching out to every relevant contact that I had—multiple people in the UN, foreign reporters, Taliban—imploring them for help. Even before the car door closed on Sapai, foreign media was drafting stories about the raid. From the back seat, Sapai could hear the constant buzz of Sargar's phone. The Taliban official was being told he had gone too far, even his colleagues could see that; it was written all over the news. After a few minutes of arguing, he angrily turned to Sapai. "You're going home," he said. "But keep your phones off until the morning." Sargar wanted it to appear, Nafay later thought, that Sapai had in fact been detained.

That night, Sapai had a late dinner with his family He assured his wife that everything was going to be fine, a line, as a journalist, he had often repeated to loved ones. The next morning, partly in a bid to prove to his anxious wife that everything was really okay, he went back to work, joined soon by Nafay, who'd also been released within a few hours the previous night. Aman, still in detention, would arrive later.

With Jahid and me on Zoom, the TOLO team held a meeting to discuss what could replace the soap operas—a sketch comedy show set two hundred years ago, before even the British invaded Afghanistan? A documentary about the wars that led to Afghanistan's independence?—it was harder, now, to imagine any programming that could possibly adhere to the Taliban's shifting guidelines. After Aman was released, I called my Taliban contacts, fuming over the treatment of my colleagues, and although

they were annoyed that I referred to Sargar as a "child," they had
to agree that his behavior was hotheaded and eventually he was
demoted, removed from any work having to do with media.

Our head of news knew he had been lucky. He stood by his decision to run the story, and to write the copy himself. But he was
shaken, he told me. What would happen next? For the first time
in his life—through six decades that began with a peaceful childhood, and since then witnessing coups, a civil war, the Soviet
and American occupations, two Taliban regimes, and the mass
exodus and return and exodus again of refugees in his country—
Sapai wondered if he would now have to finally leave Afghanistan. Thousands of miles away in Austria, I imagined, not for the
first time, whether we would have to close the Kabul offices of
Moby forever, and if we did, what we would be leaving behind.

CHAPTER 2

ARIANA AIRLINES

DUBAI, 2002

In March 2002, the only airline running commercial flights in and out of Kabul was consistently rated among the worst in the world, used in decades prior, with some trepidation, only by aid workers or businesspeople daring enough to set up shop in a Communist and later Taliban-run Afghanistan. A few decades earlier, during the relatively peaceful 1960s and 1970s, Ariana Afghan Airlines had been Afghanistan's premier airline, and had for years been part owned by Pan Am, shepherding thousands of Western tourists, with their scruffy hair and backpacks, in search of figurative and literal highs in the exotic East; opening up the world to well-to-do Afghans, who could themselves now leave Kabul for New Delhi or Istanbul or Frankfurt, where visas for Afghans were issued freely. Decades later, the airline had been reduced to two aging 727 jets and a harried, threadbare staff, unable to cope that day with the throng of Afghans descending on them at the Dubai airport, begging to be let on a flight. Among them were my younger brother Zaid and me.

Neither of us had been to Afghanistan since 1978, when I was twelve years old, and Zaid was nine, and we fled with our family in the wake of a coup d'état, first for Japan, where my father worked as a diplomat, and then, after he resigned from the diplomatic corps in protest of the 1979 Soviet invasion of Afghanistan, Australia, where I graduated from high school and tried, a few times, to finish university. My personal story involves many moves to many different continents, some of them in a rush, at least one in a panic, and several encounters with violence. But in the context of my country, what happened to me is ordinary, even enviable. We were only one family in an entire generation of Afghans forced to leave, and we were lucky; we didn't become refugees, like the millions of Afghans who crossed the eastern border and eked out a living while stuck in camps and urban slums in Pakistan, but relatively privileged political asylees, with two educated, working parents and a welcoming Australian community to cushion our fall.

Even before our exile, my three siblings and I—my brothers, Zaid and Jahid, and our baby sister, Wajma—had lived only part of our young lives in Kabul. I hadn't even been born in the country; my parents had me while my father was posted on a diplomatic mission in London years before the coup. We were adaptable, and I easily felt at home wherever I was, something I still take pride in. We learned to speak Japanese and then, after moving to Melbourne, Australian English. Although I admired the effortless Australian drawl, I never fully let go of the American accent I had acquired at our schools in Tokyo, which I thought made me seem a bit worldly in our new suburban life. Regardless of how we sounded, we all always felt fundamentally Afghan.

Our attachment to Afghanistan as our homeland was in a strange way strengthened by our physical distance from it. My parents spoke Dari, the Afghan dialect of Farsi, and cooked rice with Afghan spices. They read Afghan poetry, discussed Afghan politics, and listened to Afghan music. My uncles had once owned a business recording and distributing music, a complement to their main venture importing electronics, and they told us stories of Afghan musicians, both folk and pop, in their heyday in the '70s, who they took me as a young boy to see in concert; the most important birthday gift I have probably ever received in my life was a cassette player when I turned eleven or twelve, and I dreamed of visiting the music studio one of those uncles was in the process of finishing when the coup d'état upended everything.

Afghan friends came over weekly to talk politics in my parents' small drawing room, conversations that only grew more rousing the more closed off and inscrutable the country became. Eavesdropping was my favorite after-school pastime, and it became how I formed most of my early ideas about my home country, ideas that were no less passionate for being secondhand; I got into trouble a lot in school, but the instance I remember most vividly was early in my Tokyo high school when I was reprimanded by my speech and debate teacher for refusing to talk about anything other than Afghanistan.

We lived as though our lives in Australia were only temporary, and yet there was an unspoken assumption that we would never be able to go back home. For my parents, this was a daily struggle we never quite understood until we were old enough for them to tell us. My father hated the endless commutes to jobs he felt were beneath him. My mother worked long days to keep our household afloat, starting as a teacher before opening a bakery and catering operation in Melbourne. As connected as we felt to our country, the longer we stayed off Afghan soil, the less claim it seemed we had to our Afghan identity. And losing that felt like a slow death.

By 1996, when I turned thirty, the closest I had come to returning home was by living across the northern border in Uzbekistan. I had moved there, I told people, to take advantage of the post-Soviet business opportunities. And it was true that I had grown utterly bored in Australia, and London, where I had lived for a brief time, making a good salary as a banker, and that compared to the Melbourne suburbs where I'd whiled away my teenage years, Tashkent felt euphoric, a place of transition as it emerged from the Soviet years. It was also true that I started a business when I got there, however halfheartedly, buying and selling any commodity I thought could do well—electronics, pantry staples like sugar and cooking oil. But when I failed miserably at the business, only ever making enough to keep things afloat month to month, I wasn't really bothered. I stayed in Tashkent for four years, barely breaking even, just to be close to Afghanistan.

Uzbekistan looked and smelled like the Afghanistan I remembered. The trees were familiar, blooming bright purple in the spring. Like Afghans, Uzbeks have an almost mystical attachment to the mountains and the sunrise and sunset they create—colors like knives slicing through the city. I bought dried fruits and nuts from the Tashkent markets; the taste brought me back to my grandfather's orchard, just north of Kabul, where I had spent so much of my childhood. You could calculate in your head the amount of time it would take to get to Kabul—two days of driving through daylight southwest through Samarkand and crossing the border if those borders had been open to the casual traveler, which of course they were not.

In Tashkent, I could get news that was coming out of Afghanistan, which in the mid- to late 1990s with the Taliban in power rivaled North Korea as a hermit state. I was interested in meeting anyone—politician, intellectual, or fighter—coming through or from Afghanistan, with any information, but Tashkent was no Peshawar, overrun with Afghans, and once the Friendship Bridge at the border was shut down in spring 1997, even fewer managed to come through, making use of a slow and expensive privately owned barge that crossed the Amu Darya. Still, I did what I could to gather information, inserting myself into conversations with strangers, trying to blend in; everyone smoked, so I started smoking. I began making connections at embassies and NGOs and foreign businesses—a lot of the seconds-in-command at the embassies were in their early thirties like me—eventually following those connections to Washington, DC, and London.

Islam Karimov, the president of Uzbekistan, had a vested interest in Afghanistan, seeing the rise of the Taliban as a threat to his country's national security. In an attempt to help quell the fighting, a regional priority, Karimov hosted peace talks between warring parties in Tashkent. Nothing substantial came out of it, but it drew leaders and information across the border, and while the vats of cooking oil failed to sell at a high enough margin to make me anything close to a rich man, I sat in front of my computer, compiling what I heard into a newsletter, which I emailed to everyone I knew, whether they cared about Afghanistan or not, and which I called, rather unimaginatively, the "Afghanistan update."

One of those US State Department friends introduced me over email to Ahmed Rashid, a Pakistani reporter who would go on to write what is still the most important book on the Taliban, and we became fast friends. Ahmed was one of the many people I spoke to who regularly went inside Afghanistan, and the only writer I knew who had the courage to question his country's intelligence agency, whose support and influence over the Taliban were becoming apparent, about what they were doing on the ground. He had an unsurpassed understanding of the Taliban in an era when no one really cared to or knew how to look very closely.

The news I did manage to compile was always horrific. I feel foolish now saying that any of it came as a surprise. When the Taliban was sweeping through Afghanistan and after they took over Kabul in September 1996, without any real understanding of what was happening on the ground, I naïvely assumed they would realize that they were not up to the task of governance and reinstate the monarchy. If they didn't bring back the king, I expected that they would try to institute something resembling the traditional jirgas, a local variation on participatory democracy, something that made good on their claims to represent the people. My father had nothing but disdain for the Afghan

Communists, who he blamed for his family's exile and who he was certain had led Afghanistan to ruin. Because of this, like many Afghans, and in fact like the American government, he initially invested hope, however warily, in the mujahideen during the '80s who seemed strong enough to defeat the Communists. Later he simply wished for anything that might put an end to the civil war. But the Taliban of the 1990s, once in power, didn't care about all the different ethnic groups and political affiliations who made up the country. In fact, they seemed intent on destroying it.

Refugees who'd found shelter in Uzbekistan sometimes snuck back into Afghanistan, at great risk, to attend to a dying relative or settle a land dispute, and they might return to Tashkent with stories of a dictatorial regime ruling with a brutal interpretation of Islam. The Taliban, they said, watched you anytime you left the house. If you were a woman, you couldn't walk alone. "They would ask us questions about Islam," they said. "And if we didn't know, or didn't agree with them, we could be arrested." Almost all Afghans are Muslim, but the sect, the manner of practice, and the degree of devotion can differ. I identify as a Muslim. Islam provided a structure to my family, especially when we were so far from home. One of my beloved great-uncles was a hafiz, an honorific given to a Muslim who has memorized the Koran. That said, if either of us had been in Kabul during the first Taliban regime, I have no doubt we would have been thrown into jail.

A terrible drought during those years left most of Afghanistan impoverished and close to starving; evidence of hardship, arduously catalogued in human rights reports, was impossible to ignore. Still, after many of the foreign aid workers who published those reports were forced to leave by the Taliban in summer 1998, even news of the suffering became harder to access. The northeast was partly and tenuously under the control of the

Northern Alliance, the strongest military opposition to the Taliban, and their fighters would cross the border with information. They told me that the sporadic fighting was brutal and bloody. Reporters, the few who cared to investigate stories about Afghanistan, traveled in and out across the Pakistani border in the south, and Northern Alliance territory via Tajikistan. These rare pieces of vetted news along with the bits I gathered from other sources, such as reports by the human rights organizations that remained on the ground, began to paint a picture for me of Afghanistan under Taliban rule.

People were starving. There were no jobs, and no money. Many Afghan farmers in the north survived by growing poppies, despite the Taliban's draconian ban on the narcotics trade. We heard about Afghans being executed in the Kabul football stadium, or being punished with amputations because they were hungry and had stolen food. And so they became too petrified of an unforgiving regime to transgress. This gave the illusion of order, of security. People used to say that under the Taliban, no matter how hungry you were, if you found money on the road, you wouldn't pick it up out of fear that you would be punished for stealing. These were stories told in whispers, carried across the borders, and catalogued among the Afghans living as refugees into the lore of the Taliban.

By now, the horrors of that first Taliban rule are well known. Famine, public executions, massacres, and expulsion of ethnic minorities from their villages. A capital city reduced to a fraction of its size. Women disappearing from public life. Dynamite strapped to centuries-old Buddhas in Bamiyan, destroying them and a part of Afghan heritage. Only three countries—Pakistan, Saudi Arabia, and the UAE—recognized the Taliban as Afghanistan's lawful government; the rest of the world almost completely disengaged, out of disgust or disinterest. And there I was being fed details in bits and pieces, sometimes hidden in propaganda, sometimes reluctantly told weeks or months after the fact, occasionally coming over email from Ahmed Rashid or another reporter, while I sat in the middle of nowhere Tashkent, pretending to care about the price of cooking oil. It was maddening.

Two years after I closed my commodities business for good and reluctantly moved back to Australia, I watched the Twin Towers fall on CNN. Practically overnight, Afghanistan went from being a forgotten place to the center of the universe. Taliban crimes, particularly their persecution of girls and women, would no longer be the fodder of despairing newsletters by obsessives like me or human rights organizations, but headline news, the subject of speeches delivered at the UN, the promises made by a First Lady. In the weeks after the attack, every big news outlet in the world sent a reporter to try to get into the country, or at least to provide dispatches from neighboring countries. After the initial shock and horror of 9/11 wore off, my next thought was, *Now we can go back.*

ZAID AND I pushed our way to the front of the crowd surging against the Ariana desk. "There are no tickets." The airline employees shrugged apologetically. Flustered, they seemed to be choosing people at random, anointing them with seats. Afghans themselves, they understood the desire to return. But there was only so much space on an airplane. "You'll have to wait a few days," they said. "Then we can get you on."

Back then, Terminal 2 was the pathetic, withered branch of the newly glitzy Dubai airport. While most of the airport was a luxury shopping mall, luring travelers in with thick clouds of designer perfume, Terminal 2 offered a McDonald's and some vending machines. It hosted short flights to poor, often war-torn, countries; I used to affectionately refer to it as the "terror terminal." Once I saw a group of men on a connecting flight from the

Maldives, well dressed in loafers and blazers and colored slacks, wide-eyed and appearing lost. I still laugh remembering the way they looked at us—as though a bunch of Afghans, Pakistanis, and Iraqis, some of us in traditional clothing, yes, but quite a few of us in loafers and slacks and blazers ourselves, were intergalactic travelers, something out of the bar scene from *Star Wars*. But I would come to love Terminal 2 before its big renovation many years later. The constant delays and the close quarters with little to distract meant you could arrive there alone and land in Kabul hours later with three new business connections and a handful of new friends.

Zaid is a few years younger than me, hyperengaged with the world and blessed with an excellent memory and a gift for storytelling. By 2002, he was a decade into what had become a thriving law career in Melbourne, and he reveled in arguing for what he thought was right, usually getting his way. Unlike our youngest brother, Jahid, who is a bit more skeptical, particularly when it came to politics, Zaid and I are both optimists, sometimes excessively. We share the same assumption that things will work out in the end, possibly because unlike our younger siblings we remember the day of the coup, and that we all made it out of Kabul safely. That's not to say either of us is naïve. Zaid is animated, often ebullient, but he sees the world as a lawyer does. Justice can prevail, but you have to be prepared to fight for it. Sometimes, in that fight, you have to get creative.

That day in Dubai, Ariana was back in operation and the Taliban regime had been toppled, Kabul looked fairly intact in the news coverage, and American officials were glowing about how quickly they'd succeeded; beauty parlors were reopening when moments before women could not leave their homes unless wearing a burka; NGOs were scoping out buildings to establish offices; the UN was sending investigators to chronicle Taliban crimes, itself a declaration that those crimes were in the past.

But I knew how Afghanistan worked. Things could change any moment. If we didn't go back now, who knew when we would be able to return? Through a family connection, Zaid and I got a meeting in the airline manager's office, where we set out to charm him. "Your son-in-law is a family friend in Melbourne," I told him. "Can you believe it? Uncle, what a small world."

"Oh yes," he said. "You're right, he knows your father." It was the kind of conversation Afghans had a lot in exile. The script changed, but the content was more or less the same. "I think in Kabul my cousin knows your cousin," someone would say. "And I think my father also knows his cousin," another replied. "I think they went to university together, possibly, or their cousins did."

Every connection had meaning. Our relatives both lived in Pakistan; they both worked for the government; we went to the same school; we have the same family name. Our mothers' mothers lived on the same street in Kabul; we were originally from the same village; we loved the same Persian poems; we ate the same food; we left for the same reason and eventually returned at the same time, fighting for a seat on Ariana Airlines.

My father has a large blood family, and also a vast chosen one. The kinds of conversations like the one we had in the manager's office, establishing connections that could go back generations, are both lighthearted and profound. In Afghanistan, everyone has a cousin, everyone is a cousin, friends who become so close that the word "friend" hardly seems sufficient become uncles, sisters, brothers, aunts. Although we had no idea that day that we would start a media company, it wouldn't be long before Moby itself would become a family, and not in a false corporate retreat way but in a full-throated Afghan way. "Here." The manager offered us tickets for the following day. "You're up front, as well."

The old plane was full beyond capacity. People crowded the aisles, shoving their bags into the overhead bins and pushing the groaning doors shut. Children much too old sat on the laps of parents and siblings, the seat belts straining to contain them all. Flight attendants, having given up their seats to customers, clung to the door handles during takeoff.

Zaid and I sat up front, where passengers were allowed to smoke. I matched my seatmate cigarette for cigarette. I cannot remember what he told me when I asked him why he was returning to Kabul. He was going back to claim some long-lost piece of land, or to visit a relative's grave, or to find a job in the new government, or to start a business, or just to live; he was going back to do all of the above. Everyone had urgent business to settle in the home they hadn't seen for years.

Over the Persian Gulf and then Iran, the flight was uneventful. Passengers opened up newspapers and books. Music leaked out of headphones. Mothers quieted their children with sweets. Zaid and I talked about what we would do when we landed, mundane, dispassionate things that could calm our nerves—who was coming to pick us up, whether we had all the right papers to pass through immigration, checking for our Australian passports one more time. I noticed the fabric on the seat in front of me was fraying, and the ashtray on my armrest needed to be emptied.

I had flown over Afghanistan before a few times as a teenager and later as a young businessman taking long flights from Australia. I've always been good at passing the time on airplanes, sleeping or reading. The moment we were over Afghanistan, however, I would wake up suddenly, put my book down, become alert to the world outside the airplane window. It was like an alarm went off.

I'm like my father; I resist being overly sentimental (sometimes I succeed, sometimes I don't). I dislike unnecessary use of metaphors. Life itself is descriptive enough. But there was something supernatural in those alert moments on the flight, something that compelled me to lean over and look out the window, scanning for a break in the clouds so I could see the land below. The Afghan mountains always astonished me. I remembered them from my childhood. Our house in Kabul had been at the foot of a large hill that swooped up steeper and steeper into one of those mountains; you couldn't walk for long in one direction without losing your breath. I hadn't walked on that block since I was twelve. On a red-eye from Australia to Uzbekistan, I had once seen bursts of colorful lights on the ground below and thought for a moment that maybe they were fireworks—a wedding, perhaps—until realizing that they must have been bursts of artillery fire, some battle somewhere in my homeland thirty thousand feet below me.

Shortly into the Ariana flight, the captain came on the intercom. "We are now in Afghan airspace," he said, in English and Dari. All at once, the plane fell quiet. Next to me, grown men in beards and poorly ironed brown three-piece suits choked back tears, the gray smoke from their cigarettes collecting around their heads. If there were babies on the flight, they somehow knew to stop screaming. The clouds were thick outside the window. I watched for the mountains to come into view, and then we skirted their white tops on our descent into Kabul.

CHAPTER 3

RETURN TO KABUL

I was surprised to find that after all those years I could direct the car from the Kabul airport to the home of a friend, where Zaid and I were to stay for the week and, we hoped, come up with some kind of a plan. The city had grown in our absence, but crudely, splintered by conflict and stifled by poverty. Soviet-style architecture had replaced some traditional homes, and these newer buildings were sagging with neglect. Much of the west of the city was in ruins or completely flattened, one of many visible signs of the many conflicts the country had endured—the two coups that led to the Soviet invasion that led to the resistance by the mujahideen that became a civil war that led to the Taliban taking over and then this, the American invasion that people like Zaid and I were calling a liberation.

Old roads were paved but falling apart, and they took us away from the airport and into town, past a small restaurant, a big cemetery, the government office where my father once worked, the US embassy, until recently closed. Kabul University, where my parents met, looked empty, unloved. The roads near my mother's childhood home, a traditional house with a large garden lined with white flowers, were choked with rubble. In just a few years, her old street would boom with commerce, becoming one of Kabul's hubs for textiles and tailors. But in those early days, there was hardly enough electricity to power a sewing machine.

The chaos of the airport, and the joy once the plane landed— grown men bending to kiss the tarmac, weeping through customs—had not prepared me for how listless Kabul would feel that week. The sounds I remembered so well from my childhood, of kids playing football in the street, buses speeding down the road, produce sellers yelling from the sidewalks, were all muted. Even the spring colors, those purples my mother would always say bloomed only in Kabul, appeared dull. Qargha Reservoir, just outside of the city, was almost completely dry, the result of several extra-hot and -dry summers, and had become a symbol of the absence of vibrancy under Taliban rule.

When the car neared my childhood home, I ignored the impulse to look down our old street as we passed. I didn't want to be reminded, not yet, of my old home. That first week it was enough to just be there, spending time with other Afghans, their sense of humor, the food, the culture. Zaid and I drove from corner to corner, taking photos and videos of practically everything we saw to send to Jahid, Wajma, and my parents back in Australia. ISAF, an international peacekeeping force of around five thousand people, was in charge of providing security in the city at the time, but I saw militias, including former Northern Alliance fighters, positioned around the city. The Americans and, soon, their British allies were engaged in combat with Taliban and Al Qaeda fighters in the provinces, with people in Kabul clearly delighted to see the Taliban gone.

No matter Kabul's condition, Zaid and I were elated to be there. That first night, we had dinner with friends, sitting on cushions on the floor in the traditional Afghan style, eating food I remembered from my childhood, the flavors somehow more pronounced and delicious. We talked for hours about the future of a country we had only just arrived in and that we all arrogantly imagined we could shape into anything we wanted. In 2002, Afghanistan felt like a blank page, and everyone was arriving with their own ideas of how to fill it.

More than 350,000 Afghans had already returned from refugee camps and cities in Pakistan and Iran, and another million and a half would do so in the coming months. Their lives over the years since they had fled Afghanistan had been full of hardship and precarity, and they were coming back to claim small parcels of land or resurrect small businesses. For them, whatever life awaited them in Kabul or the provinces must have seemed better than what they had left behind in exile. In comparison, Zaid and I were the privileged ones. We had some means; we had been leading comfortable lives in Australia and we both had our jobs and lives back there in case things didn't work out. In those early days we met only a few other Afghans like us, who had money and plans, however abstract, to invest in our country. It was important that Zaid and I come up with a good idea quickly, we realized, so that we didn't come off as wealthy Afghans, swooping in to make a quick buck off the country's liberation. We had already met some such characters, and their many international counterparts, do-gooders and mercenaries alike who, unsure of what to do, were devising ideas for hair salons and foreign restaurants that even we, even in that hopeful moment, could see were outlandish.

We wanted to believe in the possibility, and yet the country was so limited by so many things—lack of certain skills and expertise in its labor force, slow trading, no reliable electricity or water—and parts of the country were still enmeshed in conflict. Our ideas came quickly and were just as quickly shot down. Embroidered textiles, known for their intricate patterns, would be difficult to produce at any quality and scale, without access to the most skilled workers, who might not yet have returned. Music recording, one of the many businesses my family had established in the 1970s, seemed impossible to resurrect in the immediate wake of Taliban rule, when even listening to music had been illegal. The Afghan superstars who had come through my uncle's half-finished studio were dead or in exile, and because of the conflict, an entire generation of Afghans hadn't been trained in traditional music or singing. Most of the orchards we visited on Kabul's outskirts, once so bountiful with fruits, had suffered for years from neglect and drought, and with the livestock depleted, we couldn't envision jump-starting the once-flourishing Afghan lambskin trade. We briefly considered reviving the same uncle's cotton cultivation business, but quickly realized that the country lacked the basic infrastructure and water needed to get that off the ground. We had no experience in hospitality, so opening a hotel wouldn't work, although those were clearly needed, with the influx of international journalists, aid workers, and UN bureaucrats. A catering business sounded intriguing, notwithstanding the fact that none of us knew a single thing about cooking and I, for one, dreaded the idea of pretending as I had for years in Tashkent to care about the price of cooking oil.

Nothing would be easy. Afghanistan is landlocked, dependent on border traffic, and yet crossing the borders in some areas where conflict was ongoing was still treacherous; the Taliban had been bad at governance, but they knew how to fight and were still doing so in the hinterlands. Electricity, available in urban areas alone, was generated with imported diesel, outrageously expensive, rationed, and unreliable. Our airports were basically nonfunctioning. The highways were in shambles; there were no trains (even today there are no passenger trains in Afghanistan). The more we thought about what Afghanistan needed, the more impossible it seemed to do anything.

We grew up loving Afghan almonds. Maybe that could be a business? In the 1960s and 1970s, Afghanistan had been a major exporter of nuts and dried fruits, mostly to the Indian subcontinent. Even after the economy tanked following the Soviet invasion, the ensuing civil war, and the Taliban takeover, agriculture remained Afghanistan's most important sector, with the majority of Afghans working and making a living off farm work. Plus, those nuts and fruits were the flavors of our childhood. Zaid and I had been delighted to see the almonds, anemic-looking compared to fat, uniform American almonds, but so much sweeter, for sale in the Kabul markets. "We can start small, with a few dozen trees," we said, remembering our grandfather's vast orchard north of the city, where we had spent most of our weekends stealing fruit meant for the market, just like our mother had when she was a kid. "Maybe we can set up a system to help other farmers export their goods." We were convinced that the Afghan economy could recover over the coming years if Afghans took advantage of the foreign investment, including the development aid that was starting to pour in, and created sustainable local businesses.

With at least one idea that seemed somewhat feasible, we tried to set up meetings with anyone interested, officials from the newly established interim government, farmers, manufacturers, anyone who could help us get some kind of business going, but even the simple act of arranging places to meet rubbed up against the chaos of those early days in Kabul. Most Afghans had no phones at the time, whether mobile phones or landlines; the first mobile network would be launched in April 2002, although with very limited offerings, with Internet access to follow only much later. Foreign correspondents relied on satellite phones, government and UN officials on donated bulky orange Ericssons, and the general populace needed to buy pricey calling cards. The muscle memory that had guided us from the airport that first day faded as we navigated parts of the city that had drastically changed. We were frequently getting lost on Kabul's bumpy roads, which with each passing day became more and more glutted with cars.

We missed important meetings. Or we might be offered a meeting with someone vitally important only to realize that important person had no knowledge of the meeting, or didn't exist at all, a character hastily created out of thin air as a networking tool by someone too eager to please. In the morning, we might make a date with a minister, perhaps someone who had just returned from abroad and, like us, was struggling to adjust to the demands of the new Kabul, only to be left sitting at the agreed-upon restaurant, annoyed and a little embarrassed, with no way to track down our missing lunch date.

Sometimes, the disorder and social lawlessness drove you crazy. Other times, it worked some kind of magic. You could cold visit a high-ranking minister and wait until he chose to meet you. You could insert yourself into conversations you probably had no business being in, learn a little, then weigh in like an expert. With our fluent English and Dari, and our family connections, we were able to meet dozens of foreigners that first week and try to convince them we could be useful to them, and sometimes they appeared to agree. "Our younger brother Jahid speaks perfect Japanese," we told a newly returned Ashraf Ghani, to which he nodded enthusiastically and said, "Oh yes, that could be useful dealing with Japanese donors," even though we all understood that those Japanese donors would likely speak English. Outside of the restaurant where one minister stood you up, you'd run into a different minister, join them for dinner in a nearby hotel, and through them make lunch plans the next day with their friend, a consular officer or a military advisor or an assistant to Hamid Karzai, the head of Afghanistan's interim government.

In the evenings, people gathered in what was left of the abandoned embassies and guesthouses, or in the residential homes that people were quickly converting into placeholders for new embassies and guesthouses. The Intercontinental, built in the late 1960s as Kabul's first luxury hotel, became a favorite meeting place for coffee, overlooking the irregular rectangle of the drained swimming pool and the panorama of the city below. This was a few years before a mediocre renovation would try, and fail, to restore the hotel to its glorious past, and long before militant attacks would abruptly jolt it back to reality. Electricity flickered on and off in the lobby, but the hotel was filling up with foreigners. In 2002 Kabul, anything could happen.

Hundreds of journalists either living in or passing through Afghanistan would craft their narratives of the American war from these Kabul hotels and guesthouses. In the very early days, the stories were almost exuberant, and often black-and-white, portrayals about the Americans' quick victory over the "evil" Taliban in Kabul. They were also about the Afghan nation getting a second chance, largely echoing the message President George W. Bush was sending from Washington: the United States as the savior of Afghanistan, rescuing its people from the horrors of a brutal regime, rescuing its women from a brutal culture. In these articles, Afghans tended to welcome the foreign troops and celebrate the fall of the Taliban; gone was the antiquated religious and political movement that had been oppressing the Afghan people, and here were the modern, enlightened foreigners and returning Afghans, eager to rebuild the country.

There was something made for Hollywood about that narrative. It is certainly based on a true story, albeit an overly simplified one that presents the Taliban as a monolithic enemy, operating in the shadows. Still, it was hard not to get swept up in the hopefulness of that time, in the feeling that the country was being reborn with everyone in Kabul working together toward a shared goal. We wanted it to be true. In this story, Afghans were heroes too.

IT WAS STILL my first week back in Kabul, and we were still seriously considering an almond exporting business, when I visited Sayed Makhdoom Raheen, a friend of my father's from his government days who had spent the Communist and Taliban years in exile and upon his return been appointed the minister of information and culture in the interim government. In my father's telling, Raheen was a character straight out of the sartorially wild 1970s, who had a PhD in Persian literature and was a friend of the king, and who as a young man had embraced the style of the time, wearing audacious bright red three-piece suits and platform shoes, with an antique gold-plated pocket watch, a piece of costume jewelry with some sentimental value, tucked into a breast pocket.

By 2002, the minister, now much older, had toned down his look but still cut a striking figure. Over a pin-striped suit and patterned necktie, he wore a Western-designed, ostentatious coat of thick lambskin. On anyone else, it would have looked ridiculous, but Raheen was so commanding and so confident, standing at maximum five foot six, he could have pulled anything off. He had a great memory for poetry, and used to recite it at length, particularly, I would come to find once we became friends, after work hours, when the worries of the ministry faded and the pleasures of socializing took over. Those who knew him would joke that you never wanted to interrupt the minister when he slipped into reciting verse, which he often did.

The Bonn Agreement, overseen by the United Nations, had been signed in December 2001, establishing an interim government with representatives from all the main ethnic, geographic, and religious factions in Afghanistan, and an emergency Loya Jirga, Pashto for "grand council," which was to meet in summer 2002 to select a president for the transitional government. Within the agreement were several exciting, aspirational statements for a reimagined country. The justice system would be rebuilt in accord with Islamic principles, Afghan legal traditions, and international standards, and overseen by a Supreme Court. A new constitution was to be drafted, a human rights commission to be set up. The agreement stressed the importance of women participating in the political process. Karzai, a champion of the anti-Communist mujahideen and member of the educated elite, was named interim head. Many of the officials taking part in the new government I knew from my time in Uzbekistan, or through my family.

Somewhat buried in the larger proclamations about national reconciliation, peace, and democracy, the Afghan parties had agreed to the importance of freedom of thought and expression and a free media. Bonn had reinstated the 1964 constitution, which declared these rights "inviolable"; the new constitution adopted in 2004 would reaffirm this language. By the time that the US invaded Afghanistan, however, television had been banned for several years and the only media available was Radio Afghanistan, which had been prominent in my childhood, but under the Taliban had been renamed Radio Voice of Sharia and where programming consisted mainly of religious recitations, moral education, and Taliban pronouncements. Historically, the state news media hadn't served the people, or the truth, really; rather, it existed to bolster those in charge and frighten those who might dare oppose them. It hardly mattered, though; most people in the country didn't have electricity, never mind a television.

Raheen, though, was thrilled, and during our meeting wouldn't stop talking about the possibilities. "This constitution will mean huge changes for culture in Afghanistan," he told me, shifting his thin body excitedly toward the edge of his chair. "Think about it—if media is free, we could do what we want with music, television, real news. Afghan news, Afghan shows, made by Afghans."

"You and your siblings are looking for something to do, right?" he asked me. I nodded. I hadn't yet brought up the idea of almonds or lambskin or embroidery. The minister grew serious. "You should start a radio station," he said.

For a moment I was so taken aback, I didn't know what to say. Kabul was full of possibility, but not always of optimism. I thought of the silence in the city, how dark and quiet it became when the generators were turned off. I thought of the crushed buildings in Kabul, the unexploded ordnance and land mines throughout the country, the refugees returning by the hundreds of thousands. A few days before the meeting had been Nowruz, the Persian New

Year. Nowruz of my youth had been joyful, albeit almost always rainy, as it meant the season of visiting my grandfather's orchard was about to begin. Around Kabul, people celebrated in different ways, flying kites, hosting large outdoor meals, staging concerts. As a city, we always welcomed spring after long, snowy winters.

That first Nowruz back in Afghanistan, I had been busy in meetings and didn't plan to celebrate formally, but I still woke up with a sense of excitement. It would be the first Nowruz since the Taliban's expulsion from Kabul, and I had heard that a celebration had been arranged in the football stadium, which had only a few years before been used for public executions. It was inarguably a time of transformation for Afghanistan, and Nowruz, like any New Year celebration, is about transformation, renewal.

Driving to a meeting, I passed over Wazir Akbar Khan hill and was suddenly caught in a swarm of people, thousands it seemed like, blocking my car. They carried nothing in their hands, and no bags. I couldn't hear much conversation, and certainly no music. I didn't see anyone selling kites. It was too cold to picnic. Would there be fireworks later that evening? I hadn't heard of any scheduled. Later I would read in the international media about vibrant celebrations near the football stadium, and I would wonder if the scenes, which I did not witness, weren't perhaps exaggerated by an overly excited foreign reporter, the type whose stories belied the toil of real recovery from the Taliban. Afghans, from what I saw, might have felt free that Nowruz. But they didn't know yet what they could do with their newfound freedom.

As my car inched closer, I watched the crowd. Their faces were blank. They walked silently and barely seemed to notice where they were. Once they reached the top of the hill, they simply turned around and started walking back down. I pulled over and rolled down my car window. "Why are you here?" I asked a man who seemed to be walking with his family.

"No reason." The man shrugged. "Maybe just to look down

at the city. Maybe there's something to do. It's Nowruz." He resumed walking. I drove to my meetings, honking gently at the people who strayed into the road, annoyed, disappointed.

Now I see that Nowruz for what it was: a display of courage by a city of traumatized people. The year before, it wouldn't have been me honking, but Taliban militants driving where I drove, yelling at the people for leaving their homes, men and women and children together, for being out on the hill for a holiday they had banned because it originated in a pre-Islamic era. It was daring enough that first Nowruz just to go outside, pull your body up the hill, and then walk back down into the city and go back home. In the coming years, the Wazir Akbar Khan neighborhood would become part of the Green Zone, which grew bigger and more fortified, housing more government buildings and embassies, and where ordinary Afghans would have to show papers in order to get in. I see now that the walk that day was evidence of a transformation.

In that moment, though, driving to my meeting, I had been confused, almost bereaved, by what I saw as their strange behavior. Later, in the guesthouse where we stayed, I described the people to Zaid as "zombies." Bonn Agreement or not, the scene did not leave me feeling confident that the country was ready for what Raheen proposed.

"Why would we do that?" I asked the minister in our meeting.

"Because now, you can," he replied.

Media hadn't occurred to us. But Zaid and I had to admit that it seemed a bit more compelling than investing in almonds. After the meeting with Raheen, I brought up the idea to everyone I knew, waiting to see if the proposal was so far-fetched it made them laugh and being surprised, and encouraged, when it didn't. I mentioned it, in passing, to Ahmed Rashid, the Pakistani writer whose definitive book on the Taliban had been published, a harbinger, in March 2000. A few days later, he called me from DC.

"I was having dinner with Andrew Natsios," he said. The then-head of USAID had arranged a meeting while Rashid was in the US to talk about his now much-feted book. "I told him you were interested in founding a media company."

"I am?" I replied.

And that's how it happened.

CHAPTER 4

BUILDING THE RADIO

After the meeting with Minister Raheen, we forgot all about the almonds. We rented a two-story home along a busy road that would soon be filled with restaurants and stores, about a kilometer away from the US embassy, in what would become one of the most fortified neighborhoods in all of Kabul. The house was nondescript, one in a line of nearly identical homes built for technocrats and professionals before the civil war and suffering from years of neglect. It had been previously rented by the BBC and its renovations made it somewhat habitable. Still, an overgrown lawn hid trash and rubble, the iron railings around the front terrace had rusted, and the inside was a museum of dust.

Jahid, growing more disillusioned with the corporate world in Australia, had taken a leave from his finance job in Melbourne, bringing a little bit of money to invest and a great deal of his brand of measured enthusiasm. He indeed lent his Japanese language skills, and background in business, to working for Ghani, then the head of the Afghanistan Assistance Coordination Authority (AACA), which helped secure and distribute aid for early development projects. Jahid admired Ghani for how enthusiastically he listened to the ideas brought to him by young Afghans, and because my brother found, in the older Afghan, an ally in shooting down the condescending stereotypes so many of the foreign aid workers brought to their meetings—"It's like they expect a guy in a turban, not a suit," Jahid complained to us. Whatever time he didn't spend at his new job, we spent together, building the radio.

We slept shoulder to shoulder on the cold tile of the first floor while transforming the second floor into a makeshift studio, with the help of Timmy Byrne, a presenter and station manager of an Australian radio station called KISS 90 FM, who was between jobs and whom we convinced, somehow, to help some novices start a radio station in Afghanistan, a place I gathered that he knew little about but, in classic Aussie fashion, considered a good adventure. KISS 90 FM had been Melbourne's most popular independent dance station, known for music that was as loud and aggressive as the DJs who played it. It was the kind of station a young person might turn on in the car to annoy their parents, and even though we expected Afghans likely wanted something more traditional than dance music, Timmy could help us bring to life the kind of station we envisioned: a shock to the system.

A small team got to work on the upper floor of the house, tearing down a bedroom wall and building a plexiglass barrier between the on-air talent and the producers, soundproofing the other walls with hundreds of egg cartons bargained for at one of Kabul's open-air markets, chickens squawking in the background while we told the confused shopkeeper, "No, no eggs, not today." Out of space, we enclosed one of the balconies with crude wooden walls to use as an expansion for the studio. When the landlady, an Afghan expat living somewhere in Europe, visited the house later that year, she nearly had a heart attack. "What are you doing to my beautiful building?" she cried. "Don't worry," we said. "We'll fix it before we leave."

While Jahid worked to build out the studio and Zaid, ever the lawyer, helped parse the evolving media laws, I endured the endless meetings needed for us to get a broadcast license, a bureaucratic procedure in a land improvising with new bureaucratic procedures, which no amount of optimism could make less painful. My first stop, at the recommendation of Raheen, was the new head of the state-run Radio Television Afghanistan, a former

Northern Alliance leader who, the story goes, was so bitter and stubborn toward his rivals even within his own group that during the civil war he had torn the passenger seat out of his military jeep so a fellow militant whom he despised wouldn't be able to sit beside him. The fighter turned media chief took one look at me, declared me a waste of time, and kicked me out of his office.

Seven or eight new radio stations were already on air in Kabul, funded by NGOs and Western governments, playing news and talk. Most of them had received bigger grants than us, while, aside from the USAID grant, the majority of our money came from our personal bank accounts. The USAID grant of $228,000 had come with surprisingly few conditions, save for some guidelines about free expression and the need to hire women. But most of our money was our own investment, and we were determined that eventually we would be financially viable.

Raheen had been appointed minister in part because, as a loyalist and a member of the old guard, he provided some continuity and expertise. But like all of us, he was struggling to navigate new terrain, and not get stuck in the battle between urbanite returnees, who were more closely aligned with the pre-Soviet governments, and the more conservative mujahideen. Although my connection to him helped me get meetings with people like the head of the RTA, it did not prevent me from getting kicked out of those meetings. In those early, already-competitive days, we encountered a lot of resistance to our idea of a free media wherever we went. Members of the old guard, less open to new ideas than Raheen, fretted over the introduction of a radio station that might be, as they put it, "unsuitable for Afghanistan," founded as it was by Afghans who had grown up outside of the country. I made it my practice to sit and listen to them, drink a cup of tea, and nod my head, and then as soon as the meeting ended, forget everything they had said.

Radio Voice of Sharia, which had reverted to its original name,

Radio Afghanistan, naturally didn't want to give up its long-held monopoly in the country, although they didn't say so outright. After those meetings, I laughed with my brothers. "They play the lamest kind of music," nothing modern, if we were lucky some Afghan pop from the 1970s, but certainly none of the Western or Turkish or Indian music that young Afghans truly liked. Although RTA was being rebuilt with help from the BBC and other foreign entities, we found them easy to ignore. The same was true of the American donors and do-gooders, many of whom also liked to worry about what the Afghans were "ready" for, like parents sending their children to school by themselves for the first time. Eventually, Raheen and I realized that without any streamlined system for issuing broadcast licenses, we would have to set one up ourselves, and we did.

It may seem cocky to say, and I'm sure people had that impression of us at the time, but we hated being told there were any limits to our vision. "Afghanistan can't handle a totally free media," I was told, by representatives of foreign governments, by Afghans who had returned from Europe or the US, by heads of NGOs. *Can't handle what exactly?* I wondered. And which Afghans are you all talking about? Afghans who had grown up outside the country were arriving or returning with dynamic ideas about the purpose and range of media, and with diverse opinions about movies, music, news reporting. Afghans who had lived under the Taliban were hungry for something new. The idea that Afghans weren't ready to hear music on their radios made me laugh. Everyone goes crazy for music, I reasoned. That's why the Taliban had to ban it.

Radio was the best kind of idea: simple but revolutionary. I recall the term "no-brainer" being thrown around a lot those early days. Women on the radio? No-brainer. Call-in shows for the morning drive? No-brainer. Under the Taliban, the punishment for being caught with banned music could be severe and violent, but Afghans still managed to find a way to listen. They smuggled cassettes from Pakistan through checkpoints hidden in the upholstery of their cars, bought them on the black market, and closed their windows and curtains at home before playing their Michael Jackson and Ahmad Zahir tapes at a low enough volume. Would these Afghans tune in to a radio station after so many years of being deprived? Definitely a no-brainer.

WE NAMED THE station Arman, the Dari word for "hope," and started hiring. Immediately, we received hundreds of applications, from both men and women. Very few of the applicants had any radio experience, but then again neither did we. Our collective inexperience could be a virtue, we reasoned; we wanted to start something totally new, with people who could speak and understand both Pashto and Dari and hadn't been trained on the flowery, almost Shakespearean Dari of the state radio. "They don't say, 'give me a glass of water,'" Zaid joked. "They say, 'Would you please be kind enough to pass me that glass of beverage of the clear variety?'"

We planned a soft launch, with some Afghan, Indian, and Western pop music DJ'd by young Afghans who could speak informally to one another, channeling the dialects of the people, in Afghanistan's two official languages. Dari, the lingua franca, was used in higher education and business, the language spoken by most people in Kabul, while Pashto, a grammatically complex language with its own rich literary history, was now unfortunately associated with the Taliban. Language, which also signified ethnicity, had divided us—and not only under the Taliban; the British and Soviets had both recognized and exacerbated this division. Pashto had been the language of my ancestors and my mother tongue, but by the time we were born our family had been in Kabul for so long we barely spoke it and learned little in school. But in the new Kabul, on the new radio, both languages would be given equal weight. Just as importantly, from the very first broadcast, we wanted men and women in the studio together. Obvious, we thought, but revolutionary.

We interviewed in panels, inviting a handful of nervous applicants at a time into the grassy garden of our house-turned-studio. Most were young, and shy when confronted with the newspaper we gave them to read. They answered our questions as though trying to pass a university exam. We looked for applicants who loosened up after a moment, who spoke to each other with some ease, who had nice voices and strong opinions about music, movies, politics—really, anyone with a voice agreeable enough that a taxi driver wouldn't turn them off during rush hour.

We met Afghans who had returned from Pakistan with stories about passing time in the deplorable condition of the refugee camps or slum-like city housing with Indian films and soap operas. We interviewed people who had grown up in Iran watching banned shows via satellite TV—these stories would be instructive many years later, when we established our own Farsi satellite network, to be broadcast in Iran and the region. We met Afghans who had never left the country, who described collecting musical instruments at home and forming a family band to fill the quiet hours after dinner.

Afghanistan is a large country, and incredibly diverse, with more than twenty million people at the time (over subsequent decades, the population doubled) and nearly twenty different ethnic groups as well as tribal and kinship affiliations, whole handfuls of languages and regional dialects and accents, and, though nearly all Afghans are Muslim, a wide range of religious practices, customs and traditions, as well as political opinions, international loyalties and animosities, tastes in music and movies and books, eye and hair colors, and manners of lining those eyes and styling that hair. It's true of any nation, and yet, when a place is written about mostly in the black-and-white terms of war and liberation, it sometimes feels important to say it again: one cannot generalize about a country like Afghanistan.

Aside from often oversimplified accounts of tribal and sectarian clashes, that diversity often gets diminished in the media coverage of the country, and it had rarely been reflected in the composition of the government. Discord—between villages and provincial capitals, weak central governments and stronger local leaders, international forces and those who fight against them—has historically made it easier for certain families, descendants of the monarchy or those from powerful tribes, to maintain power with little input from the majority of the people. From the beginning, we wanted our radio station to reflect the real Afghanistan in all its complexity.

In the process, we also had to acknowledge our own family's claims to power and status. We'd come from merchants and traders, scholars and poets, and we had connections to the royal family and many former officials who held positions across many different governments. As children, we were often reminded that my mother's father was a direct descendant of the founder of Afghanistan, Ahmad Shah Durrani, whose tribe ruled the nation for two hundred years. We didn't merely love our grandfather; in our household, he was almost mythical, strong and commanding in the stories people told about him, gentle and kind in my memories of him from my childhood. When he died, I was six or seven, and the grief was unbearable. We had assumed he would live forever.

My relatives owned land, and although some had connections or aspirations outside of the country, everyone kept one foot in Afghanistan; on my mother's side, boys were sent to Germany and, on my father's side, to Turkey or the US to study with the expectation that, once they graduated, they would come back.

We come from Kandahar in the south and Paktia in the east, and have some strong roots in Kabul, but by the time I was born, almost everyone in the extended family had long since moved to Kabul, not yet the metropolis it is today but already the biggest and most vibrant city in Afghanistan. Kabul is a melting pot of tribes, languages, and cultures, and being from the city is an identity all its own.

"Democracy" was already a buzzword in those days, even before the US changed its goal for the war from capturing Osama bin Laden and dismantling Al Qaeda to the unspoken one of nation building. My own feelings about the war itself and how it was conducted would change over time. And whatever a general or diplomat meant by democracy, whether they said it on the battlefield in Helmand province or from the embassy in Kabul, that changed as well over the years. Over two decades, this word deployed so repeatedly appeared to lose its meaning. But not for us.

TO START, WE hired nine people, three women and six men. Only one of them, a young man named Massood Sanjer, had any media experience. Massood's family was from Paghman district, west of Kabul, but he was born and raised in the city. He was just leaving high school for university when the Taliban took over in 1996, and, even though most families he knew were fleeing to Pakistan and even though he couldn't imagine what his future held under this new government, he was determined to stay in Afghanistan. While he studied architecture at university, he took up a part-time job as a news reader for the Radio Voice of Sharia. For five years, Massood read bleak pro-Taliban propaganda disguised as news on the radio, perfecting his timing and voice and building his confidence. His exceptional command of English, honed by a love of Western movies and a smattering of formal courses, meant that for five years any English speaker anywhere in the world who was interested in the official news out of Afghanistan would have heard Massood deliver it. He didn't know what the work would lead to, but he stuck with it. "You had to have hope that one day it would matter," he told us at his interview.

Massood was plucky. He studied, read the news, collected his small paycheck, and after dinner his was one of the many Afghan families playing music with the curtains drawn. After the US invaded, he worked as a fixer for several papers and then for Fox News, a well-paying job he gave up by joining us. Being a part of an Afghan media company was always the dream, he said to us. He shared very little about his life under the Taliban, but showed us photos from his days at Sharia radio, sitting in front of an old microphone wearing a turban and a beard, photos he still keeps on his phone today.

Of the dozens of women who came to be interviewed those first days, Sima Safa was one of the few not accompanied by a male relative. There were no men to take her; Sima's father had died of a heart attack in Karachi, where they had lived as refugees since 1996, and her brother, a doctor in Pakistan, refused to return to Kabul. He had tried to stop Sima and her mother, who suffered from a calcium deficiency that made her prone to fainting, from returning as well. "What if Mom has an episode?" he asked her. "What will you do in a country full of men?"

Sima's hands shook so much during her interview that she had to lay the newspaper flat on the desk in front of her in order to read it. She sounded calm, though, with a voice as clear as a bell, in both Pashto and Dari. "We thought you were just showing us that you could read something far from your face," Jahid joked, when she confessed that she had been too nervous to hold the paper.

Our nine new hires showed up early the first day of work. Before we started, we took a group photo in front of the house, tall weeds sprouting up the front of the small, cracked terrace. They look nervous, the men in button-down shirts and slacks a size too big, blazers more suited for a funeral, and the three women dressed in black and dark brown, loosely tied headscarves revealing a few inches of dark hair. In the photo, Sima's head is down, but she's looking directly into the camera.

Sima and Massood brought notebooks and pens. While they ate lunch, they listened to recordings of KISS 90 FM and NOVA 100, another commercial Australian radio station that Jahid, Zaid, and I had been listening to recently, known for a slightly more mainstream Top 40. Timmy stayed for a month, helping them untangle and imitate the host's banter. We sat on the floor, throwing out ideas for shows. Someone suggested a sports bulletin, although Afghan sports had withered under the Taliban. Another suggested a comedy show, perhaps satirizing the government, hilarious in its growing pains. We sketched out ideas for news programs, bulletins that would play between DJ sets, and call-in shows, maybe even to a psychologist or psychiatrist, which would be a novelty in a society where people didn't tend to share their private problems with strangers.

Our only two chairs were situated in front of our only two mics. While the rest of us brainstormed, two people would practice hosting a show, one person acting as the guest—a minister or a football star, an American businessperson, an activist—and the other the host, asking questions. Sometimes, they pretended to be DJs, filling the time between songs with jokes. "Have you heard the one about the soldier?" Massood asked Sima, speaking into the dead mic.

"I don't think so," Sima replied. "Why don't you tell me?"

"He was bragging about being in a war," Massood went on. "'Oh, look at me! I cut the feet off of five people!'"

"The feet?" Sima replied, smiling. "Why the feet?"

"That's just what his friends asked," Massood said. "Why didn't you cut off the heads? And the soldier said, 'Oh, someone else had already done that.'" Sima laughed so hard she nearly fell off the chair.

WE WERE BARELY sleeping, so we hired someone to help us with daily chores like cleaning up and brewing the strong tea that kept us going. Jan Agha had never been outside of Afghanistan and, when we first met him, he didn't seem entirely sold on the idea of a media company succeeding in Kabul. "I thought, it's impossible that Afghans could make something like this," he says. "It must have come from another country. Everyone I knew felt the same way." But he needed a job, and he had a connection to draw on. "My uncle once worked for your father, making tea when he worked in the foreign ministry," he said. When we returned to Kabul, Jan Agha's uncle tracked us down and brought along his nephew and his son, Yar Mohammad. We hired them both.

Jan Agha is handsome, tall and imposing but with cheekbones so high and so prominent they appear carved onto his face like a Greek statue. He grew up in Salang, on the foot of the Hindukush, about seventy miles outside of Kabul—a formidable distance in those days over badly laid roads—in a poor family, without any access to education or work outside of hawking goods at the local market. Their lives were structured not around the changes in state power but around the daily grind of poverty. Many of the applicants told harrowing stories of their lives under Taliban rule, but when we asked Jan Agha, he shrugged. "To tell you the truth, our lives didn't change all that much," he said.

When he started working for us, Jan Agha's family would pester him with questions about what on earth was going on in that two-story house. "It's funded by the Aga Khan, isn't it?" a cousin said. "Where are you going with all those egg cartons?" his mother asked. Jan Agha shrugged. He had no answers. He didn't know where the money came from. He wasn't entirely sure, at first, why we were attaching the cardboard to the upstairs walls, or what each piece of equipment was for. (To be fair, actually, only Timmy knew for sure how to connect the microphone to the amplifier, or when to hit the sound delay.) But soon, like the rest of us, Jan Agha felt like he was in the middle of something important.

Jan Agha is tough, a former mujahid who'd fought against the Soviets, and although he was hired as an assistant and janitor, he soon took over the place. He had an almost pathological sense of responsibility to how the office looked, and would chastise the other cleaning staff for any refraction, no matter how minor. During the week, he slept in one of the studios. He liked for people to think he did so to be always on call, but really, his home was much too far away for him to commute back and forth. He was so commanding, and so certain of his place within the company, that the staff started to call him "Jan Agha Mohseni."

He also has a wicked sense of humor, which he preferred to direct at the power-drunk and power-hungry, whom he openly disdained. One day Moby's head of security arrived at the office, slouching onto a couch like he owned it, his gun propped on the armrest. "Get me a coffee," he barked, not looking at Jan Agha.

"How do you like it?" Jan Agha replied, knowing that coffee would have been a status symbol, a foreign taste that the head of security would have ordered only to impress other people in the office.

Thinking for a moment, the head of security glared at Jan Agha. "I like it how Saad Mohseni likes it," he growled. A moment later, Jan Agha returned with coffee so bitter and so strong, so different from the mild tea the man was used to, that he took one sip and, without thinking, spat it out onto the floor.

When Jan Agha was sick, we paid for his hospital care, arranging for him to be transferred from the second-rate facility where he had checked himself in to Kabul's top private hospital. When his son fell ill, the company sent him to India for treatment. After a few years, when Jan Agha told us he wanted to go on pilgrimage to Mecca, we paid for that as well.

Jan Agha stayed through everything. He pinned those egg cartons on the walls. He learned how to use the equipment. He tested his voice behind the microphone, calm and deep and introspective, particularly when he talked about Afghanistan.

He celebrated, however baffled he might have been by the content, when Arman FM first went live. He listened like the rest of us as taxi drivers blared the pop music from their windows so entire streets could hear. He made cup after cup after cup of tea for the staffers who couldn't believe what was happening, the government officials who visited to complain, and me and my siblings working until well after midnight.

Three years after he was hired, in 2006, Afghans protested in the streets of Kabul after a truck leading a US military convoy crashed into multiple cars during rush-hour traffic, killing at least five civilians and injuring many more. Rumors spread around the city about American soldiers shooting directly into the crowd that had surrounded the convoy. By then, Afghans living in Kabul were tired of the foreign military presence, of the billions of dollars of aid money they heard were pouring into the country but that did not improve their lives, of the dispatches from family living in the provinces, where air strikes had killed innocent civilians and the Taliban insurgency was raging. Afghans did not expect anyone to be held accountable. They filled the streets near the US embassy, prevented from reaching it by blockades of Afghan police officers and soldiers, and chanted, "Death to America," and "Death to Karzai." Soon the protests turned into riots, spreading through the city, including to the streets around Moby.

Jahid, Zaid, and I called a meeting. Most of the people we sent home, but some of our reporters went to cover the protests. Essential news staff had to stay in the office to produce the news for our radio and TV stations but, of course, we worried for everyone's safety. At that point, Moby had not suffered any major attacks. But we knew that many Afghans thought that our company was full of foreign agents, and even if the protests didn't arrive on our doorstep, the Taliban had recently become increasingly violent, using suicide bombings and IEDs, in the countryside, and they might see the chaos in Kabul as an opportune moment to infiltrate and attack. Even our security guards were scared, and they were right to be.

Jan Agha arrived at the meeting brandishing a gun. "I borrowed it from the head of security," he said, winking. While we evacuated the office of everyone but essential staff and the chants outside grew louder, Jan Agha positioned himself at the front gate, then still a flimsy metal gate typical of residential homes, holding his gun visible. That day, no one attempted to break into our offices, and eventually the crowds, as well as me and my siblings, went home. To make sure everything was okay, though, Jan Agha stayed put, just as he stayed in 2016 when a Taliban suicide bomber attacked a bus full of our employees, just as he stayed in 2018 when two of our journalists were killed while reporting on an explosion, and just as he stayed, nearly twenty years to the day he was hired, when the United States withdrew from Afghanistan.

CHAPTER 5

ARMAN LAUNCH

It started with a little music. Nothing fancy, nothing we had to think too much about—American pop, Bollywood hits, and singers like Ahmad Zahir, the "Elvis of Afghanistan," whose voice had been the soundtrack of 1960s and '70s Kabul before conflict squeezed the country of people and, incredibly, even when music was eventually banned. A soft launch broadcasting one CD of music—that was our goal for the first week. Jahid burned around twenty songs onto the CD, not giving the individual tracks too much consideration, thinking only that it would be a good way to test our signal before starting the real programing. And yet so many people listened on that first day, and things went so much more smoothly than anyone could have predicted, that Arman FM launched on April 16, 2003, about as softly as a nuclear explosion.

There was no such thing as a trial run. We scrambled to keep the air from going dead. Anyone passing by the studio who didn't immediately freeze when they saw a microphone was asked to talk into it, about whatever they wanted. Security guards and drivers came in to discuss the weather. Janitors shared details of their commutes to work that morning. Brand-new producers, without an ounce of experience, told stories of their youth in refugee camps. Some recited poems and jokes. They read lists of songs they planned to play or had played already, or favorite songs from the heyday of Afghan music. People so often said things without thinking into a live microphone that Timmy teased us that we had become experts at using the twenty-second delay button.

We had already hired a small staff to begin digitizing cassettes and CDs of Afghan music so that we could play it on air; shop-keepers began to complain to us that because of Arman FM, they lost their business selling cassettes of traditional music, all they had in stock, in one week. "Everyone wants the stuff they hear on Ar-man," they complained. We played international pop music with brief interludes for talking—I occasionally came on during the Top 40 countdown, using the stage name "Ahmad Popal," loosely named after my maternal grandfather's family name "Popalzai," hoping that if they saw the boss speaking so informally, the new DJs would follow suit—and soon the chatter between songs was as popular as the music itself. Within a few months we had expanded outside of Kabul, feeling a bit like explorers staking our claim with a radio antenna—as well as a transmitter to distribute a signal, a generator because there was no electricity, fuel to run the genera-tor, and a guard to protect it all—instead of a flag.

Turns out, Afghans want to hear ordinary people on the radio discussing ordinary things. They want to hear both of their of-ficial languages, and they want to hear those languages spoken in the accent they acquired as a refugee, or with the inflection of their cousin who had never left the country, in the way they speak it at home around the dinner table. And, contrary to the hand-wringing by the international community about whether Afghans were ready for a free media, our listeners really—more than anything, it seemed—wanted to hear women on the radio. Any complaints we got at first from conservatives complaining were outweighed by the praise we received from our listeners. Within six months, polling showed that three of our five most popular DJs were women.

Figuring that, like in Melbourne, morning drivers would want something catchy to listen to on their commute, we quickly devised a call-in show that could be broadcast during rush hour. On its own, it was not a revolutionary idea. But for Kabul at that time, it was evidence greater than any new NGO moving into a new office that the city was changing. We cast Massood and, to balance his cheekiness, the more conservative and serious Sima. Another no-brainer.

When Arman FM launched in spring 2003, I was in Australia, still working under the delusion that I could split my time between Kabul and Melbourne. "You've got to get back," Jahid called me. "This is some crazy stuff." Jahid had already quit his job at the AACA, which he had become head of after Ghani was appointed finance minister. The US had just invaded Iraq, and suddenly the fight for development resources had become backstabbing and political, and my brother wanted no part of it. Although Jahid wouldn't leave the development world immediately, I could sense his enthusiasm for Arman, and that he was beginning to believe that it was via independent media that he might make a difference in the country. I packed immediately. "I'll do some work remotely," I told my colleagues in Melbourne, but deep down I knew I was done with banking forever.

Kabul had changed immensely in the year since I'd first arrived. International donors and organizations were pouring into the country to establish schools, promising to achieve a higher level of literacy, for both girls and boys, than all prior Afghan generations. The city was beginning to seem safe, even hospitable and bustling. "People are starting to relax," Jahid told me. Men, once obligated to groom themselves according to the Taliban's rules, had shaved their beards and walked around the city proudly showing their pale chins and cheeks.

With Jahid having chosen to settle down in Kabul, Arman became a true family business. Jahid is much more introverted than Zaid and me; when he speaks, he is controlled and thoughtful, sometimes disarmingly patient while waiting for a response.

Unlike us, he can be a bit of a pessimist, guarded and skeptical. And yet he had embraced his work with the interim government, coordinating aid. Unlike Zaid and me, who only worked informally for the government as advisors, it took Jahid a couple of years to become fully disillusioned with government and aid work and move on to Moby full-time.

The three of us spent hours driving through Kabul over the coming months and years, through the logjam of intensifying traffic, documenting what we could of the changes in the city on our state-of-the-art camcorders and digital cameras. Bombed-out sites were taken over by construction crews that built schools and shopping malls, and new embassies and hotels and offices for NGOs, all eventually surrounded by high blast walls. Those spaces were filled with thousands of new staff, their drivers and janitors and housekeepers, and also security contractors hired by foreign governments to do the work that locals weren't trained to do.

Business owners looking to profit off the expat community's homesickness also soon poured in, bringing restaurants specializing in food that would have once seemed impossibly exotic in Kabul. We suddenly had Tex-Mex food, Lebanese food, and a French bakery. South Korean soldiers, aid workers, and missionaries preceded Korean restaurants (as well as one of our earliest foreign hires, a great technician named Phil Chung) until 2007, when the Taliban hijacked a bus carrying a group of missionaries from Kandahar to Kabul, and most South Koreans were compelled by their government to leave Afghanistan. A proper Thai restaurant opened in the same neighborhood as Moby, run by one really entrepreneurial Thai woman who also did the cooking. The foreign workers, from embassy staff to cleaners, were like a convoy of nomads, traveling from place to place together. Instead of following a spice route, they followed conflict.

In the beginning, there were so many journalists packed into this one city that we used to joke that every reporter in the world was there, even gossip columnists. And hundreds of thousands of Afghans, most of them returning from Pakistan and Iran, were back after a lifetime away as refugees. From the many glorious vantage points on Kabul's hilltops, the city spread out like a patient on an operating table, construction crews pounding buildings together, cars snaking along the crowded streets, smoke from new restaurants billowing into the gigantic Kabul sky.

During those years, Kabul had begun to feel nearly cosmopolitan. You could hear a dozen languages in one restaurant. Chicken Street, so called because it had once been a poultry market, was again alive with shops selling handmade rugs and jewelry, with some of the same shop owners as the 1970s, or their children, once again marketing to foreigners. Smaller hotels and guesthouses opened their doors to journalists and temporary workers.

It was an ecstatic time to be in Kabul, and I think that all Afghans, to some extent, were getting a little carried away. We liked hearing people say that Afghanistan had changed. We drank the Kool-Aid. Why not bask in thirty seconds of positive fame in the spotlight? Even when Zaid, Jahid, and I were stopped by a security guard in front of the Ariana Hotel—an old-school Western-style hotel, from 1945, it had become CIA headquarters, the ballroom converted into the not-so-inconspicuous "Tali-Bar"—and told to erase all footage we had taken in the proximity, we somehow found the enforcement of these rules comforting. The guard's stern diligence was a sign of stability, a commitment to the US-led project that was promising to transform the country.

It's not that we wanted the international community to stay forever; Afghans are famously a fiercely independent people. But we knew that before the internationals left, there needed to be huge changes within the Afghan government and its security forces for stability to take hold and last. Even then we feared that if Afghans could not trust their own institutions, whoever the Americans left behind in Kabul would just start fighting one another again.

WE TRIED HARD to forget that we were total novices, and instead chose to believe that because Arman FM had become so popular so quickly, we could learn how to keep it going. Before we launched, because it seemed like something a professional media company would do, we conducted a survey of one thousand households in Kabul, trying to gauge how popular our station would be compared to the news offerings like BBC or state radio. A few weeks later, we were shocked by the results. Almost everyone we polled said they wanted to listen to documentaries or religious programming. "We prefer not to listen to music," they said.

The survey results sounded to me like total nonsense. "They are giving the answers they think the government wants to hear," I complained to my siblings. "Or they're worried about what might happen to them if they gave the wrong answers," Jahid replied. Both the Communists and the Taliban had run police states, where authorities could drag you out of your home and lock you up: under the Taliban, because you listened to music or because you didn't go to the mosque enough; under both governments, because your preferences were out of step with what those in power permitted; or for no reason at all. Afghans had been conditioned to please or, more profoundly, to fear what could happen if we displeased authority.

We received plenty of criticism, of course. Initially, it was aimed at our hosts' colloquial way of speaking, which the educated elite looked down on. Then, it was about the pairing of women and men, the easy, informal way Sima and Massood spoke to each other, telling jokes about war, Sima mocking Massood for his vanity, Massood mocking Sima for her accent, the audience teasing both of them, everyone laughing. A newspaper published a cartoon with a man and woman together in bed, the caption reading, "Arman FM DJs."

But we heard Arman's chatter and pop music everywhere we went—taxis, stores, restaurants—much more than we heard the BBC reporting on the war, and certainly more than we heard the struggling RTA. Afghanistan was a country of young people, and what young person doesn't want to listen to music? We decided to conduct our own informal surveys, to try to sidestep whatever fear or cultural boundaries were keeping listeners from telling the truth. We joined other families in the parks for picnics, eating the food they ate, playing cards, and taking note of the music they listened to. We talked to taxi drivers until their heads hurt. We became close with Mirwais, a particularly chatty Moby security guard with an obscene hernia and a serious lack of talent for shooting a gun, who would regale any Moby executive he saw for ten minutes with his opinions about our programming. "This is our audience," I'd tell the other company higher-ups, when they complained that a guard was voicing his opinions. "We should listen to him."

Everywhere we went, we found clear indicators of Arman's popularity. In the airport, workers offered to help expedite me through long lines at immigration if I would ask one of Arman's DJs to dedicate a song to their wife. Letters piled up in the Kabul post office; Sima had already received dozens of marriage proposals through the mail. "This guy wrote an email today," our sister, Wajma, after she also left Australia for Kabul, said. "With a long lecture about how anti-religious the music we play is, and how terrible the types of conversation people have. Then, he wrote, PS I have a song request. 'Shalala Lala' by the Vengaboys."

In the mornings, I would go running in Ghazi football stadium, early enough that it was still dark, and a security guard would have to open up the gates to let me in. Alone, running in circles along the perimeter of the football pitch, I would count each cloud my breath made in the cold air and try not to think about the ghosts of Taliban brutality that kept most people away until the sun came up. I knew that people had been killed where I now jogged and stretched, where I listened to pop music through my headphones, where I dreamed of producing a show about football when a decent football league didn't exist yet in Afghanistan. Anyone in that stadium at that hour would have felt haunted by the recent past. But you do what you can to get over it. You have to. You want to run; you want to explore. You want the city to be new again. If you tried to avoid every part of Kabul where something terrible had happened, you would never leave your house.

And now, I reminded myself, things did seem different. By the time I had finished running, the stadium would be full of young men jogging together or kicking a soccer ball back and forth. Some mornings I would chat with them. "What kind of music do you listen to?" I'd ask. "What radio station do you put on in your car?" But other mornings I would just sit on the bleachers, drinking my water and watching the groups as they moved in calm circles around the track. There was something comforting about all those people, Afghans and internationals, stretching and exercising. They were not oblivious to the brutal recent history of the football stadium—some had probably lived nearby while it happened, others had scoured the news for stories about it in Peshawar—but instead of avoiding it, they chose to confront that history and move on. That bravery and optimism gave me confidence that we were doing the right thing.

Before the city became too dangerous, and Moby a stated target of Taliban violence, I took endless, aimless walks around Kabul by myself or with a single companion, eventually a bodyguard or two, and at the end within eyeshot of an armored car. I trudged up the hills along narrow, residential streets lined with identical concrete homes set behind metal gates, built for employees of governments long past; along wide, busy boulevards where drivers would pull over beside small restaurants to buy kebabs and savory stuffed flatbreads called bolani on their way home; by markets crowded with vendors manning their stalls piled with tomatoes and pomegranates, melons, and grapes, listening to the chorus of prices trying to drown out the call to prayer.

With a friend, I could walk for hours, to the shops, the parks, see what people were wearing and listening to, often on a Friday, when people were more relaxed and eager to engage with strangers. We'd listen as an old man told rapturous stories about Afghan music from his childhood, swaying to the memory. We'd shake our heads in shared frustration when a shop owner yelled at a speeding SUV. "They do that all the time," he'd complain. "Those warlords or rich guys with their convoys, they don't care about people like me."

You could tell a lot about a changing city by what was for sale in a small shop. Markets were flooded with products that had been previously unavailable, and more people were there with the means to buy them. Sweetened condensed milk usually meant people were drinking more coffee, which nodded to the international presence. Imported cheese nudging out the local varieties indicated a wealthier clientele. Once, in an audacious moment, I asked a shopkeeper about feminine hygiene products, and listened for ten minutes while he enthusiastically described the buying habits of international women, talking until my companion, red with embarrassment, asked if we could move on.

Everything in those early days told us that the formal survey we'd commissioned was wrong. Afghans wanted to listen to music. Later, when I met Tom Freston, he compared our venture to some of his experiences at MTV, when Christian conservatives from the American Bible Belt protested what they saw as a corrupting force, just as older, more conservative Afghans were pushing back against Arman. It doesn't matter what the surveys say, or how loud the voices are in opposition, or where the change is happening, Tom said. In the end, youth wins.

LATER THAT APRIL, the month we launched Arman FM, we hosted a kite-flying festival on a hill in the city that is host to the grand mausoleum of an assassinated king. Kite flying had been banned under the Taliban, and it was a hard rule to flout; kites, no matter how private the location of the flyer, are designed to be seen from a distance and, in Kabul, meant to fight one another. Crushed light bulbs are glued to the strings so they become sharp enough to slice through an opposing flyer's string, and make their kite fall to the ground.

We advertised the festival on the radio, offering free kites emblazoned with the logo of Roshan mobile, our first major corporate sponsor. Remembering the listless march of people up the hill for Nowruz the previous year, we advertised constantly, hoping we might draw enough of a crowd to qualify, if not as a real festival, at least as a celebration, an introduction to future gatherings.

Nothing, certainly not the surveys that suggested Afghans wished to stay inside listening to BBC documentaries, could have prepared us for the crowds that showed up that day, on the hill with the mausoleum. Thousands of people arrived at once, mobbing the Arman staffers who were handing out the kites, in their eagerness pushing against the tables and ripping some of the thin paper off the frames.

DJs who had gone to work the event called us in a panic. "We can't move," they said. "Everyone wants to meet us, to talk about what we are going to play." The crowds were friendly, ecstatic, but they were still crowds. The city was new, open, expanding, but it was still Kabul. Eight of our DJs, unable to move the bus through the crowd, had to walk an hour down the hill, ditching their Arman FM gear for nondescript scarves. Others stayed, turning the music up over the ruckus, amazed by the scene. It was a bright day, and I made my way slowly down the hill. Watching people as I passed, I immediately saw that the crowds, however rowdy, were joyful.

Later, a journalist friend showed us how to count people in a dense crowd by multiplying the number of people in a square inch of a photograph with the total number of square inches. "I think there are over a hundred thousand," he told us. We were astonished. The Kabul police had warned us in advance that they wouldn't be able to handle a large crowd, but we still hadn't considered hiring our own security. *It's just radio*, we had thought.

CHAPTER 6

CLEANING UP THE CITY

Listening to Sima and Massood on the morning show during those early years felt like listening to a brother and sister sitting around the table, teasing one another. Sima made fun of Massood's thick black hair. "For sure, it's fake," she said, while Massood took to describing Sima, who was still shy when not behind a microphone, as monstrously big and powerful, like a character from a tall tale. "Nearly seven feet tall," he said. Taxi drivers, recognizing Sima's voice when she got into their cars, would turn around in disbelief. "I thought you weighed three hundred pounds!"

We had no call screeners; Kabul didn't even have landlines during those days. Soon enough, we began acquiring mobile phones, and after an enterprising listener discovered Massood's personal number and shared it around the city, he started receiving call after call from locals eager to share their experience of Kabul, mostly during show hours but sometimes, to Massood's annoyance, at two in the morning. While an assistant answered the phone, Massood and Sima responded to the callers on air. "There's traffic on the way to the foreign ministry," one caller would say. "There's a pothole in the road out of the city," another reported. "Where are all the police?" another driver complained. "It's chaos on the streets!"

A week after the morning show debuted, the Kabul central post office, essentially unused during the Taliban period, was flooded with hundreds of letters from readers, most effusive, some asking

Sima for her hand in marriage, others begging to know what she looked like. "Take a photo with her and send it to me," relatives of Moby employees would whisper as they left for work. "You work at Arman?" a security officer would ask at a checkpoint. "Before I let you through, what does Sima look like?"

"Seven feet tall," we would always say. "Three hundred pounds."

Sima and Massood had a magical friendly chemistry, but the morning show really took off when they were joined by the worst driver Moby has ever employed. Humayoon Danishyar, my cousin, had studied sculpture at the Kabul School of Fine Arts. In 1992, when the second civil war erupted and battle raged in Kabul, he was nearly forty years old and had been making a living as an artist, after having served his compulsory military service. Knowing that he needed to leave, and anticipating, like many, mass casualties and a takeover of the government by one of the Islamist factions, he destroyed all of his work—large, abstract sculpture, photos of Kabul street life, paintings featuring women—before militants could do it for him and took his young family to Pakistan.

In his years in Pakistan, Humayoon felt watched. Police constantly checked to make sure his documents were legal and up to date. He moved frequently—no one wanted to rent to refugees—and worked selling jewelry in a market that catered mostly to Afghans. He went to Afghan restaurants, sent his children to schools that were run by Afghans and taught in Dari. And he assumed he would never return home.

Although Humayoon was more than a decade older than me, I felt close to him and his family growing up, a connection that was actively fostered by my parents. My mother frequently wrote him letters after he moved to Pakistan, asking after his kids, whose lives were so different from her own. Later, when I talked to him directly, I usually wanted to know one thing: Did he have any sense of what was happening in Afghanistan?

Humayoon always told me whatever he knew. He treated me as his peer even though he was not only older he had also endured so much more, while I was a privileged college dropout with a faint Australian-American accent. Humayoon's parents were still living in Kabul, and he had some sense of what their lives were like, although they carefully censored their letters to him, and he did the same in his replies. It took weeks to receive the letters anyway, since they were sent via Afghans crossing the border, and by then any news of the country was old.

In the mid-'90s, around nine months before the Taliban came into power, Zaid and I flew to Pakistan to visit Humayoon, staying for a few nights in a hotel near his apartment in Islamabad. He hadn't seen us since we were children, when Humayoon would take me on the back of his bicycle to football games, entertaining us with his wild, inexhaustible humor. He was the type of person who rarely seemed glum. But when he saw us that first night in Islamabad, he seemed to suddenly realize the time that had gone by since he took a sledgehammer to his sculptures, and piled his young children in the back of a truck racing to the border, he and his wife covering the children's ears so the gunfire didn't scare them. "Time passes quickly for refugees," he told me.

In September 2002, during our second visit to Kabul, I called him on his mobile phone in Islamabad. "Hey," I said. "We're starting this business. Would you come join us?"

Humayoon said something like, "I'd be delighted!," which made me laugh. "You sound so formal," I told him. "Like a Brit accepting an invitation to tea."

"Well, I'm serious," Humayoon said. "Of course I'll come." Without much money, he had been waiting for a viable way to get back. "When would you need me?"

"How's tomorrow?" I said, half joking. It took my cousin two days to return to Kabul.

KABUL WAS NOT yet a good place for an artist to scrape together an income. But Humayoon knew his way around the city, and began to drive us, in part because he needed the work and was family, and in part because we wanted to spend time with him. Humayoon is hilarious, with a fondness for double entendre and a magnetic personality that could shake the rigidness out of a steel rod. He has a way with people. More than once he talked his way through a military checkpoint with a funny story, the Afghan policeman's ready gun shaking from laughter.

"Kabul feels peaceful," he told us over dinner one night in the office. "But that peace is eerie." He worried about Karzai bringing former mujahideen commanders into the halls of power, because he saw what we saw, that those men had assumed positions in the palace close to the interim president and seemed to have his ear. "What if there's another war?" he worried.

"That used to be an apartment building." He would point out the window as he drove, gesturing toward one of the many flattened buildings. "That used to be a school. My cousin got married there." He wasn't prone to melancholy but returning was hard for him. He described those early days as a roller coaster. "It's the happiness of returning to your country," he told us. "And the sadness of seeing that country destroyed. The happiness of seeing your family after so long. And the sadness of worrying that the new government will bring the old guys back to power." Mostly, though, he told us, sitting in the Arman office while Jan Agha brought us cup after cup of tea and Sima and Massood practiced in the studio, "It's the happiness of feeling like you can help rebuild."

I don't think that Humayoon will mind me saying he was a truly awful driver, the kind who seemed to go suddenly blind when confronted with a street sign or a wandering pedestrian, who every four or five days would bring the car in with a new dent claiming the traffic median came out of nowhere. It was partly due to his terrible driving, and our desperation to get him off the road, that he ended up as one of Arman's most beloved hosts, as much of a household name, according to one internationally funded poll, as Hamid Karzai himself.

In the beginning, my cousin would call in to Sima and Massood to report the traffic, so animated that he could make the story of a fender bender sparkle. "Hey, avoid this intersection, it's full of police. Be careful of this particular road, someone really needs to fix these potholes, what is anyone in government even doing?" Like Massood, listeners got ahold of his phone number, and soon people started calling him with their own traffic news, which he passed along, cradling his clunky mobile phone against his shoulder, shouting jokes at Sima and Massood. Eventually, not wanting to let down any callers, my cousin juggled a dozen mobile phones and even more SIM cards, and started taking grainy photos of his drives, so the hosts could include more detail.

"Why don't you go into the studio and describe it yourself?" I said to him one day. He happily took his place in the DJ's empty chair, much more confident with a microphone than a stick shift.

Not long after, Humayoon arrived at Arman to deliver a script, but when he got there the studio was empty. He walked through the office, looking for anyone, until he finally found Timmy. Our consultant was panicked—the studio shouldn't be empty; the airwaves shouldn't be quiet. "We don't have time to find anyone else," he said to Humayoon. "You'll have to read it." Afterward, Timmy called me. "Humayoon has a really good voice," he said. "He should be on the radio full-time."

Humayoon was comfortable on air, perhaps too much at home. He was an Afghan patriot who had a deep skepticism of and well of resentment against Pakistan, where he had felt dehumanized. One day, without our knowing it, he got behind the microphone to air his grievances.

"Pakistan would destroy Afghanistan if it could!" he shouted into the mic, uncharacteristically inflamed with anger. He continued, citing the Pakistani military and intelligence services and their history of interfering in our politics and providing a safe haven to the Taliban, and how we as a country now had the chance to become truly independent. Humayoon has always been a bit conspiratorial—he's not alone, even Karzai was prone to it—but, as often happens with conspiracy, there was a general truth behind what he was saying. Pakistani interference in Afghanistan is real, and with each heated declaration he became more animated, his voice louder. It wasn't until he began referencing Afghan poetry, though, that things became truly incendiary. "You don't know how brave you are until you are in a war," he recited. "You can't imagine your own strength until you fight for your country." Young men started calling the studio. "We are packing bags for the border," they told Humayoon.

My cousin is prone to exaggeration. It's part of what makes him such a commanding storyteller. When he recounts that radio broadcast now, you'd think he had summoned a militia to Jalalabad to fend off an imminent Pakistani invasion when, in reality, all he did was stoke a few teenage tempers in Kabul. But he did have power behind the microphone. "You need a show," I said, laughing. "But you have to be careful. We can't use the radio to send people's sons to war."

Kabul was growing at breakneck speed, Afghans moving back from the places they had lived as refugees or relocating from the provinces, where reconstruction efforts had yet to begin in earnest and there were fewer opportunities. For these transplants, the city could be exciting, but it was unfamiliar and perhaps hard to make sense of, with both the ghostly remnants of an authoritarian state pummeled by war and the exuberant early days of a promised better future.

Practical matters fell through the cracks. Who oversees trash collection? Why was this well suddenly dry? How do I file paperwork for my new job? This road is falling apart; we have been without electricity for two weeks; the traffic outside our living room window is becoming unbearable; the school is still closed. War or no war, people still want running water and a school to send their children. Fighting or no fighting, people still hate traffic jams; they still want reliable city workers; they still want to know why they should pay taxes.

There was no way of getting accountability from public officials at institutions that were learning how to function in this new Afghanistan, where there was a shortage of skilled labor, where development money was starting to pour in and disappearing just as fast. People were starting to grow frustrated with the judiciary and the police, which were proving to be ineffectual or corrupt or threatened into submission by warlords and other strongmen. The international security presence, in some ways comforting for those of us living in Kabul, would become increasingly unbearable outside of the city.

Humayoon joined Sima and Massood on a new call-in show we named *Cleaning Up the City*. Starting at 7:00 a.m., three times a week, Kabul residents could call the hosts to give news about traffic, gripe about garbage collection, ask for romantic advice, and express their worries about the transitional government, the American troops, the increasing violence in the provinces, and, when these happened, the Taliban attacks in Kabul. Not receiving any clarity from their government or the international donors, Afghans called Arman FM.

Massood, Sima, and Humayoon did more than listen; they made the show into something like a live investigative newsroom for issues as minor as a leaking pipe and as dire as early signs of corruption. If someone called about trash piling up on the street, they would dial up the head of sanitation. "Can someone go to collect the garbage?" they'd ask, and, often, someone would. "My kid's school allows bullying," a parent would report, and Massood would keep them on the line while he tracked down the principal. A taxi driver called wanting to alert other drivers to a con he had just fallen for. "A man got into my car carrying two ducks," he said. "At one point they were making a lot of noise, so he asked me to pull over so he could dump them on the side of the road. I said, no, don't leave them there! I'll take them. But when I got out of my car to get the ducks, the man drove my taxi away." Humayoon had to cover his microphone to laugh. "Yes, yes, sir," he said after he had collected himself. "Thank you for letting the people of Kabul know about this dangerous crime."

"Well, it *was* a carjacking," I said to Humayoon later, although I was also laughing. In the scheme of things that were happening and had happened in Afghanistan, a crime like something out of a children's book, involving bothersome ducks and a gullible driver, was good comic relief.

As the city expanded and the problems deepened, the complaints grew more serious. Listeners reported attempted bribery at the airport, a hit-and-run, a kidnapping. A young couple called. They were from different ethnic groups and were in love. "Our families won't let us marry," they said. "But if we can't, we will kill ourselves." There were stories of corruption, where what the officials reported was happening in their grant reports was the exact opposite of what was being witnessed on the ground. "They said they are building a school here," said a listener calling from a town north of Kabul. "But we haven't seen a single brick." Massood called the construction company that had been contracted to do the work. "If there's no school," he asked them, "then where is the money going?" When a wedding party was bombed by US forces, the groom's father called *Cleaning Up the City* to mourn his murdered loved ones, and the three hosts wept with him.

"We are fighting the Taliban and there's no ammunition," a soldier called one morning from Helmand province. The minister of interior happened to be at Moby, preparing for an interview on a later show. In those early years, much of the insurgency was being fought against by both the military and the hapless Afghan police force, which the interior minister oversaw. Massood pulled him into the Arman studio. "Can you tell this young fighter when he can start using his gun?" he asked the minister. Another call came in right after, from another soldier, also in Helmand, who hadn't been paid his salary in six months. "What sort of minister are you?" he said. "Bragging on the radio about everything you do for the country. You have to take care of the people who fight for you." The minister squirmed uncomfortably, promising the soldier his salary, telling the other soldier stationed in Helmand to expect a helicopter of supplies.

Sima, Massood, and Humayoon shared the almost superhuman quality of not being awed or frightened by people in power. They could call a minister, a judge, the head of Kabul security forces, and ask them hard questions straight from the angry mouths of listeners. "I have a person whose only job is to answer the phone when Sima calls," ministers used to joke. "You should see their face when it's her on the line; they are terrified." While the show vehemently condemned corruption and thuggery, the corrupt thugs in question couldn't help but pay attention to our hosts. One such fan, a story goes, after kidnapping a Moby driver, shouted his ransom demands into the driver's phone. "I want to meet Humayoon," he said.

Even if they didn't like the hosts, which many must not have, they were forced to listen. "Officials don't hang up when they hear that it's us," Massood said. "They want to clear their names." Ministers put on Arman in the car, telling their drivers, "If you hear my name, turn it up."

ONE MORNING MANY years into the show's twenty-year run, Massood's phone rang in the studio. He handed it to Sima, who as show producer screened the calls while Massood and Humayoon co-hosted. "I'm a baker," the man on the line said. He was speaking quickly, in a hushed tone. "You can't use my name. And please don't put this call on the air. These men are dangerous."

Sima retreated from the microphones into a back room, an unusual move. On *Cleaning Up the City*, Massood liked to say, there was no behind-the-scenes. When Sima picked up a call, she usually did so close enough to Massood and Humayoon that the microphones could pick up her conversation; the studio was small enough for listeners to feel they were eavesdropping on every part of the conversation. When she called a minister or a security official, she explained out loud who she was trying to reach and why before dialing the number. "They're not picking up," she would say. "We'll keep trying."

Now she was speaking softly. "I'm by myself," she said to the baker. "What happened?"

The night before the baker had been passing through a checkpoint in Paghman district, outside of Kabul, when he heard women screaming from inside the checkpoint office, a small, tiled room set right upon the road median. Three men walked toward his car as he stopped it, and he immediately sensed that he was not supposed to be there. "I'm a baker," he explained to Sima. "I'm up very early and I need to pick up my supplies before I start work." Most people were still asleep while he did his morning chores. Whatever was happening at the checkpoint seemed to be timed for when they thought no cars would be on the road.

Taking the phone back into the studio, Massood called the head of security in that part of Paghman. It happened to be close to Massood's hometown, and the official picked up right away. "We got a call about some women screaming at a checkpoint last night," he said. "What happened?"

The head of security went quiet. "Nothing happened," he said. He hung up.

For a few days they couldn't get any more information. The

baker had described the men as well known in the area, powerful and feared. They were rumored to be former mujahideen, in and out of jail many times, strongmen that people assumed had connections in government. No local wanted to say anything against them.

But Sima couldn't stop thinking about the call from the baker. He had been terrified; he said that he knew the men, or at least their type, and what they were capable of. And yet whatever he heard coming from the checkpoint office had been bad enough that he had called Arman and risked being identified on the radio. Why were the women screaming?

The next day, a few minutes into *Cleaning Up the City*, Sima got another call. Massood and Humayoon watched her again take it into the back room, closing the door. When she came back into the studio, she was crying. "It's a doctor at the hospital," she said. "He's treating the women. They were raped. He doesn't want his name mentioned."

Massood took the call on the air. "They brought the women in last night," the doctor said. "One of them is pregnant, but she was beaten so badly, we're not sure the baby is going to survive."

The story was a defining moment for Arman. Our hosts wouldn't let it go, even when the authorities appeared to show no sign of arresting the men. Every day for a week Sima, Massood, or Humayoon brought up the story on air. "Remember the attacks on those women in Paghman?" they said. "Still, no one wants to do anything. No arrests have been made, even though the attorney general knows who the men are." They called the office of the attorney general, asking, "What is the latest? What progress have you made finding the men who did this?" Listeners lost patience; they started asking to be put on the line with the government authorities. "Come on, you have everything, proof, names," they complained. "Why haven't you made any arrests?"

Because of our hosts, as well as that brave baker and doctor, a crime that would otherwise have been hushed became national news. Even though they were told the same thing every day by the attorney general's spokesperson, they continued to call. When they received threats on their own mobile phones, they aired those threatening calls on the show, and continued to talk about the story. After a few weeks of trying, they convinced one of the victims' brothers to talk about the case on air. Relatives of the alleged rapists called in as well. "My son isn't like this," one of their mothers said. She was crying. "We are even hearing from Karzai's office that we should stop pushing the story," Massood told me. "They say, if you don't stop, no one will want to go to this place. But we don't want people to go to this place, while these men are free."

About ten days after that first call, seven men were arrested. A televised trial—Afghanistan's first—followed within days, and a month later five of the men were executed and the other two given life sentences. We felt triumphant that the men had been caught, but more ambivalent about the gruesome sentences; human rights groups likewise made their disapproval known in their reports. Massood didn't visit the area for five years; he was so scared of retaliation from people who knew him from Arman. Sima, more than ever, was relieved that throughout the years we hadn't given up telling people she was seven feet tall and weighed three hundred pounds, as fierce and imposing as her radio persona.

PART II

CHAPTER 7

EUROPE, 2022

The senior official would not back down, and I was determined not to lose my cool. It was hard enough, at this point, to hold the interest of Western policymakers on the topic of Afghanistan. Their minds had drifted to other pressing problems, and they had closed the door; many couldn't even bear to look through the window. I had learned all too quickly after the disaster of 2021 that if the foreigners I was trying to talk to about Afghanistan felt berated or criticized or backed into a corner, the conversation would be over before it even began. "I'm not going to engage with the Taliban," she told me, sitting stiffly on the sofa. "Never."

"Why?" I asked, although I knew what she would say. I had heard it as a striving young businessman in Uzbekistan, digging for firsthand details about what was going on across the border, then in Australia, at the dinner tables of political exiles like us. These days, nearly two years after the US withdrawal from Afghanistan, I heard it all the time, a reaction to terrible cruelty that was unwittingly cruel itself.

"We cannot engage with the Taliban because of what they're doing to girls and women," the senior official told me. She seemed pained; it wasn't an easy thing for her to talk about. "We don't have to engage with people who don't respect our values."

Since the withdrawal, I have not been back to Afghanistan, but traveling constantly, from London to Oslo to Delhi, trying to keep Moby, and Afghanistan, on the world's radar; securing partners for our new projects, particularly educational programming that we hope will help prevent Afghan girls from falling too far behind while the Taliban uphold their ban on girls' secondary education. I've implored high-ranking international government officials not to turn their backs on a country they had invested so much in, and had professed to care about, but that they now seemed to be dismissing as a sore spot, as hopeless. The future of the people, I would argue, requires engagement. It is the only way to ameliorate the misery for Afghans who could not flee, who remain in a country that has since then been choked by sanctions and an ever-worsening humanitarian crisis. Our education programs would help the girls the senior official professed to care about, but they require rational engagement with the Taliban government.

For the past two years, I'd traveled from capital to capital, NGO to NGO, donor to donor, trying to make a case for safeguarding the gains of the past two decades, which I had seen take hold most tenaciously in Afghan civil society, sometimes because of, and sometimes in spite of, foreign aid and investment. "It's the greatest and most lasting thing to come out of the twenty-year war," I'd say. "It's the legacy that Afghans have created for other Afghans." Supporting institutions like the media is one of the best ways to help Afghans out of poverty and away from the riptide of extremism, I'd insist.

Those conversations didn't always go smoothly. I found myself, bewildered at an embassy reception or think tank meet and greet, comforting Western politicians as they confessed to feelings of guilt over the way the international community left so suddenly, abandoning Afghans. "It's not your fault," I'd tell them, as though they were a child and Afghanistan a glass of spilled milk.

I'd started to feel like an aging actor at a Hollywood party, once attractive and now making a case for my own relevance. It used to be that combating Islamic radicalism was a top global priority, and now people seemed to have given up. There've been so many other things to worry about—climate change, Russia's invasion of Ukraine, China, the pandemic and related financial crisis, the migrant crisis (as Western countries tend to label it), Gaza—and there's also the bitterness of acknowledging the Taliban's victory, their own defeat. The Americans had created an enemy, lost to that enemy, and then left. Once the Americans decided it was over, most other countries also quickly fell in line.

"Look at what we've achieved with ISIS," experts and diplomats and government officials would say at these forums and panels and receptions. "We fought against their brutality and won."

"Sure," I'd reply. "You were also part of a forty-two-nation military alliance that was defeated by a group with far less money, and far fewer weapons," I couldn't help reminding them, a group that many of them moreover were willing to make a deal with at the American-led peace talks in Doha.

Sometimes, I'd frame the argument in a way that might capture an American's attention, invoking the polarization in American politics and the need to engage with those you disagree with the most, even those whose views you despise. I'd not be entirely successful; no one was eager to see the parallels. "We just had to cut ties with the Taliban," American officials would tell me. "We had no choice." If President Ashraf Ghani had stayed and provided some kind of a window dressing for a transitional government, maybe there would have been space for negotiations. But Ghani had fled. I can't cry over spilled milk either.

Disengagement with the Taliban now, and condemnation of their policies, can certainly seem justifiable, even ethical. While the Taliban leadership has, at times, sent mixed messages and even seemed eager to gain international legitimacy, at other times it seems that their stances on women's rights, on education, on minority rights, on inclusive governance are just as rigid and uncompromising as ever. The Taliban government faces a panoply of challenges; hard-line pronouncements alone cannot feed a starving people or provide them with homes and jobs, let alone respond to the effects of global crises like climate change. Sanctions and the freezing of central bank funds were measures imposed to put pressure on the Taliban, but it is the Afghan people who've suffered.

Haven't we learned, time and time again, that disengagement with a totalitarian regime only punishes the people who live under that regime? "If your intention is to make the Taliban suffer," I'd tell the people I meet, "let me assure you, as someone who talks to them and to people on the ground every day, they are not suffering." Look at the leadership: No one is malnourished. Off the battlefield and in the Arg, the presidential palace in Kabul where the senior leadership meets, they have only fattened up. The rumor around Kabul is that if you have a wedding or any kind of gathering, you better be prepared for some Taliban fighters to come in uninvited expecting a full plate. Meanwhile, an Afghan family of ten might have only one breadwinner left, with everyone else unemployed.

"Listen," the senior official told me. "We give a lot of money on the humanitarian side."

"For years, you threw money at the country like it was full of beggars," I said as patiently as I could manage. "It'd help someone for a year. But your commitment needs to be a bit more serious than that."

At that point, the official lost her cool, stiffening a little in her chair, raising her voice slightly. I wondered if her assistant found it ironic—the stoic European showing her temper while the Afghan, someone from a country they thought of only as a place of war, stayed calm, on the outside at least.

"We don't want to legitimize them," she said.

"It's too late," I replied. "You legitimized them to the world and to Afghans when you supported America's talks with them, and decided not to stick around, and by doing that, you allowed them to take over the country. For the sake of the Afghan people, I ask you not to turn your back on Afghanistan."

SINCE THE US withdrawal, I talk to my contacts within the Taliban regularly—they are high-ranking officials in Kabul and the provinces who consider themselves to be pragmatists. I try to get a sense of where they may be open to debate and some compromise, and they, in turn, want to know what's planned for Moby—what stories we are reporting on, whether they could get on a panel Arman or TOLO is hosting or have one of their press conferences covered. Unlike their original iteration in the 1990s, this new cadre of Taliban are much more media savvy; they, too, are part of the Internet generation. These self-described pragmatists are eager to have the Taliban government recognized by the international community but confess to being unsure of how to get the leadership—older and doctrinaire—in Kandahar to budge on any issue.

For obvious reasons, sanctions come up again and again in these conversations; lifting them, my contacts tell me, would be part of what they refer to as "confidence-building measures" that could be the beginning of negotiations. Without that possibility, they see no reason to come to the bargaining table. Sometimes, they express fury about their image in international media, or they want to argue about a TOLO story that they feel has been unfair to them. Often, they are wrong. Sometimes they have a point. As the world has receded from Afghanistan, and as both international and local media coverage have diminished, it has become even more important that Moby continues to operate in Afghanistan, sending reporters across the provinces in an effort to give the world some kind of view of the ordinary Afghans who might otherwise be forgotten.

A recent United Nations Security Council report about the

Taliban having a close relationship with Al Qaeda and providing it and other terrorist groups a safe haven in Afghanistan had the pragmatists particularly worried. "If the world believes the report, it will delay lifting sanctions," they say correctly. I bring up human rights and women's rights again, an impasse that they created themselves. "Unless you show real effort to be more inclusive," I say, "these governments won't budge on sanctions."

The Taliban government has been ruling with fear, ratcheting up restrictions on women's rights, including their right to work for international organizations; it has detained journalists and harassed aid workers. Reports on executions and public lashings in the provinces and in Kabul have been frequent. Yet it is against the backdrop of this physical and psychological violence that it becomes even more important to engage with the Taliban, to better understand what various groups within the group are thinking and debating. As I always say, they are not a monolithic organization, and Afghan society is not the same society as of the '90s. The international community cannot simply lecture, they cannot only threaten and punish or pull away and expect the Taliban to behave differently as a result. The Taliban were not vanquished by NATO forces, and twenty years after being routed from Kabul, they prevailed again. They see themselves as the ultimate survivors.

Many of the people my colleagues and I speak to within the Taliban can be fairly described as thin-skinned. They don't like being criticized, and they don't like being ignored. They rage over the decades of violence they've endured, and smart over what they view as ongoing disrespect; they crave recognition as the legitimate representatives of Afghanistan more than anything else. And they are angered by the constant assailing of their education policies. During the twenty years of American presence in Afghanistan, the subject of girls' education became a point of humiliation for the Taliban. Many are reacting to a familiar pattern: the international community comes in, builds a school with a grab bag of donations, slaps on the decals of various international NGOs, and congratulates each other on opening day. "If the Taliban were still here, these girls would not be able to go to school," a Western official would declare at the ribbon-cutting ceremony. Rather than making education an Afghan project, we let foreigners with their own agendas take victory laps around our schoolyards.

The Taliban would then look at those schools and say, "This school isn't Afghan. They aren't teaching our values. We won't allow it to remain open." And, sure enough, when they took over in August 2021, one of the first decisions they took was to stop adolescent girls from going to school. Their approach to education, for both boys and girls, is about exerting control. Hundreds of religious schools have been built across Afghanistan since the Taliban takeover. Most are for boys, though, according to their Ministry of Education, girls of all ages should be allowed to attend these madrassas.

Their view of themselves as real Afghans responding to oppressive regimes or foreign influence can be traced back to their origin, emerging in the wake of the decade-long Soviet occupation that left the country ravaged, and during the disorder and brutality of the 1990s civil war, when ordinary Afghans suffered daily abuse, theft, and corruption. Many of the fighters then were young men who'd been indoctrinated in madrassas while growing up as refugees in Pakistan. They saw themselves as a righteous movement, and after disarming the warring militias and bringing much of the countryside and Kabul under their control, the Taliban compelled all Afghans to live under their puritanical interpretation of Sharia. It was in this harsh fashion that they brought law and order, and what might have looked to many like something resembling a relative peace to much of the country.

In the 1990s, the Taliban were led by Mullah Muhammad

Omar, an ascetic village preacher based in Kandahar who'd make the fateful decision to not hand over Osama bin Laden to the United States after 9/11. After his death in 2013, Mullah Akhtar Mansour, a relatively worldly leader, took over until his death in an American drone strike in 2016. Since then, the group has been led by Mawlawi Haibatullah Akhundzada, a religious scholar of the most conservative ilk, and well known as someone who does not brook dissent. A recluse like Mullah Omar, Akhundzada is said to reside in Kandahar province, not watch TV, and only receive news reports through BBC Pashto. As far as we know, he has visited Kabul only a few times since 2021. During the years of battles with the Americans and the Afghan National Army, his authority was kept in balance by the Taliban commanders; the tactical decisions regarding when to fight and where and for how long were at least as important as enforcing the extremist ideology that distinguishes the Taliban. As it became clear that international forces were itching to leave, he also authorized his political deputy, Mullah Abdul Ghani Baradar, to negotiate with the Americans in Doha, while he stayed behind the scenes in Pakistan.

But after Kabul fell, and the day-to-day military operations took a back seat to questions of governance and religious law, Akhundzada ascended to his full authority, presiding over gatherings of religious scholars, and appointing ministers who have all pledged their allegiance to him. Government began to transform according to his conservative views; in the Taliban cabinet, for instance, the Ministry of Propagation of Virtue and Prevention of Vice has been revived and the Ministry of Women's Affairs eliminated.

From the outside it may look like the Taliban will surely lose its grip on the country, their theocratic certainties pitted against the needs and wants of some forty million Afghans. On the ground, however, it's a deeply complex scenario in which an organization comprising several different viewpoints contends with the rigid views of their leadership, not to mention shifting regional politics, and what steps need to be taken to achieve international recognition. They face pressure from Afghans who have fundamentally changed over the past twenty years, who demand that schools reopen and women be allowed to work; they worry about Afghans who might join IS-KP if they see the Taliban as weak. Unity, no matter these internal debates, is paramount to their survival. Millions of dollars had been spent over two decades—by both the US and the former Afghan governments—trying to fracture and weaken the movement, to no avail, and now that they had won, the Taliban leaders were certainly not going to lose their standing by infighting. And engagement, in my view, is the only way to make life better for the Afghans who live under them.

When we meet in person in the UAE or Qatar, we often discuss girls' education. Even as we develop our education programs at Moby—hour-long radio shows, thirty-minute TV shows for those who can access them online or by satellite, terrestrial, or cable—it's crucial that we do our best to predict the Taliban's leadership reaction at every step. The shows, hosted by Afghan teachers who are now out of work, teach subjects that would be easier to defend as important, even to the Taliban, like chemistry and biology taken directly from the Afghan curricula, rather than potentially more controversial subjects like history, literature, or civic education. The shows follow the established curriculum for these subjects to the letter. Technically, we aren't breaking any of the Taliban's rules or testing any red lines, although those rules and red lines change daily and according to whomever is enforcing them.

Many of the Taliban members my colleagues and I speak to insist they want girls to be educated. They understand that the issue is the number one reason preventing most other governments from engaging with them. They tell me they have daughters of their own who attended schools in Pakistan and Qatar. But they do not know how to push back against the policies set forth by the leadership in Kandahar, without splintering their ranks and unity. They describe the ways they try; they make assurances that they will continue trying. Still, after these meetings, I often feel like the foreign officials I meet on the road, frustrated by the lack of positive action, angered by the continuing disregard for people's basic rights. I wonder what exactly is the point of these pragmatists describing their more moderate beliefs to me when Afghanistan's girls have now been out of secondary school for years now. Is it all bluster? Am I wasting my time?

The defense minister, the son of Mullah Omar, the movement's founder, travels to Doha, in an apparent effort to connect his government with international powers and perhaps move the needle toward negotiation and a lifting of the pressures at home. But still those girls sit at home. A conference is organized in Tashkent in July 2022 with Taliban pragmatists, but later that year the Taliban ban women from working for international NGOs and then the UN. (Many women, the sole breadwinners in their families, continue working at these aid organizations, despite the official ban, because of engagement with Taliban at a local level.) My contacts call me, and I try to keep an open mind, as Afghanistan plunges deeper into a humanitarian crisis, but still women remain banned from parks, forced to cover themselves head to toe, instructed not to leave the house to go far without a male companion (another rule that is inconsistently enforced and often defied, at least for now). A hard-line higher education minister is appointed, and he bans women from attending even the gender-segregated classes at universities. And another school year begins without girls above sixth grade.

The culture minister, Khairullah Khairkhwa, refuses to talk to me directly, but through intermediaries I hear rumors of his efforts to challenge conservative leadership. "If all of his decisions are going to be vetoed at the top, why even bother having an information and culture minister?" I blurted out in frustration to some of my contacts, knowing it might make it back to Khairkhwa. By early 2023, Moby's news bulletins and current affairs shows on TOLO had run over a thousand stories about girls' and women's education; we find clerics to put on the air who will condemn the ban along religious lines; we question, gently, members of the Taliban when they try and fail to justify the ban on live talk shows and panels.

We'd also broadcast several shows around the first anniversary of the American withdrawal. We invited Taliban officials on air, asking them to offer a cohesive vision for the future of the country, which they stumble over. We prepared exclusive interviews with the minister of mines and petroleum, an important figure for Afghanistan's economic prospects. The brother of a Talib who was killed in a US drone strike came on air, and so did John Bolton, President Trump's former national security advisor. We hosted a panel of prominent Afghan women's rights activists about all that they've lost over the past year; TOLO's host covered her face with a mask, but we did not compel our guests to do so. The rest of the time we filled with historical documentaries about the nineteenth- and early-twentieth-century wars fought between the British Empire and Afghanistan.

And, in the meantime, we were building the studios in the basement where we planned to produce the new educational programming. The set looked nicer than a typical classroom in a Kabul public school, bright and cheery, transformed between shoots from an elementary classroom to a middle school. Professional teachers with several years of experience host the shows. Many of them are women who have lost work since the American withdrawal. In between the lessons, the plan is to broadcast educational entertainment—game shows and spelling bees, *Sesame Street*–type shows for young kids, and science experiments for the older ones. Each day we hope to run educational programming with four to six hours of original content on a dedicated channel.

Since 2007, we've broadcast our entertainment and news channels via satellite as well as terrestrial and cable, to make sure Afghans beyond Kabul can also access our shows. Afghans, as resourceful as ever, find a way to watch what they can. In some Kabul neighborhoods, one household buys a satellite dish for the entire street, and ten homes connect to it via rudimentary cables. In the provinces, villagers use one of the hundreds of local cable operators across the country. Those with access to the Internet can download shows off our app, which is available thanks to lessons from the days of distance learning during the pandemic, and a quarter of the population is said to have access to the Internet via their phones. By January 2024, we'd begun airing the educational programming, hoping for the best.

As I have for twenty years, and ever more profoundly since 2021, I live with two opposing visions of Afghanistan's future in my head at all times. In one, the educational programs work. They make Afghan girls feel less alone, and their parents less anxious. Afghanistan doesn't fall behind as precipitously as it otherwise would, and when things improve—in whatever way that happens—Afghan children and teenagers are able to pick up where they left off. The programs, in no way an alternative to schools, are a temporary Band-Aid and only need to be used for a short period. It is not hard for me, as an optimist, to imagine such things happening.

I can also just as easily imagine everything going wrong and our new programming harming the people we are trying to help, putting new pressure on them, shining a light where they would prefer to stay hidden. Some nights, as I lie awake and think about Afghanistan, I fear there is no bottom to this worst-case scenario. Life only gets harder for millions of Afghans. There are more women begging in their blue chadors on the streets, their babies lying on blankets beside them as evidence of their desperation. With caches of weapons and droves of experienced fighters sitting idly in the provinces with nothing to do, no jobs, no school, no money, no wives, Afghanistan becomes Somalia. The country fragments. The Taliban continue to get harsher and more violent in their struggle to maintain power. Afghanistan is again a nation of refugees, many of whom will never see their home again. I try not to let my mind go there.

CHAPTER 8

TOLO TV

KABUL, 2004

In the summer of 2004, nearly three years after the US invaded Afghanistan and toppled the Taliban regime, the country was preparing for its first democratic presidential election, scheduled first for July, then September, and finally for October. Karzai was the clear front-runner, handpicked by the Americans at Bonn, backed by the Loya Jirga, and the incumbent as interim president, but Afghans still looked forward to voting day as a turning point in their nation's history and a time of celebration. At Moby, our news team prepared to cover the elections on our new television station, which we had named TOLO, which means "sunrise" in Dari. The only problem—well, one of a few—was that technically TOLO didn't exist yet.

Arman FM had been such a hit that people immediately started talking about expanding into television. Most everyone in the office wanted it, with the exception perhaps of Sima, who was adamant that no one should know what she looked like. Minister Raheen considered it the logical next move. Jahid, Zaid, and Wajma saw the potential too—Jahid would soon start overseeing our operations in Afghanistan and later become COO, leaving government work behind—and even my parents, though they were busy in Kabul with their own chores and social lives, agreed that it made sense. At first, although chief pragmatist wasn't my natural role within the family, I tried to keep our feet on the ground. "Hold on," I said. "People don't even have electricity. How are they going to watch television?" With radios, I reasoned, you can use batteries. If you have a car, you can listen in your car, or on the bus or in a taxi.

It's not as though the story of a new Afghanistan was going unreported. Quite the opposite; if anything, it felt like there was a journalist for every civilian in Kabul, crowded into the press conferences held at the Intercontinental, lining up in the waiting rooms at the Arg, embedding with the US troops in Kandahar. Many were doing an admirable job of capturing a complicated and constantly changing picture. Some were less capable, but they seemed to be enjoying themselves in Kabul. I made a point of meeting as many foreign journalists as I could, inviting them to have coffee with me in the Moby office, or I would go to parties with them in the evenings, feeding them tips and linking them to government sources, trying to right the ship if I felt a story was being overlooked or reported poorly. I like to think that I sometimes succeeded and that they came to appreciate my takes. I valued their perspective as well; many of them are still friends. Often, because I was working too much to travel, they would provide dispatches from the parts of Afghanistan I didn't get to see, the places where the presence of NATO troops was already less of a liberation and more of a nightmare. It was sometimes easier for a foreign reporter to travel to far-flung places, and it was often good for us Afghans to see Afghanistan through their eyes, unblinkered by nostalgia or wishful thinking. Their perspective could be brutally clear, if sometimes reaching too starkly black-and-white conclusions.

At the beginning, there was a brightness in much of the international media coverage about Afghanistan's prospects. So much money was pouring into the country, and if that money was channeled correctly, the hope was that it could be transformative. The Taliban state had collapsed, international forces were finishing off its fighters in the provinces, and there was the emergence of a new political order, one that could mirror established democracies around the world. Or so they wrote.

The world, we felt, was ravenous for news about this extraordinary project, this transformation of a mostly forgotten country. Every media outlet imaginable appeared to have opened a bureau in the city and sent some of their best and sometimes most daredevilish correspondents, many of whom, when I met them, would tell me that covering the American war in Afghanistan was the most extraordinary experience of their careers. "Why?" I always wanted to know. Each had a different answer—the political journey of the country, the opening scenes of the War on Terror, the liberation of Afghan women, the diversity of tribes and ethnicities, their preconceptions already upended by a little travel and study—some answers being more abstract than others. "The sky in Afghanistan is so . . . high," *New Yorker* writer Jon Lee Anderson told me. At first, I wasn't sure exactly what he meant—the mountains, the sunsets, perhaps the elevation going to his head—but soon I came to understand. Afghanistan is a place where, contrary to what outsiders may think, people feel free. The landscape compels you to, no matter the geopolitics and disputes unfolding on the ground. Even today, when people ask me to explain the magnetism of my home country, I quote Jon Lee Anderson.

As Afghans, we invested hope in this early rush of media coverage. We were now the center of the universe; we were pressing the reset button on decades of war. Twenty, thirty stories were being published a day around the globe about Afghanistan—on the Battle of Tora Bora, men shaving their beards, girls going back to school—and I gorged on them, especially when I was back in Melbourne. I presumed everyone did. After I moved to Kabul, it seemed to me foreign journalists never tired of hearing about life under the Taliban, even when the survivors themselves got a little sick of telling the stories or pulling up the photos of them wearing turbans to show inquisitive reporters. Arman FM itself would become a story. Reporters were fascinated by this upstart radio station, and the impact something as simple, but also as revolutionary, as pop music on the radio had on the city. It was a feel-good story about a new Afghanistan. But there were horror stories out there too.

In December 2001, Carlotta Gall of the *New York Times* reported that dozens of Taliban fighters, Afghans and foreigners, had been killed after they surrendered to Northern Alliance forces led by General Abdul Rashid Dostum. They had suffocated to death in the sealed metal shipping containers in which they were being transported to prison in northern Afghanistan, with no food, water, or fresh air. In May 2002, she reported that a mass grave had been found in the area by forensic investigators working for Physicians for Human Rights, and in August *Newsweek* did a cover story, "The Death Convoy of Afghanistan": the article described how hundreds of Taliban prisoners had been asphyxiated in "what could well qualify as war crimes"—later estimates said nearly two thousand had died, with some being shot by their guards, in these containers—and asked questions regarding the involvement of General Dostum and American special forces who were in the area at the time. Dostum was a key American ally, soon to become a high-ranking defense official in Karzai's administration. Years later, with human rights groups still asking the US military to conduct a proper investigation into the crime, the *New York Times* reported that Dostum had been on the CIA payroll, which explained, in part, the reluctance among US officials to take action.

I followed the story, like everyone I knew, both when it was first reported and over the years as more details emerged. From the beginning, what had happened didn't sit right with me. The facts of the story had been reported and vetted by human rights investigators. But where was the outrage? "It's mass murder," I said to Zaid. "It doesn't matter if they are Taliban; no one deserves to suffocate to death in a container. Why aren't people angrier about this?" Back then too, I favored amnesty for all Afghans, regardless of affiliation or crime; I thought it was the only way to move past the desire for retribution, the only way to unite the Afghan people.

A genuine rage among Afghans over the mass killing of the Taliban fighters only materialized after the reporting on the American effort to protect Dostum. But the anger was directed at the Americans, who, it seemed, were once again using subterfuge to shape the war narrative. There was little grief expressed for the people who had been killed in such a horrific way, no fretting about the example it set for our incipient justice system, no confronting our own inhumanity, no awareness of our own bloodlust after so much trauma. There was no acknowledgment on Afghan state media that many of these Taliban fighters were also Afghans who did not deserve to die in such a gruesome manner. Or maybe, because so many of our stories were being written about us rather than by us, those feelings were simply going unreported.

We wanted our news station to reflect every aspect of the country and its people, and our first democratic presidential election in October 2004 seemed as good a place as any to start. The election, we decided at Moby, needed to be reported by Afghans, in Dari and Pashto, by reporters on the ground in Kabul who knew the city and for whom it wasn't just a news story. They would be voting too, but they would be professional in their coverage, not partisan like state media and some other outlets tended to be. We could do that on Arman, where we'd been developing a strong news team. Still, we knew that radio coverage could not compare to seeing the election day play out on a commercial independent Afghan television channel like the one we were envisioning. I came around to the idea. By the time I did, we had six months to launch TOLO.

THE FIRST TELEVISION studio was crammed into the same house as Arman FM, downstairs from the radio studio in what was once the dining room. We sat reporters around a small round table, where they would interview guests; we already had a lineup of politicians, academics, and experts for the week around the election, all eager to present their views on an Afghan TV channel. With the help of a USAID grant, we began constructing a makeshift studio in the downstairs dining room, which we outfitted with what lights and cameras that Jahid, forever our family's quiet autodidact, had sourced from Europe and then waited for what seemed like years to receive.

In addition to foreign journalists, Kabul was overrun with foreign consultants, usually funded by the US government and offering their expertise to Afghan start-ups in all fields under the sun. Most of them arrived armed with lots of technical knowledge, but little understanding of the local context, history, or languages, and their work could sound like a punch line to a dark joke: an agricultural consultant travels to a rural farm with a sack of seeds only to discover the farm had been a poppy field that had been poisoned by a counter-narcotics team; an education consultant brings textbooks in the wrong language; media consultants visited Moby with earnest mission statements about media as liberator but no reporting experience in countries like Afghanistan.

Our company policy, unspoken of course, was to rebuff these consultants, as kindly as possible. Their attitude, so solicitous, was, at best, condescending. Working with a USAID grant, the consultant would usually be an American who'd never reported on Afghanistan before or listened to Afghan music or even spoken to an Afghan person. Their advice offended our correspondents who had been on the ground since the war started, tireless in their pursuit of accountability from the governments that were meant to represent them. The consultant would hang out in Kabul for a few months, and talk a lot—about employing women, which we already were, or how the media could strengthen democracy, which was a word the consultants threw around with abandon and which Afghans knew had arrived in their country at the barrel of a gun. Then they'd leave, bill the US government, and soon we'd hear from them again offering yet another training session.

We chose to hire our own private consultants. Ashley Schwall-Kearney, an Australian news producer, and Dominic Medley, a Brit who had already done some media training work in Afghanistan, flew in and began to help training our staff in how to cover elections, from talking to voters in line at the polls, to scheduling interviews with candidates, to keeping track of the results as they came in on election day. We also began the process of hiring television journalists, looking for people who seemed comfortable in front of a camera. Some came from Arman FM, but most were new hires. Because the growth of TV journalism in Afghanistan had been interrupted by wars and the Taliban ban, there was an underestimation of what Afghans could achieve in that field. We knew, though, that even under the most difficult circumstances, aspiring Afghan journalists had figured out how to advance their craft. Interviewees would come to us describing their education: "There were no books in Dari on journalism," one young man told us. "And no journalism teachers."

"How did you study, then?" we would ask. The answer was usually the same. "We watched CNN, the BBC, when we were in Pakistan," they said. More recently, they tuned in to the state-affiliated TV channel, which, without other options, most Afghans who wanted news in Dari or Pashto watched, but it was replete with propaganda, and with a quilt of clips bought from international networks. Still, the new reporters came to TOLO eager to prove themselves. They searched for news wherever they could—online as Internet cafes became more affordable, through contacts they nurtured even when they had no outlet to publish, on the streets in their neighborhoods; in Afghanistan, there was always something happening.

Before we launched TOLO TV, we sent teams of journalists out to report on stories. Often, they returned with impressive work: investigations of small-scale corruption, street interviews with people worried about the election being postponed, stories about local businesses opening on the ever-crowded Kabul roads. Sometimes, those practice runs turned into impromptu journalism lessons. "I want to do a story on kids who are swimming in really dirty water, in the cold, in the Kabul River, without any adults watching them," one reporter said. "It's very dangerous." It was an example, she said, of how a generation of the city's children were potentially getting lost in the chaos of development and conflict. It was a story that an Afghan, familiar with the city and its mores, would report better than a foreigner.

A producer approved the assignment, and the reporter returned with excellent video—a half dozen children, unsupervised, shivering in the filthy river waters of Kabul while the city roared around them. "How did you find them?" the producer wanted to know.

"They were just hanging out by the water," the reporter replied happily. "They didn't want to swim, but I gave them a little bit of money and they went in." She was proud of her resourcefulness. The producer brought me the report. Later, we had a meeting about journalistic integrity.

TOLO TV LAUNCHED just a few days before the October 2004 election. We kept it simple; there wasn't time to do anything too elaborate or to send reporters from Kabul city to the provinces. Stories outside of Kabul came to us via international networks, and we ran their headlines as chyrons on our channel while our presenters summarized what they were seeing. It sounds clichéd to say that it was better than nothing, but that's the truth; it was enough for us to be covering these stories in Afghan languages, on an independent Afghan TV channel.

Inside the city, there were plenty of stories for our reporters to cover. Voter turnout was huge, ardent, and in some places—it's painful now to remember—practically ecstatic. Reporters interviewed Afghans lined up at polling stations, and we cut between them and the studio where guests joined our presenters at round tables. The election was being held on a Friday, part of the weekend in Afghanistan, and while voting was not mandatory, people looked relaxed, and seemed happy to vote, to talk to our journalists, to describe their feelings, and later to hold up their index fingers, stained with indelible purple ink, to ensure they would not try to vote again, for our cameras and all the others that were crowding the polling stations that day.

We told our reporters that they should think of the BBC and CNN as our competitors, even though we knew that our setup compared with those international giants was virtually from the Stone Age. We simply didn't see the other local private stations as any competition at all; to us, they seemed too beholden to those in power, too scared to push the envelope or too underfunded to try. Reporters from RTA appeared stiff and unapproachable; they parroted whatever those in authority wanted them to say, and their segments made the day, which was so joyous, seem about as exciting as a traffic jam.

"Talk to the voters like they're your friends," we told our TOLO reporters. "Ask them how they're feeling. Don't worry about what we'll think back in the office." The story, we told them, wasn't who was going to be elected president. The story was that Afghans, after the decade of civil war and Taliban tyranny, followed by nearly three years of an interim government put together with the help of international forces, were finally voting again.

Our cameras captured the mood on the street. A woman took a long bus ride through traffic with her young children in order to line up at her polling place. A young man had recently turned eighteen, just in time to get his voter card a few weeks prior. The lines were massive, slow but happy. Many had been refugees until recently who thought they might never set foot in their country again, never mind vote in an election. And although there were mixed feelings already about the American invasion, which had precipitated these elections, in general Afghans were showing they had faith in the process by turning up to vote in such high numbers.

The TOLO studio wasn't yet connected to an AV van, the way international outlets were. Instead, a cameraman would record a reporter interviewing someone waiting in line to vote, then give the tape to a colleague who would stuff it into a bag and rush it back to the office, speeding on a motorbike or sweating on a bicycle to avoid getting stuck in traffic. They arrived winded, triumphant, as though they had been escorting the crown jewels through a crowd of thieves. We reviewed the footage as quickly as possible before putting it on air. There was no avoiding a substantial lag, but what we got from our reporters that day was realistic, intimate, and Afghan.

TOLO was live. The lights stayed on and hung in place where Jahid had overseen their installation, the studio walls didn't come crashing down, no guests canceled at the last minute, our fuel-run generators and backup UPS system lasted. No one complained about our reporters approaching them in line, no fights broke out between people debating key issues on air, no presenters said regrettable things, no reporters lost their train of thought, or at least not so much that they broke the rhythm of reporting. The day felt like one of the cartoons I would watch as a kid, all of us running around on the streets of Kabul, rocks and anvils falling out of the sky, denting the sidewalks, making our enemies cackle, and somehow, by some immense stroke of luck, none of them landing on our heads.

I was so consumed by work that I didn't manage to leave the office until much later that afternoon to vote, taking those left at Moby along with me—my three siblings, security guards, drivers, anyone who also hadn't had a free moment to cast their ballot. Company vehicles left the office in a caravan toward Zarghona High School, about ten minutes away along the main road. Zarghona is an all-girls school, an imposing building that would be barely large enough to accommodate the thousands of girls enrolled there when the Taliban, nearly two decades later, would stop them from attending secondary school. During the week, the students would squeeze behind long desks, shoulder to shoulder in classrooms with pistachio-green walls. Over the years, journalists, TOLO included, produced countless stories from inside Zarghona school.

By the time we arrived the crowds our reporters had been tracking all day had mostly dwindled, and we were able to enter quickly through the school's green metal gates. Reporters, having gotten their stories, had also left. Analysts were already predicting that Karzai was going to win by a wide margin. It took a while for votes to be tallied, and for the official result to be announced, and although there were allegations of fraud and irregularities, investigations did not unearth anything that would have overturned the results. All things considered, it was a clean, hopeful election.

Subsequent election days, whether presidential or parliamentary, would not feel as celebratory. For those, we would go to vote as early as possible in the morning, getting it over and done with, feeling like we were simply doing our duty as Afghans. But 2004 had been different. We savored that election, going to the girls' school at the end of the workday like voting was a piece of chocolate we saved until we had finished the rest of the meal. It was so smooth, it should have been boring, but every step felt profound. We showed our voter cards to the poll workers, took our ballots, chose our candidate, inserted the ballot into a plastic box, and had our fingers stained with purple. We left feeling satisfied, even triumphant. That's how I would describe Kabul in those best moments, early in the forever war, as Americans would come to describe it—not just full of hope, but full of a hope that you could, for a brief moment, take for granted.

CHAPTER 9

WAJMA

My sister, Wajma, was born in 1974, just a handful of years before we would be forced to leave Kabul. As the youngest, and the only girl, she was doted on and adored—my father made no secret that he had always longed for a daughter—and, in many ways, held to different standards than her older brothers. There are parts of her experience as an Afghan teenage girl growing up in Australia, and as an Afghan woman helping her brothers run Moby in Kabul, that she did not tell any of us about until years after she decided to leave Kabul for good.

At the time, to be fair, there was little chance to talk about our feelings. Like all of us, Wajma worked sixteen-hour days and slept only as much as absolutely needed. Our projects together as a family were consuming, and often euphoric—Wajma did tell me that working at Moby was the first time in her adult life she was excited to get up and go to an office. But I also didn't want to ask her questions about her experience that would seem overly blunt or facile. I didn't want to presume that her time there was defined solely by what was hard about being a woman in Afghanistan. I knew that it wasn't. Still, there is no denying that none of us experienced Kabul the way Wajma and my mother did, just as our fathers and grandfathers and uncles and male cousins all had a significantly different recollection of the country they lived in than the women in their families.

Our mother, Safia, grew up in an Afghanistan that was both oppressive for women and, by comparison to life under the Taliban, full of opportunity. Girls went to school, and some of them graduated from Kabul University and worked in government and elsewhere; the 1964 constitution recognized equal rights for men and women. And yet in a conservative society it was expected that women of all social classes, regardless of education, would marry, have children, and stay at home to raise those children. In many families and in many parts of the country, that expectation was strictly enforced by male heads of family or village leaders, long before the Taliban or their fundamentalist interpretation of Islam had materialized.

My maternal grandmother exists mainly in the memories passed down to my mother by older relatives and friends who knew her before she died, quite young, the second wife of my maternal grandfather. A Pashto speaker from the unrelenting mountainous southeastern part of Afghanistan, she was said to be very beautiful, but sad and self-isolated, known to spend hours gazing out of a window at seemingly nothing. Her father, my great-grandfather, had been murdered when she was a child; we didn't know why or by whom—some kind of local grudge or in a burst of violence—and the tragedy of his loss further toughened the already tough women, members of the Zadran tribe known for loyalty and forbearance, he left behind. My great-grandmother was said to carry a gun anywhere she went because, with no male heirs, it was her obligation to avenge her husband's death.

My grandmother seemed to wish to be left alone even while she was surrounded by those she loved. By the time she died, she had learned only a little Dari, but enough to communicate with her children for whom Dari, through schooling, had become their primary language.

My mother was raised more lovingly by her stepmother than by her own mother. But the happy childhood she remembers is mainly owing to her father, a striking figure with intense blue eyes whom she remembers as gentle and patient, and who doted on the children he had with both his wives. He raised my mother and her sisters to be strong women, never subservient to men, and although he was devout and hoped his daughters would say their daily prayers, he did not monitor them to make sure they did. When I was growing up, my parents replicated this nondogmatic approach to Islam.

My grandfather gave my mother her sense of self-worth. When my father, about to assume his post as a diplomat in London, spotted my mother, eighteen years his junior, on the Kabul University campus where she was studying, and shortly after asked her father if they could marry, he was told it was "up to Safia"—at that time in Afghan society, it was nearly a revolutionary way of thinking. It was partly at the excitement of living abroad—since Ariana Airlines' founding a decade prior, my mother had dreamed of becoming an airline pilot—partly because she liked what she saw in my father, and partly because she was allowed to make the decision for herself, that only weeks later they got married. Busy with her studies, my mother had not really thought about finding a husband or having children, but tells us motherhood felt natural once we arrived: three boys first, each a couple of years apart, and then the longed-for Wajma, her only girl.

Wajma's search for her identity as an Afghan started earlier and revealed itself differently than it did for Jahid, Zaid, or me. Most of her early memories of Afghanistan are vaguer than ours—she was only four when we left for Japan—laced up tighter inside our parents' own recollections of our home, our street, their friends. Or they are simple, visceral—the taste of freshly peeled pine nuts, shaking a blanket full of fallen mulberries and then being tossed around in the blanket herself, watching Ahmad Zahir perform at a concert while eating ground chickpeas out of a paper cone. "The fruit in Kabul isn't like fruit anywhere else," my mother would tell her, chopping up some peaches in our Melbourne kitchen. When Wajma asked what that meant, of course there was no satisfying answer. "It's just better," my mother would reply, and even though it had been so long since she tasted Afghan fruit, Wajma felt that she agreed.

Growing up, Wajma would consider her own Australianness, weigh it against that of her friends at school, and find it lacking. She didn't look exactly like most of the kids in our predominately white neighborhood, she didn't eat all the same food at home, where she spoke mostly Dari, not English. Even though my parents were remarkably progressive for Afghans of their generation, Wajma was still, as the only girl and the youngest in our family, raised in a manner that was more conservative than most of her Australian female friends. At the same time, when she thought about Afghan women of my mother's generation, she found herself freer, more adventurous, much more independent. Children and marriage were abstractions, there for her only if she should choose them. Wajma traveled alone, once for a long time with just a backpack. While I prided myself in being a chameleon from a young age, feeling at home most anywhere in the world and brushing off any signs of awkwardness, Wajma was more interested in exploring the world in order to discover who she truly was away from the big, broad strokes she had been painted with at home: Afghan, Australian, daughter, sister, woman. Thinking about Afghanistan—like the rest of us, she longed to travel there, just to see it as an adult—Wajma arrived at the following conclusion: "In Australia, I'd never really felt totally Australian. So I must be very Afghan."

WHEN WAJMA HEARD that Zaid and I had gone back to Kabul in March 2002, she was on month two of a four-month backpacking trip. Immediately, she made plans to join us. "I should be there," she told my mother.

We may have worried about her from the get-go, although my

stronger recollection is feeling that of course Wajma would come. We had the same parents who encouraged us to be similarly adventurous and curious, the same upbringing, the same attachment to our homeland. "Come for a few weeks, Wajma," Jahid told her. "See it for yourself."

My mother, also unsurprisingly, opted to accompany her and so, at first, Wajma experienced Kabul through this homecoming, twenty-five years in the making. She was honored to watch Safia Mohseni's unforeseen return to her homeland, which transformed her. In our eyes, our mother had always been unflappable. When the gunfire that accompanied the 1978 coup d'état sent her school-age children running into the streets in fear, she was at home, waiting for us, solid as a tree. When our father resigned from the Afghan foreign service while we were living in Japan and we had to vacate the embassy's apartment, it was my mother's friends who helped us find a new, more affordable place to live in Tokyo. When we needed money in Australia, she got a job as a teacher, then left that job to run a bakery and cafe, which she could do in her off hours, eventually taking a better-paying job as a consultant. The home she made with my father was bright and happy, welcoming to a constant stream of friends and visitors. We only realized much later in life how difficult those years were for her, and how in spite of her experience living abroad as a diplomat's wife, she nonetheless struggled to make it work in Australia.

Back in Kabul, Wajma would point out that our mother seemed different, more fully herself. She wept over the changes she saw in the city, even the positive ones, but Wajma had also never seen her more confident and assured. In her own city, speaking her own language, she filled every room she entered. She talked to everyone—taxi drivers, shop owners, strangers on the street—as though they were long-lost relatives. It felt to her that they were.

Wajma waited to feel the same way, to settle into her identity as an Afghan. Her Dari, which she had thought was fluent, didn't get her very far while haggling for jewelry on Chicken Street. Another Afghan expat, who would become one of Wajma's many close friends in Kabul, teased her for her accent, imitating the Australian twang that infiltrated her Dari. "You have to give me a better price because I'm translating for her," the friend joked to a shopkeeper, pointing at Wajma. It brought back memories of a trip to Pakistan that she had taken as a teenager to visit some family. "Is she Afghan?" a shopkeeper had asked our cousin, nodding toward Wajma. "Yes," he answered, "but she was raised in Australia." The shopkeeper looked at my sister knowingly. "Yeah, I can tell," he said. "It's the way she carries herself." It was just a moment, but one that she now realized she had brought with her to Kabul, a little pebble rattling around in her shoe, just big enough to make her uncomfortable. Undeterred, she vowed to improve her Dari.

The liberation of Afghan women, and the hope that they would recover from those dark years and thrive once the Taliban were gone, was one of the loudest parts of the rhetoric underpinning the US invasion. Every media outlet produced stories of Afghan girls and women navigating their new freedoms—going to school, going to work and also to the beauty parlor, running in and voting in elections. The coverage was excitable and breathless in its tone, with Arman and TOLO being no different from the international press. Certainly, by now we know that protecting and promoting women's rights was hardly the reason behind the American-led war; at best, it provided moral cover for the invasion, as it did for extending the occupation. That doesn't mean it wouldn't have been a worthy goal unto itself.

At Moby we tried to take concrete steps to help advance women's rights. We hired as many women as we could, at all levels; even a portion of our security staff were women. Through our programming, the Afghan public listened to women cover local politics on the radio and then watched women question people in power on TV; they were exposed to women doing excellent work, and it seemed to take only a split second before the discomfort at such female presence in the public space turned into devotion. We instituted a company policy that discrimination against any employee because of their gender would lead to immediate termination. Social change is inevitable, but it happens in an irreversible manner only when it's accepted by the public. The media can play a role in bringing that about, we thought, but it has to be organic.

Even during that first visit, though, Wajma could see that we hadn't taken it far enough. "You need a female voice in the boardroom," she told us, and six months later she was in Kabul permanently.

WAJMA MOVED HER suitcases into one of the many bedrooms in a house we had rented without much thought aside from security and proximity to the studio and offices. Our house was, to put it bluntly, ugly, vast, and lacking in character, built for an extended family who could have transformed it into a home, not for four perpetually exhausted siblings who mostly saw each other at work. Situated on one of Kabul's main roads, we could smell the exhaust from minibuses and hear the sound of car horns while sitting in the common rooms. The pollution only worsened as the city grew, but the government was unable, or unwilling, to widen the roads to accommodate the monstrous traffic, and soon we found ourselves stepping out the front door into a giant, smelly traffic jam.

Zaid, Jahid, and I had moved in with little furniture, at first sleeping on mattresses without bed frames and sitting on the floor on cushions in the drawing room, more out of laziness than cultural adherence. Wajma only bought a bed frame when, one year after moving in, she woke up on the floor to find a scorpion crawling on her stomach.

We were so consumed with growing Moby, and so connected as a family through our work and our return to Afghanistan, that we barely noticed how inhospitable our home must have seemed, or noticed it at all. Years later, Sarah, an Iranian-American designer I met in Kabul, who would later become my wife, had to remind me that parts of the house were actually lovely. One room, she said, was covered in hand-painted wallpaper—birds and flowers against a light blue background. "If you say so," I said with a shrug.

Wajma felt a little silly living with her brothers, as though, even as she turned thirty, she were back in her childhood home. But she was overjoyed to be in Kabul, where she'd last been a toddler, to no longer be working as a project manager for the Australian yellow pages, "a cog in the world of marketing" as she had so often complained about being. That her colleagues in Melbourne thought she was crazy for making the move—the general reaction in Australia when any of us mentioned our new home—only made her more confident that she was doing the right thing.

Melbourne had become stifling, but for Wajma, Kabul was ripe with possibility. Everything felt fresh; people seemed open to new things. She could experiment in her work and explore, insert herself into new situations where she could push the creative boundaries, so unlike her work experience in Melbourne marketing firms, where hierarchies were strictly enforced. Compared to Kabul, Melbourne felt lifeless. I could relate to her eagerness to step off the corporate treadmill.

At first, Wajma eyed jobs at the UN. Most young women like her, educated Afghans who had lived abroad prior to 2001 worked at the various NGOs expanding throughout the city. A handful had already become friends. Soon, though, Jahid, who had tried his own hand at non-media work, convinced her to come to Moby full-time, where she took charge of the public service announcements that aired on Arman and TOLO. Funded by organizations like USAID or the UN, they were lucrative for Moby, keeping the business afloat in the early years before we managed to secure major corporate sponsors. The content guidelines, though—about personal hygiene, family planning, education—were preachy and saccharine, sometimes downright offensive, the kind of subject matter that could make our viewers change the channel—exactly what we didn't want. Wajma was given the nearly impossible job of making the PSAs both engaging and culturally inoffensive.

Like Jahid, Wajma can be soft-spoken and introspective. But at work, she was confident, deploying her keen ironic wit and, like any good marketing consultant, her eye for creative messaging. She and Jahid excelled at spinning those tedious messages into PSAs, figuring out how to work creatively around societal and cultural restrictions. When the Ministry of Defense asked us to work on an anti-narcotics campaign—drug abuse was soaring among young men in Afghanistan, including soldiers and police—and sent Wajma a three-minute sermon from a popular imam railing against the grievous harms, both physical and spiritual, of heroin addiction, we all rolled our eyes. "We can't put this on air," Jahid said. "This kind of moralistic stuff doesn't work. Plus, it's boring." At Jahid's suggestion, Wajma spliced up the sermon into shorter bites, attaching them to equally short messages delivered by ordinary Afghans—representing neighbors, colleagues, family members whose opinions actually mean something to ordinary Afghans—that scolded the drug dealers for being, as the ad went, depraved enough to make money off other people's addiction and misery. "Afghans really care about what their neighbors think about them," she reminded the ministry officials as she crafted the PSA. "Trust me."

An NGO asked Wajma to advertise contraceptives without

mentioning two words—"sex" and "condom"—and without suggesting, in a country where women are expected to have many
children, that smaller families are more desirable. Wajma wrote a
script about how a more manageable family unit makes it easier
to buy food, pay rent, lead a more comfortable life. It was a powerful message, based on research, not propaganda, and soon my
sister took over much of Moby branding; it was clear she was not
impressed by what we had come up with so far. When she saw the
proposed logo for TOLO, a bright sun bouncing in the corner of
the screen, she grimaced. "It's so . . . big," I recall her saying. She
hired a designer to redo it, and soon founded Lapis, an in-house
advertising agency that created and supervised most of Moby's
branding work.

Sometimes, your family are the easiest people to take for
granted. We were all working so hard, and in such close proximity, that we drifted apart. We didn't think very much about how
the other person was coping unless it had some effect on Moby.
Jahid and I struggled with the pace of networking required to
keep a new media company going. At times, Zaid wondered if his
law career would stagnate if he stayed out of Australia any longer.
Wajma, also ambitious, worried occasionally that she was living
in a fantasy world, that once she left Kabul she might find that her
work for Moby didn't translate outside of Afghanistan. The least
combative of the four of us, she grew annoyed with her brothers'
constant sparring.

We all worked at all hours and would spend the evenings networking or socializing or staying until dawn in the office—for
men, and non-Afghan women, the options for what to do each evening in Kabul were nearly limitless. At the beginning, adjusting to
the constraints and freedoms of her new life, Wajma often found
herself alone in our big, ugly house, in her sweatpants watching
junk TV—*Grey's Anatomy* became a source of comfort—in a state
of limbo between the expat and Afghan communities. There were

not very many Afghan women returnees like her, who were educated and had connections in the West, and who also planned to
make a life in Kabul long term.

But she did make several close friends, mainly Afghan returnees who worked for NGOs or at embassies. They explored together, new restaurants and shops in the city, the views from the
surrounding mountains, day trips to the rural outskirts to pick
fruit with our mother—Wajma recounting the horror and delight
of passersby seeing a young Afghan woman climbing a tree—and
where once she and a friend, sore from sitting in a car on bumpy
roads, jumped out to race through a field to a distant river.

On weekend trips, Wajma and her new friends would sometimes get into small amounts of trouble, forgetting, perhaps,
where they were. In Bamiyan, where the beauty of Afghanistan is
on full display alongside the ruins of giant Buddhas destroyed by
the Taliban in 2001, armed security discovered Wajma and three
friends sleeping at an illegal campsite in the middle of the night,
and after some tense negotiation begrudgingly allowed them to
stay, but only until the sun came up. Still, it was her right to
explore. Her brothers were doing it, so why couldn't she? Wajma's Dari improved, she left the house more for social events, and
she began to feel, if not truly Afghan, whatever that meant, then
closer to her Afghan self. In those initial days, she was happy to
wake up early and walk to work.

So enamored was my sister with rediscovering her homeland,
and helping to reshape its future, that the fact of her being a
woman in Afghanistan was, at first, pushed into the back of her
mind. The most sexism she experienced in those early years came
from the international media, which tended to cut her out of their
coverage of Moby and our family endeavors. By the Moby staff,
she was treated as an equal. To her surprise, she felt more conservative than most of her female colleagues, who were accustomed
to their daily choices—what to wear, how to get to work, whether

or not they would or could go to school—being acts of rebellion and bravery in and of themselves.

But while she spread her wings, we grew more nervous. I'd always been against Wajma moving to Kabul permanently, although I never told her that. It had nothing to do with her abilities, which were prodigious, or how much we needed her, which was a lot. I had great optimism about the future of Afghanistan and the future of Moby, but I didn't have my head in the sand. As a woman, Wajma would be exposed to challenges that were harder than the ones we brothers experienced. I knew that while she was in Kabul, I would spend a lot of time worrying about her. I was concerned that her being there would distract us from growing the company. I hate admitting that, even today. In those days, the company was all I cared about.

It was obvious that Wajma would travel with extra security, and that when my mother was in Kabul, she would do the same. When they were out shopping or visiting or exploring the city, I would constantly call their bodyguards and driver to track their whereabouts and make sure that they were safe. At first, Wajma and my mother treated it like a game, tricking the driver into leaving them alone at a market, leaving the house in secret to go on a walk in the neighborhood together. (Later, I found out that while we were calling her bodyguards to check on her whereabouts, my mother was doing the same for all four of us.) But as the company profile grew, they felt strangers' eyes on them. It rattled them to think that someone on the streets might know who they were, and soon they agreed to travel in an armored car.

We tried not to think about what could happen to Wajma if she wasn't extra careful. She could be kidnapped while out shopping or taking a taxi home from work; the year she arrived, three UN workers, two of them women, had been snatched from a Kabul street. She could be harassed because what she was wearing was not sufficiently modest or be photographed at a party with foreigners where alcohol was being served. People gossip, and their expectations of women are different, unfair. I had married an Iranian-American, yet I still worried that Wajma could be seen as being too close with foreigners, particularly when Moby was constantly accused of being a mouthpiece for Iran or the West. There were a thousand things to worry about. Wajma would have hopped on a bus with a backpack to any part of the country by herself if she could have. After a while, though, it was too dangerous for her even to walk to the market alone.

SHORTLY INTO HER time working at Moby, Wajma had been asked by an international publication to interview Afghan women about the changes they had experienced since the fall of the Taliban. She was delighted by the assignment. In the office, and on the streets of Kabul, young women were already occupying spaces that, under the Taliban, had been reserved for men, and they had ambitions to secure advanced degrees and have flourishing careers. At TOLO, many of our best reporters were young women, interviewing ministers and high-ranking officials and ambassadors. They were witnesses at the sites of bombings; they risked harm themselves doing their work. When we'd launched Arman, Sima was in her early twenties, and it took only a few weeks before ministers confessed to feeling nervous when their assistants told them Sima was on the line.

Many of the women featured in the article had dreams of living and working in Kabul. But one of the interviewees, a young woman just on the brink of university, was less optimistic about the future of the country. "What's your dream?" Wajma asked her. The young woman answered quickly, with the certainty of someone pointing out the obvious. "To leave Afghanistan," she said.

Why? Wajma remembers thinking to herself at the time. *Why would you want to leave? Fantastic things are happening here, and it's only going to get better.* She was disturbed by the woman's answer. Quickly, though, she put it out of her mind; sixteen-hour workdays are helpful at keeping one focused.

Three and a half years later, Wajma left Kabul, first for Dubai, where she would continue with Moby full-time, and then to New York to get her master's degree. By the time she left, Lapis was a powerful, lucrative branch of Moby, and Wajma was exhausted by the work and felt cloistered by the increasing security. She felt she could be of good use to the company in Dubai, where she would also have more personal freedom.

She hadn't thought about the young woman, and her desire to leave the country, in years. Then suddenly, years later in conversation with a foreign journalist, it came rushing back as vividly as if it had happened the day before. Wajma found herself again face-to-face with that disillusioned young woman who so quickly had come to suspect the promise of liberating Afghan women that came attached to the international presence, and who admitted without guilt or sorrow her eagerness to leave Afghanistan at the first opportunity. The young woman was young but smart; she saw things clearly. She had lived through the civil war and the first Taliban regime; it was too risky to trust the promises the new Afghan governments and their international partners made to women.

Wajma, on the other hand, had an Australian passport. She could leave anytime she wanted. "Was I ever so arrogant?" she wondered to a friend, remembering how surprised she had been at the young woman's answer. "Or so naïve?" What did she really know about other Afghan women, whose views of liberation were much more nuanced and more complicated than anyone seemed willing to explore at the time, or since; of her work in marketing, which couldn't be about forcing change in minds that were not hers to change; of herself as an Afghan, so attached to a place that had shaped her from a great distance; of a homeland that cannot always be home, ever more so for its women?

CHAPTER 10

BAD TV

Naim Sarwari spent the first Taliban regime in the Radio Television Afghanistan studios—squat, plain boxes that had been mostly unused since the group took over and banned the music and entertainment programs that were once filmed there. While radio broadcast began in 1925, it was not until 1976 that grant money from Japan helped build the rudimentary studio and transmitter buildings in what was then the outskirts of Kabul. Two years later, the first television station, with programming all in color, was launched by the state-owned Radio Television Afghanistan. In the beginning, there were a few hours of music, news bulletins, and children's programming each day and, after the Soviet invasion, propaganda films and war songs.

After the Taliban took over in 1996, they shut down Afghan state television, renamed its radio arm Radio Voice of Sharia, and canceled all the music entertainment programs that had been recorded in those studios, shutting their doors indefinitely. Even the news bulletins went on hiatus. But for whatever reason—some vision of the future should the poverty and violence of that period miraculously vanish, a wish to one day use the studios to disseminate their own propaganda, or maybe just a protection of the country's resources, in whatever form they came—the Taliban regime was intent on preserving those studios and every piece of aging equipment inside of them, retaining a few employees to oversee the upkeep.

Sarwari—everyone calls Moby's affable head of production by

his last name—has never lived outside of Afghanistan. By the time the Soviet forces withdrew, he had already worked at RTA for five years; he stayed through the civil war years and, with the arrival of the Taliban, watched as Kabul emptied, with even more families fleeing to Iran and Pakistan. It was a frightening time to be there. Still, Kabul was home, and, unless he absolutely had to, Sarwari didn't want to leave. After a few uncertain weeks while the country adjusted to the aftershocks of Taliban rule, and needing money for his family as well as a sense of purpose in the midst of all the uncertainty, Sarwari agreed to return to work at RTA, where he received the assignment as caretaker of the studios.

Once a week, Sarwari would open the heavy doors of the abandoned studios, looking for any sign of forced entry and checking off a list to see if anything was damaged or stolen. Nothing, not a camera lens or microphone, was ever out of place, and he had the feeling that would be true even if the doors weren't locked; with the Taliban known for carrying out brutal public punishments, Afghans didn't steal very often, even though so many were out of work and starving. Once inside the studio, Sarwari would begin dismantling lights and projectors, dusting each component before fitting them back together, stowing them away in their cases, locking the cabinets and doors. It was odd work, sometimes meditative, sometimes frustrating, the equipment becoming so familiar that Sarwari felt like a child who had been given a puzzle to keep him busy. Every year that passed, the contents of the studios grew more obsolete, warped with age and weather, and still every week he tended to the equipment carefully, dusting each part, making sure they were secure, closing the studio doors tightly behind him. By the time the US invaded, and the Taliban fled Kabul, I am sure there was no one in the country as knowledgeable about the media technology used in Afghanistan as Sarwari, and we hired him shortly after launching TOLO TV in the technical operation department.

Sarwari later told us that he was surprised by our TOLO setup. "It's brand-new, but so basic," he said, sounding a little disappointed. Jahid had sourced the best transmitters and mixers and cameras we could afford, but had little idea how much we'd end up needing, never mind how to use them. Sarwari loved to throw up his hands, a frustrated expert surrounded by eager novices, telling us our requests to him were ludicrous. After so many years alone in the studios with his puzzles, it may have felt good to be the only grown-up in the room. "It can't possibly be done, Saad jan," he would say. "We don't have the cameras. We don't have the money." He was so fond of telling us that should we pursue this television show or buy that piece of equipment we would surely have to shut our doors, cast our staff onto the street, let our screens go dark, that we nicknamed him "Namesha," Dari for "it can't be done." Sarwari liked drama. And then, of course, after so much arguing and because he was so smart and the prospect of a new, free Afghan media so excited him, he would find a way to do everything we asked for and more.

"Sarwari," we would say. "Can we install tracking lights in this studio?" "It can't be done!" he would cry, and then he would do it. "How about a stage for musical performances?" we would ask, prompting Sarwari to press his fingers to his temples like an annoyed schoolteacher. "It can't be done, Saad jan," he'd say, and then, of course, he would find a way.

As TOLO expanded its original programming, we rented the house next to the one with the Arman studio, an almost identical building that was also two stories, with a large living area and kitchen downstairs and above it a cluster of bedrooms, which we began converting into offices. We built a small studio on the first floor, outfitting the largest room with what equipment we had, paid for with the money we had started collecting from businesses like Roshan mobile, one of our most stalwart sponsors, and painstakingly assembled by Sarwari and Jahid, his best student.

Inside the studio, we installed a small news desk positioned in front of a wall of television panels and asked our Arman reporters to practice sitting behind it.

I would like to say that our coverage of the 2004 election put TOLO on the map. But Arman FM had been successful because we used a commercial model and focused on entertainment. Likewise, what would soon make TOLO by far the most popular TV station in Afghanistan wasn't our fearless reporting, it was an Indian soap opera with a title that, in English, translates to *The Mother-in-Law Was Once a Daughter-in-Law Too.*

If entertainment television itself is junk food, then soap operas, cheap to produce or syndicate and addictively easy to watch, are pure sugar, and, as such, the obvious first step in building up an entertainment schedule for our fledgling station. Jahid negotiated the purchase of *The Mother-in-Law Was Once a Daughter-in-Law Too*, thinking only that it was both cheaper and more culturally relatable than Western soaps, for Afghans who'd long been fans of Bollywood films, so much so that they'd learned to understand a fair bit of Hindi.

Plotlines focused on the family, in India as it is in Afghanistan, a large and complicated but beloved and close-knit unit. Bloated with soppy romances, logic-defying crimes, and the odd medical miracle that make up a good soap, the show was still rooted in values that Afghans would recognize, and, of course, we scrupulously censored any salacious scene to keep the critics off our backs. The actresses dressed in resplendent saris that covered most of their bodies; the older ones covered their heads. The young women had strong personalities, were professionals, but also longed to get married and have families. And what could be more relatable than an overbearing—in this case, criminally so—mother-in-law? Even the tut-tutting over the more outrageous plotlines, as true in Delhi as it was anywhere else in the world, appealed to us; criticism was yet more evidence that these shows were a force, and if viewers weren't watching them on TOLO, they would find a way to watch them on international channels.

"We need to dub the shows in Dari," Jahid proposed to Sarwari once we had secured the distribution rights. "Many more people will watch if the characters are speaking their own language." Dubbing hadn't seemed possible to us; in an attempt to bring the show to market as quickly as possible, I had argued that between subtitles and the familiarity with Hindi that many Afghans have, most of our viewers would be able to follow the plotlines, which are practically pantomimed by overacting. Jahid, though, was the visionary when it came to dubbing, and he insisted. "What about all the people who can't read the subtitles?" he said. "Dubbed shows will set us apart."

Sarwari, presented with a need for new hardware, groaned in his fashion that it couldn't be done. But we stayed in the office every night until midnight, making sure that it was. A team of dubbers reported mostly to Jahid, and eventually that part of the business became a big reason for our success. Afghans were delighted to see a mother-in-law berating her son's wife in their native tongue.

Over the years, I've heard people from all backgrounds, Afghans and foreigners, dismiss our entertainment programs as frivolous. My response is, of course they are. Who could possibly take twenty-two minutes of a mother-in-law plotting to break up her son and his wife seriously? But I also argue, to anyone who cares to listen, for the inherent value of these frivolous offerings, their utter necessity in any country but particularly a country like Afghanistan, with a litany of tragedies that could consume us if that's all we thought and talked about every day. During these twenty years of Moby, it's our lightest, most escapist offerings that have had the widest viewership and most immediate and visible impact, more than the news and documentaries, certainly more than the investigative pieces, meticulously reported, that failed to unseat crooked ministers or do anything to quell American military violence in the provinces. A nation needs to hear about the tragedy unfolding in the name of the War on Terror. We gave them that daily on TOLOnews, both on the broadcast and, eventually, online. Afghans are informed. We have to be. But by 8:30 p.m., everyone deserves a little escape.

THE DARI VERSION of *The Mother-in-Law Was Once a Daughter-in-Law Too* was an instant hit; even the dubbers became stars. Stories of the show's popularity were often as dramatic, and as difficult to believe, as the show itself—the wedding that stopped playing dance music at 8:30 so that guests could watch; the mullah who, while preaching against the show's "bad women," revealed a suspiciously detailed knowledge of the plotlines; a family friend terrified by a taxi driver racing home in time to tune in. "Your children almost killed me!" he told my mother, only half joking. I like to tell people the story of how, during the 2006 riots, sparked when an American army truck crashed into and killed civilians in Kabul, I was asked by Marshal Fahim, a former minister of defense, to air more hours of soap operas in the hopes it would draw people home, and indeed by the time the show came on, the streets had cleared, probably, but not certainly, a coincidence.

Some of the most fervent critics have confessed to me that they watched the show at home—they had to, they said, in order to know what they were objecting to—and while one parliamentarian might bring a formal complaint against TOLO for some plotline they felt had crossed a line, another would deliver long speeches in which he likened his rivals to the show's villains. Karzai might have been pressured by some of his conservative allies who were unhappy with the depiction of idol worship in the show—and we eventually agreed to pixelate the scenes where characters prayed to Hindu deities—but meanwhile other allies would be also in his ear, defending us because they loved our music programming. Arguing for TOLO, daily it seemed, I quickly learned that it was useless to try to convince our critics to see value in a particular show, but rather to see the network and all its offerings, from the news to the soap operas, as a package deal. It was a lot more difficult for politicians to publicly oppose Afghan free media as a whole than it was to gripe about a single vulgar plotline.

Within a year of launching, our list of programs on TOLO had grown tremendously. Reality shows and talk shows were cheap to produce, and we relied on them early on. Late-night talk shows were hosted by local comedians, daytime talk shows focused on women's issues, and midday talk shows digested lighter headlines. While we'd built sufficient indoor sets to host all the new programs, we sometimes took advantage of Kabul's nice weather, dragging cushions and carpets into the office gardens and positioning our hosts around a spread of teapots and sweets to chat about local businesses. "It's traditional," we told officials who came for a look. *It's cheap*, we thought to ourselves. Later, our adaptation of NBC's *The Voice* was too expensive to produce for more than two seasons, but not because we blew the budget on our re-creations of the show's chairs—Seussian eyesores covered in red leather that swiveled toward the stage when a judge approved of a performance—which a local designer created for a fraction of the $20,000 we would have needed if we'd tried to import them.

We developed travel shows for Afghans who couldn't afford to, or didn't feel safe, venturing far from their hometowns. Cooking shows helped connect disparate Afghan palates. Music shows and videos highlighted new Afghan talent. Our satire shows were among our most trendy, biting back at a government that failed the people so consistently on so many levels. One of them, *Alarm Bell*, was modeled on an Australian show but instantly took on a very Afghan flavor of mockery, the star, Hanif Hamgam, channeling Karzai's haughtiness by dressing up like a twelfth-century Persian king. The authorities hated it from the beginning, although they mostly complained in secret. No one wanted to admit that they had watched the show and recognized themselves in one of the characters, and the more outspoken they were against it, the more attention *Alarm Bell* received in the international media.

We could never tell what might work and what was doomed. Everything felt like an experiment. *The Voice of Afghanistan* cost too much to produce for long, and the public never really embraced the show *Laughing Bazaar*, based on *Last Comic Standing*. TOLO's versions of *Deal or No Deal* and *Family Feud* landed with mixed results. We hit the jackpot when Wajma and Jahid suggested creating an Afghan singing competition show, and soon *Afghan Star* became our most popular, most enduring, and most controversial show. "What kid doesn't grab a tennis racquet and pretend to play the guitar?" Tom Freston said during one of our many conversations about *Afghan Star*. Not many Afghan youth were playing tennis, I reminded him, but I knew what he meant. Any person, no matter where they are from, would like to be given a chance to be admired, the chance to try for something they want, even if it means failing.

Many of our most admired figures came over from Arman with ideas for shows they wanted to star in or produce. Some were a natural fit for TV, and easily made the transition. Others stayed at Arman, which was growing still more popular as we expanded our radio programming, adding call-in shows to doctors and therapists, comedy shows, and more eclectic and diverse music offerings. Massood was so great on the radio that we kept him there at first, reluctant to spread him too thin across platforms. Sima, still unwilling to show her face to the public, opted to stay in the safety of the radio. My cousin Humayoon, though, began working on both TV and radio. He was a natural talent, quirky and charismatic, and, being older, had more gravitas and confidence in front of the camera than many of his colleagues.

Humayoon would go on to produce and host many shows on TOLO, but the most enduring was *Tea House*, a talk show that attempted to connect younger Afghans to their country's history at a time when war and forced migration had ruptured generations. The premise was simple. Humayoon would spend the week finding older Afghans throughout the city with interesting stories to tell, and bring them on air for the hour, where they would talk about their lives while, as the show's title suggests, drinking tea. If their stories had been told before—of life under this or that regime, or as a refugee, or returning after the American invasion—it was only in broad strokes, and often by an outsider, a reporter or a historian. On *Tea House*, Afghans told the stories of their lives through what had real meaning to them, with humor and nostalgia, speaking in casual Dari and Pashto, "the language of the people," as Humayoon would say.

Guests discussed the big issues in Afghanistan—the Americans, the Arg, corruption, education, all of it—but they also talked about their work and the food they liked, the smells in their gardens, local politics in small villages, music by people we had never heard of but that their parents had played on instruments they had to leave behind when they fled or forgot how to play because they stayed. Real stories often fed into tall tales, no less interesting to viewers, who gently teased them like they might their own parents and grandparents. Humayoon felt like he had missed so much during his years in Pakistan that even as he produced the show, he watched like a viewer, sometimes so interested in what the older Afghans were saying he would forget he was there to work.

Later he produced a horror show in which a team would go looking through Kabul's old and abandoned buildings for the occult, and which became too real for some of the people who worked on it. One day they recorded the show in a long-forgotten Kabul palace, practically in ruins and surrounded by dead gardens, which one of the guests used to visit as a child before it fell into disrepair. Humayoon felt disoriented the moment he entered and wasn't surprised when one of the producers, convinced his camera had picked up the image of a ghost, fainted. To this day, my cousin describes that palace as "haunted," even though when they reviewed the producer's footage, they found that the "ghost" was really just the shadow of a man holding a video camera.

The promise of those empty RTA studios, and Sarwari's meticulous upkeep of them, was realized during this period of creativity and development. Our television programs on TOLO, the lighter the better, quickly became our bread and butter and a solace for Afghans during tumultuous times. But as a job, television could be the hardest on our most talented staff. Poor Sarwari, head of the technical operation department, continued to fret about our unrealistic expectations for the equipment needed to make these shows happen. *Alarm Bell* ran for eleven years, and in the end spared no one, not even itself. The stars, which I recruited myself, Hamgam from the Ministry of Commerce of all places, where the likeable, charismatic man had worked as an advisor, became so popular that eventually they succumbed to the same low-level corruption prevalent among the ministers they mocked, and we had to cancel the show. It was replaced by a satirical show, *Laughter Network*, even more well liked and more brutal in its takedown of the high and mighty.

And Humayoon, so prolific in his talents, also sacrificed by being on television. Security guards had to be stationed outside of his house to prevent him being hounded by fans or targeted by people he had called out. He would eventually flee the country over worries that his work on an investigative crime show might make him a target of the new Taliban regime. And the letters

Humayoon received at Moby—thousands every month—took on a different tone once my cousin appeared in front of a camera. *Mr. Danishyar,* one admirer wrote, informing Humayoon of her impending wedding. *I've been in love with you ever since you started on the radio. I have forsaken all suitors because I was so in love with you. And then I saw you on television.*

CHAPTER 11

KARZAI

In the early days, there were a few ways I could think of to try to get an audience with Hamid Karzai. The president's father, a tribal leader and deputy speaker of the Afghan parliament in the 1960s, had been very good friends with my uncle Shakour Hamidzada, and Karzai grew up next door to my cousins, one of whom, Saboor Hamidzada, was Karzai's classmate and closest friend. Saboor had offered to set up a meeting, and so had friends of my father. But all of that would have taken too long.

In September of 2002, during our second visit to Kabul that year and six months before we had launched Arman FM and were, it'd be good to remember, absolute nobodies, Zaid and I took the first opportunity we could and tagged along with Sayed Hussain Anwari, a former mujahideen commander I had befriended in Tashkent and who had been appointed minister of agriculture in the interim government. After the Taliban's emergence, he had joined the Northern Alliance, and post–US invasion he settled easily into his role as minister and bridge to Karzai. By the time he took us to see the president, Anwari was a middle-aged man with slightly thinning hair and without the impressive beard he sported during his mujahideen years. He was a pleasant enough person to be around and, after two years as minister, would be appointed governor of Herat province, largely because he was so excellent at being somewhat charming to some people.

I'm not sure that modern Afghanistan has had a national leader who was truly connected to the people. Not the king, not the Communists, not the Taliban, who emerged claiming to be the voice for Afghanistan's voiceless—none of them ever really listened to the average citizen. But Karzai came close.

A Pashtun from Kandahar province, Karzai straddled many of the worlds that make up the place. His family had long been distinguished for its public service, which first took them to Kabul and then onto the world stage. His father was a tribal leader and a parliamentarian with close ties to King Zahir Shah, and his uncle Habibullah Karzai served in the foreign ministry and represented Afghanistan at the United Nations in 1972.

Few Afghans could come across as so patriotic and so cosmopolitan at the same time as Karzai. After completing high school in Kabul, he'd moved to India for college, graduating with bachelor's and master's degrees in international relations and political science. By the mid-'80s, he was in Pakistan, with his family, using his fluency in six languages to serve as a spokesman for one of the anti-Soviet mujahideen factions. He sometimes crossed the border to meet the mujahideen on the battlefield, but says that he never took part in the fighting.

Karzai's politics were similar to my father's, even though he belonged to my generation, and I felt comfortable debating him long before he had any reason to listen to me. Like my father, Karzai considered the years when the monarchy was in charge as the most stable period in recent Afghan history but was relieved when the former king renounced his throne in 2002. And he hated the Afghan Communists who imprisoned his father for three years and seized the family's properties.

Because some of them were former mujahideen who'd fought against the Soviet occupation, Karzai, like my father, at first had a begrudging respect for the Taliban, but he soon grew to despise their cruelty in power and was especially appalled by their decision to provide shelter to Al Qaeda terrorists. In 1999, his father was assassinated by Taliban fighters in Pakistan. It's partly because of Karzai's efforts thereafter to convince international powers that the Taliban were a problem, and that their links to Al Qaeda could end in tragedy in places far beyond Afghanistan, that when the US followed bin Laden into our country it was Karzai it lobbied for as interim leader.

When we returned to Afghanistan in September and Moby was not yet the full-time pursuit it would soon become, my two brothers and I took on roles as government advisors: Jahid, of course, heading the AACA and then working with the Ministry of Agriculture, Zaid and I taking temporary pro bono roles at the Ministry of Communications and the Ministry of Commerce, respectively. I turned down offers for full-time positions; the idea of working for the government, even one as crucial as Karzai's, seemed stifling. But I had high hopes for Karzai, at least early on, and before we established Moby and had a falling-out over some of our coverage that would end with us not speaking for years, we met frequently.

Karzai's office in the Arg-e-Shahi, the fortress-like presidential palace complex in Kabul, which had been built in the nineteenth century for Afghan kings, looked frugal, only the broken furniture having been thrown out and replaced with what was purely functional. The room was spotless and tidy, like Karzai himself, a stately man who never once looked disheveled and whose traditional Afghan clothing was so well tailored that designer Tom Ford once called him "the chicest man on the planet."

In that first meeting, with Anwari sitting placidly nearby, Karzai was cordial and curious. Like many interactions between Afghans in those early days, our political differences, or opinions about what might come after the American invasion, hardly mattered. It did not even matter much that he was the leader of our country and I was a young businessman fresh from Australia. "Come back for good," he told Zaid and me on that first visit.

"Rebuild your nation." Karzai probably said this to everyone he met back then, and I'm sure that, like us, most people took it to heart. He also advised that we should try to avoid upsetting the mullahs. That would prove to be much harder.

With every subsequent meeting I had with Karzai, I grew a little more confident, or more arrogant, depending on how you want to look at it. I'd speak with him about the war. I shared our plan with him to start Moby and was pleased when he professed his excitement about a free Afghan media. And I leaned on him to better define his economic policies, since as an informal advisor to Sayed Mustafa Kazemi, then minister of commerce, the Afghan economy had become my obsession. Kazemi and I had met years earlier in Tashkent, and he had become one of my dearest friends. Tall and charismatic, he exuded confidence, and in the years to come, as he served in government and then ran for parliament, he backed up his rhetoric with real action. Being around him, one had the feeling you could actually get things done.

One day, a couple of months before the launch of Arman, Minister Kazemi and I arrived at the Arg armed with copies of a plan that I hoped would help the nascent Afghan government focus on supporting small Afghan-run businesses, like Moby. I was no longer advising the government; even in a pro bono capacity, I worried it would be a conflict of interest, and I simply didn't have the time. Kazemi had agreed to let me take the lead on this, perhaps knowing the proposal, admittedly a bit dry compared to much of what was going on in the country, wouldn't immediately gain traction among the political elite without some finessing. So far, my proposal for a government-funded small business initiative—which I felt strongly was one of the country's most urgent needs—had been received with, let's say, less enthusiasm than I had hoped. I felt at every meeting that I might as well be asking Afghan officials to do the dishes. But in other circles, the ones full of smart people a few degrees removed from power, the argument went that in order for Afghanistan to be self-sustaining after the well of international money ran dry, we had to focus on supporting small, local businesses founded and run by Afghans, in all parts of the country.

I handed Karzai a two-page summary of the plan and began to read off a list of bullet points. "How can we keep Afghans in business?" I asked the president. "How can we motivate young people to set up businesses with an up-front cost of five or ten thousand dollars?" In Australia, I mentioned to Karzai, the government has a ministry that directly supports small business owners. "Could we institute the same kind of thing here?" I asked.

The president's eyes glazed over. My words seemed to get lost somewhere in the cloud of air-conditioning. Nearby, the men who now always surrounded the president looked at me warily. Somewhere in the palace, ministers and advisors were waiting to confer with him; some were former strongmen or local leaders whom Karzai had brought into his cabinet as a conciliatory gesture, hoping that sharing power would mean they wouldn't create trouble for his fledgling government in the provinces. Some were Afghans who'd returned from abroad pledging to serve the people but who over the coming years would instead stuff their pockets with runoff from the piles of cash flooding the country. Early on, the Arg had also started to swell with men who would brag about their credentials, but it was clear even then that they would only take from the country and give nothing back. "I was nominated for a Nobel Peace Prize, you know," a senior advisor once told me. "Well, it's not like being nominated for the Oscars," I said. "I could put my own name forward."

"Mr. President." I leaned forward. I was all nervous energy back then; I had not yet let go of the notion that an audience with the president could change his mind. "Let me ask you a question. What do you want for your people?"

Karzai perked up. He was, and still is, a great storyteller, and in the end, no one could say that he didn't love his country. Settling in, he reveled in his vision. He imagined a future in which Afghanistan was a regional tech hub, with elite universities, where we manufactured and exported mass-market versions of our famously beautiful textiles. We had the expertise, he reasoned, the cultural heritage, and the natural resources. People were coming back, the world cared about us, we were embarking on democracy again. The country was poised to change for the better.

I listened to Karzai. We agreed on so many things, particularly the abundance of talent just waiting to be put to work in Afghanistan, and I waited for his optimism to infect me in that moment. But it didn't. Instead, sitting in his tidy Arg office, I felt depressed. I thought about the shopkeepers I spoke to on my walks, how they shook their fists at the armored cars speeding by on Kabul's rutted roads. Already, Afghans were complaining about the government's dysfunctionality, the lack of opportunity in spite of what they were hearing about the massive amounts of cash coming into the country. They saw the men Karzai let into the Arg, the thugs and the corrupt businessmen, and they wearily accepted that power would be concentrated among the few as it always had. The voices of those Afghans mattered, but they were getting lost.

For once, though, I kept my mouth shut. I didn't say, "Mr. President, I agree with you about the textiles. But with which countries do we have a favorable trade agreement? Can we even produce cotton on our land, and if we do, will we have enough for making mass-scale textiles? How many megawatts of electricity do our power plants generate, and how much does it cost? Do we have airports in the right places? How can we convince people to stay in Afghanistan and work on these projects, or support them if they decide it's smarter to go work in the Gulf and send money home?" I didn't say anything. I thanked him for his time and left.

THE ARG, AS everyone refers to it in Kabul, is only a couple of miles from the house we'd rented, where we'd soon establish the Arman studio, and from those early meetings with Karzai we'd zip back up Wazir Akbar Khan road, pulling up to the house ten minutes later. Back then we wouldn't have had to pause for security checks before entering the compound; the company car, what passed for it, pulled right up to the front door of our villa-turning-into-office.

The city already seemed different from how it had been in March 2002. The atmosphere of hope remained. But the transformation to come would be less about liberation, and more about security.

In early September, the day after our first meeting with Karzai, a car bomb exploded in Kabul's central market near the Ministry of Information and Culture, killing nearly thirty people; a few hours later, that same day, reports came of an assassination attempt on Karzai in Kandahar. It was a reminder that the Taliban and Al Qaeda hadn't been vanquished. We were in Kabul at the time, our second visit that year, still weighing whether to move there full time as a family. "How many of these attacks can we tolerate?" Jahid asked me. "A lot more," I said to him, hating the question and what it implied. I was stubborn, then, or unwilling to see what the violence meant for the country's future and for the project we were embarking upon. Perhaps after living so many years in Australia, and having moved on from the experience as an adolescent of the 1978 coup that had so violently shaken the city, I had lost my ability to sense when peace is an illusion. "We can't just get up and walk away," I told my brother.

Over the next couple of years, there were a few sporadic attacks in Kabul, the death toll not so terrible, and so the security situation felt manageable. But then, around the country, incidents of violence began to escalate—suicide attacks and remotely detonated bombings, assassination attempts, Shia gatherings being targeted, schools too. Corruption sprouting up like mold on a piece of fruit precipitated bloodshed. It became clear that the Taliban insurgency had not been crushed; NATO soldiers and bases were attacked. Kabul too was no longer spared, with bloody attacks on hotels, government offices, and embassies growing so frequent that, once you confirmed no one you loved was hurt, you moved on as quickly as you could, the incidents filed away like stories in a news archive. In 2011, when a rocket, aimed at the US embassy, tore a hole in one of our studios, we calmly called in workers to sweep up the tiles and patch up the roof. It was early afternoon when it happened, but thankfully no one had gotten hurt; our reporters got busy with updates, and we continued with our programming.

The warlords Karzai had included in his government and then appointed governors only became more powerful, their corruption more brazen. The American response was laughably inadequate. *Afghanistan is never going to be like Switzerland*, they appeared to be thinking. *They're corrupt? There's violence? Yes, unfortunately, that's how it is, but we can't tell a sovereign country what to do about it.* Americans were washing their hands of the country even then; the plans to pull out NATO troops were being announced even as the violence escalated. People in Kabul became aware of how vulnerable they were. And the rich among them did what they could to protect themselves.

Blast walls began to go up around the city, one by one, a fortress built in slow motion, first around the embassies and ministries, then the houses belonging to the people who worked there, then restaurants where those people gathered, the schools their kids went to until those kids were shipped off to schools in Dubai, Istanbul, and Islamabad. Huge concrete slabs blocked off sidewalks, and the view of iconic buildings; they cut through neighborhoods and streets so that a ten-minute commute now took two hours. Outside of your window where you might have once seen a garden or a street now that view was dissected by blank, white walls and the increasing number of security guards hired to stand beside them. While white armored SUVs carrying ministers and diplomats skirted the congestion, driving on the sidewalks or against traffic, ordinary Afghans sat in place, fuming at the traffic the powerful had created and now so brazenly skirted.

Two Kabuls emerged. One Kabul was for the connected, the people who could instruct their drivers to shout out their windows and wedge their SUVs through crowds buying kebabs on the sidewalk. The other was for the have-nots, the disconnected, the people without wealth and power and tinted windows in armored cars. In one Kabul, foreigners lived in villas behind blast walls; in another, Afghans walked hours out of their way to avoid the parts of the city where they were no longer welcome. In one Kabul, the argument went, important people were targets of violence, and because they were important and targets, they couldn't risk spending hours in their gigantic SUVs in the middle of Kabul. "We can't wait," they would say. "We're sitting ducks." While it was true that they were at risk, it was also true that wealthy people could more easily change their travel patterns, hire guards, protect themselves. And anyone, regardless of wealth or status or nationality or connections, could find themselves in the wrong place at the wrong time.

People grew angry. On all of our outlets, including TOLOnews and Arman FM, we aired stories on the blast walls and traffic, and the people's frustration, and about their resourcefulness. Kabul was suddenly a city of bikes; our head of finance at the time, a proud older man, happily rode his to the office rather than sitting for hours in a car. We aired stories about the government's inability, or unwillingness, to do anything about it. Powerful men owned land throughout the city, and they held on tight to what was theirs; the government could not figure out how to seize it in order to widen the roads. As Kabul expanded, the will to redesign such a big city faded. I started leaving for the office at 5:30 in the morning to avoid the traffic, telling myself that at least I could watch the sun rise over the mountains, still so beautiful, casting its long light over Kabul, now a war zone.

BEFORE KARZAI CAME on TOLO for an interview, during the summer following his 2004 election, I told our journalists to ask him the same question I had posed to him in one of our early meetings. "Ask him what his vision is for the country," I told them. "But push him for some detail."

Karzai had become aware of TOLO, only three days after we launched, when one of our reporters showed up to his press conference. "TOLO?" Karzai had said in wonder. "Broadcasting from here, in Kabul? When I go home, TOLO will be on my TV?"

He cared about a free media taking hold in Afghanistan and consented to an on-air interview. We assigned two journalists to the story. Massood Qiam, our biggest early star, spoke Dari, and while the other, Nawab Momand, had only a little bit of experience as a state broadcaster, he was earnest and hardworking, wearing a suit and tie while he was on the job, even one day, years later, when hiking through a remote province to interview a Taliban commander. And Momand was fluent in Pashto. Karzai could switch between Afghanistan's two major languages without missing a beat, a practice we liked to showcase on TOLO's panels and interviews. Occupying forces had exacerbated divisions between ethnic groups in Afghanistan, but the divisions predated the occupation; when I was growing up, you spoke either one language or the other in public settings. But Karzai made speaking both languages, without snobbery or prejudice, seem like a natural thing to do.

The interview took place in the palace courtyard on a beautiful

Kabul morning. The journalists were nervous, and Jahid, Zaid, and I spent some time prepping them. We wanted the interview to be substantive but not confrontational; we didn't want to alienate the Afghan president. "Give the president enough time to answer your questions," we said. "Don't talk over him. But don't let him go off on a tangent either."

They asked him about the upcoming parliamentary elections, about how he was building his staff. They talked about the changing Kabul. Finally, they asked, "What is your vision for the country?"

Just like he had with me, Karzai spoke only in broad platitudes. "I want Afghans to be happy," he said. How that would happen, or what happiness looked like in the context of an ongoing war, even one in which the American presence, at least at the beginning, had positive impact, he did not say, and our journalists did not press him.

The next day, when his team reached out to say that we would have to do the interview again—the president looked too nervous, they said, too stiff for his TOLO debut—I urged the reporters to push him on that final question. "I want him to give some substance, and some detail," I said. "You know, the population is young, and it's going to grow, so this is how we are going to create this many jobs. Or we would like to produce engineers and doctors, but we also need to train electricians and metal workers. The workers could leave, go to the Gulf states, and send their money back. How can we create housing? Etcetera. Do you get it?" The journalists nodded. They still looked nervous, but they were eager to prove themselves.

"You've got to give a little more," I said to Karzai before the retake. "People want to hear some detail."

He nodded, but still, when they asked, "Mr. President, what do you want for your country?" Karzai repeated the same line as the day before. "I want Afghans to be happy," he said, with a smile.

In the years to come, as Moby grew, and we expanded our list of television shows and launched a channel dedicated to covering the news, my visits to the Arg became rarer. They'd lost their novelty, a blessing because between the traffic and the security the journey could now easily take all morning. Every meeting had begun to feel the same. The fruits and nuts and small talk; the carousel of corrupt advisors lounging haughtily on the couches; the well-meaning president losing his grip on the country he loved. I stopped hoping that these meetings would have an impact. I understood the limitations of everyone involved—the country's, president's, the president's advisors, my own. I put my head down and focused on Moby. I stopped getting excited at the prospect of meeting a president.

Karzai and I also started to argue more, and he lost his patience with me. He worried that our programming would further upset conservative Afghans who had made new media a straw man for all their misgivings about a new Afghanistan. "How can you broadcast this stuff?" he would say to me. "Why is this character on my television?" It will anger the religious leaders, he would tell me, it will challenge the traditional Afghan family, it will turn people against our values as a country. He was furious when TOLO reporters interviewed Taliban fighters, and we aired their grievances—about the American occupation, the corruption, the lack of accountability. "Afghans cannot watch this," he would tell me, not bothering to hide his anger.

"Mr. President," I'd reply. "People are perfectly capable of turning their TV set on and off."

"They're not," he'd say. "They might not know any better." Karzai believed in the Afghan people, but behind the scenes, he was notoriously blunt about how far he thought the country had to go.

Most presidents want to lead from the top down, and Karzai had immense respect for tradition and traditional values. But the country had changed a lot over the past thirty years. People took up arms against the Soviets, power had been grabbed by the rag-tag Taliban forces, and there had been a collapse of civil order. In the post-2001 world, Afghans wanted authority in Afghanistan to come from the bottom up. Still, Karzai sometimes thought of himself as a king. And in a kingdom, you can tell people how to act, who to support, what to watch.

"If they're smart enough to vote for you," I would tell him, "they should be smart enough to figure out what to watch on TV." There was not a lot he could say to that.

CHAPTER 12

CORRUPTION

My father, Yassin Mohseni, was not a sentimental person. In fact, growing up in Japan and Australia, I thought of him as stoic and sometimes tyrannical, even when he listened to Persian music or recited Hafez or Rumi. He was a sophisticated, worldly man who could engage on almost every subject on earth, but he never really wanted to talk about his family. His mother died when he was very young, and he despised his stepmother, who kept him at a distance in favor of her biological children. He was raised by his grandfather's second wife, whom he remembered as being an unusually kind woman.

Back in Kabul after nearly twenty-five years away, though, my father seemed at his happiest when he was revisiting his past. He spent his days meeting old friends, scouring the city for anyone he knew who had not died during the wars and those who had returned, like him. He was then in his mid-seventies, still mobile and sharp, many years away from the stroke that would eventually lead to his death in 2023.

In Kabul, my father would leave the family house after breakfast and not return until nighttime, having discovered a friend living north of the city and spending hours piecing together their childhoods. He made new friends, drinking tea for hours with academics whose work he admired, talking to TOLO reporters about a new story they were working on, arguing over lunch with parliamentarians, exploring the old parts of the city, looking at what had changed. It was largely his passion for Afghanistan that had inspired any of us to return in the first place.

My father was exceedingly blunt, particularly for a diplomat, and his anger, lasting but a moment, could be explosive. He was driven equally by toughness and curiosity. In Kabul, he immediately sought out parts of the city that I couldn't face for the entire twenty years. Our childhood home, for instance—even after a few years in Kabul I had not been able to return to its street to see it.

I could picture it clearly enough. It was a simple place, a two-story house in a well-off neighborhood at the base of a mountain, and the first property my father bought with the money he made working at the foreign ministry, and that he transformed with his meticulous gardening. Flowering plants lined the walkway beyond the wooden front gate, and huge stones taken from the mountains that encircle Kabul were displayed like sculptures on either side of the front door to the house. He made sure to find sod imported from London in Kabul nurseries, which meant we had a bright green lawn even during the dry months. In front of this characterless, square house, identical to all others on the street, built to house Afghan technocrats, my father grew a peach tree that produced fruit so delicious that family friends would come from across the city to pick the peaches, wrapping each of them individually in tissue paper to transport home.

I hadn't seen that home since 1978, the year when the sound of gunfire from the Arg, which was right next to the school I attended, sent me running as fast as I could into the streets, searching for my mother, who was working nearby at the Ministry of Planning. It was the second coup in Afghanistan within five years, this time led by the Soviet-aligned People's Democratic Party of Afghanistan. It was the first time I saw dead bodies lying in the street. Watching from our windows as tank after tank rolled into the city, I was overcome with the feeling, both childish and wise, that nothing would ever be the same again.

One of my father's colleagues, who was also my classmate's father, was executed that day, as were the president and eighteen members of his family, including the children; over the coming year and a half, thousands of Afghans were taken as political prisoners and killed. Cousins and uncles of mine, friends who were closer than family, disappeared and were never heard from again. Over the next three months, before we left for Japan, the house felt like the only safe place. "Watch what you say on the street," my parents warned us. "Don't repeat anything you hear us saying at home; you never know who is listening."

Now, in a new Kabul, I had no urge to return to that street. What would have been the point? The house represented the chaos of those years in Afghanistan. It represented my realization, at twelve, that there was nothing my parents could do to stop the violence or to protect me, that even as a child I was pretty much on my own. I saw then, running through the streets looking for my mother, that in this world, people can be taken from their offices and shot. That a system, no matter how strong or how weak, can be instantly changed through violence. Relationships transformed in a moment; one day after the coup my father returned from a meeting with a university friend, a leftist who had enthusiastically taken a job with the new Communist government, as shaken as though he had met the enemy.

In any case, the house no longer belonged to us. In 2001, while we were still in Australia, we had been told by a friend that a man had recently moved in with his family. That man, a commander, had taken it from the mujahid-turned-thug who'd simply squatted in the house since 1992, and then forged ownership papers. When we first learned what had happened, we knew that such disputes would be impossible to settle from thousands of miles away in Australia. The house wasn't worth a lot of money when we'd lived in it, and was not worth a lot now. Still, we hated the idea of our family house being stolen.

Getting the house back was a matter of honor that my father obsessed over. Struggling in Australia to find work that engaged his sharp mind in the way that diplomacy had, he thought about our childhood home being occupied by some unknown man, a criminal who, my father had it on good authority, was a kidnapper, maybe even a pedophile. "It's not about money," he told us. "It's about justice, about right and wrong. It's about helping our city fight immorality and thuggery." I think that deep down he was also imagining those peaches, the stripes of color in the mountain rocks, his young children playing in the yard, the city outside still filled with promise. He was not sentimental, but he loved that house, his Kabul house, which he'd bought with his own money.

From the moment he first visited Kabul in 2002, shortly after Zaid and I had in September of that year, my father threw himself into getting the house back. In the years to come, while we built Moby, he wrestled that property, with its peach tree and English grass, away from the man he called a squatter, spending untold amounts of money on lawyers and intermediaries. Although he had connections in the Karzai government who offered to evict the man on his behalf, my father was so dismayed by the corruption that was already mounting throughout Afghanistan, he turned them down. "We will have to play the long game," he told us.

THE FIRST TIME I understood that the corruption that had already taken over so many Afghans was also insidious in the international presence, and that it would destroy the entire democratic experiment, was in 2005, from Sarah, then my girlfriend, in a story she told me almost in passing.

Sarah grew up in California, the daughter of Iranian immigrants, and fell in love with the region on a trip to Pakistan in

2000, the year before the US invasion of Afghanistan, and five years after she had graduated from college. Sarah had a background in fashion, and she was drawn to Central Asian textiles and designs, complex embroideries spun into orange suns and purple flowers, weeks of intricate handwork going into each dress. In 2000 and the summer of 2001, she had traveled around northern Pakistan, and was struck by how the poor inhabitants of this beautiful part of the world were only able to survive by receiving international aid, and she hoped that one day she could help change that paradigm.

That one day, back then, seemed impossibly remote. In September 2001, Sarah enrolled in business school at Berkeley, devising a project that combined her love of design with her desire to help people reliant on foreign aid, like those she had seen in Pakistan. After 9/11, for her as for me, a shock that opened up a part of the world she longed to see, Sarah was able to visit Afghanistan itself in lieu of a summer internship, where she met Afghan seamstresses. For her MBA thesis, she focused on social entrepreneurship and Afghan women in Peshawar, outlining in detail the kind of business she hoped could help prop up the community of Afghan women carrying on their country's traditional work as refugees in Pakistan. Their craft, which she so admired, had gone underappreciated in exile, when, given the right investment, it could be the thing that sustained and empowered them. She won highest honors for her thesis, and an award of $30,000 to start her project.

Sarah took her award money and moved to Afghanistan a few months after Zaid, Jahid, and I launched Arman. She found a traditional tailor and set up a business in a small house, eventually moving into a factory full of sewing machines, hiring women to come in and create, on a larger scale, the kind of intricate handmade clothing, tunics, and dresses—pieces of art, really—that Sarah had first envisioned a few years earlier in Pakistan. Partnering with a local businessman who was a master tailor himself, at one point she had nearly six hundred women working in her factory.

To support an enterprise of this size, Sarah and her partner took on some government and military contracts. At one point the Afghan security forces contracted out her factory and workers to make uniforms out of American fabric for its soldiers, perhaps an odd task when you remembered that the seamstresses were from the parts of Afghanistan where those troops would go to fight, but never mind. Afghanistan at the time was built on these kinds of contradictions and part of what made it so exciting also made it surreal. Besides, Sarah had to be practical. The security forces placed large orders that allowed her to employ large numbers of people and helped her grow the parts of the business that really mattered to her.

One day a procurement officer, an American, came into the factory for a routine meeting. He was a low-level military officer, young and unassuming; Sarah had hardly noticed him in prior meetings, and she and her partner had rarely discussed him. Nothing seemed off until after they exchanged pleasantries and out of nowhere, between some joking around, he casually brought up Rolex watches. "I would love to finally have one," he said. He liked the gold ones best, he added.

My impulse was to laugh when she told me this story. It seemed so absurd, so clumsy, this soldier demanding a luxury watch from an Iranian-American designer and her Afghan business partner, discussing their contract like a kidnapper demanding ransom. And we felt suddenly so naïve, for having presumed that at least the US military was in the country for the right reasons, that they were staying on to ensure stability and train local security forces that would then keep the country secure. Somehow, and it seems crazy now to remember such beliefs, I had held on to the idea that the American military at least was resistant to this type of rot, or that there was a disciplining hierarchy within that would prevent this from happening, or—and this is perhaps the most naïve part, the part that really makes me feel like a child when I remember it—that there was some inherent goodness in the individual American soldier, a reflection of the inherently good intentions of the US military.

Corruption was a poison that eventually lay the country to waste. It was everywhere, from the very beginning, even though it took a little while for me to see it clearly. It was the mysterious foreign contractor promising a remote village a well and then delivering nothing, the politician lining his pockets, the businessman paying bribe after bribe. It was the thug squatting in my family home, and the officials who offered well-connected Afghans like my father a way to circumvent the legal bureaucracy. The American military's contractors, who brought billions of dollars into the country with minimal accountability structures in place, were deeply, unfathomably corrupt. And so, sometimes the corruption took the form of the individual soldier asking for a gold Rolex; other times it looked like the $70 million highway construction contract that gets subcontracted so many times, with money pocketed at each step, that it ends up costing three times as much, and it buckles and breaks after just a few years.

After the story about the soldier and the watch, I started hearing stories of corruption almost daily. On a visit to the mayor's office, an official told me, casually, like recounting what he had for breakfast, "I have to pretend to take money, so that no one singles me out as a troublemaker." An acquaintance told me about a judge who kept a cash-counting machine under his desk just for bribes. Each checkpoint before a flight out of Kabul International Airport was an opportunity for extortion, some nervous travelers, worried they will miss their flights, choosing to hand over a wad of cash to immigration and security officials. Tom fumed when an airport worker had tried to charge him to bring through souvenirs he had purchased on Chicken Street.

We heard stories about the colleagues of a dead soldier demanding goods from his widow before they would hand over his pension; ministers expecting large bribes; village leaders extorting a little money from a middleman sent to arrange the construction of a well; strongmen profiting from the development of stolen land. Parliamentarians running for office simply to get immunity from criminal prosecution, winning with votes they bought with money they stole. Politicians offered TOLO producers money in exchange for favorable coverage ("Buy some airtime and run ads," I would tell them. "That's how you get elected."), and businesses tried to bribe us to be featured on the news. When we turned down cash from a businessman who had been happy with one of our programs, he sent a box of mobile phones to the office.

Although they were never formal employees, my parents were fanatical—at once useful, annoying, and amusing—about telling us to make sure that Moby stayed clean, from keeping track of things as simple as the vegetable orders that came through the cafeteria to making sure nothing was being skimmed off the top. There was ballot stuffing in the elections, fraud in the courts, chaos in the banking laws. Ghost wells, ghost schools, ghost women's centers, a country being built on empty promises.

Even the well-meaning media consultants who passed through Kabul year after year started to feel like a variation on corruption. The huge organizations they work for win US government contracts, saying they have the skills and expertise to help develop the Afghan media sector. They come to Kabul and do a workshop on, say, how to report on women's issues; they travel around a little bit in the country, and wax a little philosophical on the power of the media and the need for women's voices. Then they go back to New York or DC, send the government a bill, and report to their donors that they are building capacity, helping these unskilled Afghan journalists figure out how to report on

Afghanistan. It still happens, albeit largely outside of the country, today.

Afghans became depressed about this state of affairs. "Is this the country we deserve?" we wondered. Like many other parts of the world, Afghanistan had gotten embroiled in the politics of the Cold War, and what followed—the Soviet invasion, the civil war and outflux of refugees, abject poverty, mass radicalization, the complete repression of women—was unbearably grim. You can't blame people for taking what they can get when the opportunity presents itself, or a nation, seeing a sudden mass influx of cash, for collecting what it can before the spigots dry up. Of course, at a certain point, people need to take responsibility for their own country, need to account for the choices they made and figure out what went wrong and why. Many of us were perhaps too starry-eyed in the beginning, thinking that Afghans have been given a new chance, that the American presence and the American money would set the country on a better course.

Sarah and her partner had been shaken by the exchange with the American procurement officer. The military contract was a big one and would mean a lot of jobs for a lot of people, and it was hard to accept that, as prevalent as corruption was, it might infiltrate their business, which was founded on a vision of ethical and equitable production of goods. When a different American officer showed up at the next meeting, they were relieved that they might be able to forget it ever happened.

AT MOBY, CORRUPTION became as big of a beat as the war itself. We conceived of our radio and TV stations as places where people could come forward and expose any wrongdoing they were seeing. Before we even launched TOLO TV, we interviewed Ramazan Bashardost on Arman. Bashardost was Hazara, a historically oppressed and disenfranchised ethnic minority mostly based in Afghanistan's central provinces. He left Afghanistan following the 1978 coup and, after a few years as a refugee in Iran and Pakistan, made his way to France, where he lived for two decades, acquiring multiple advanced degrees, including a doctorate in law. In 2002, he returned to Afghanistan and began working for the Afghan foreign ministry.

Bashardost was soft-spoken in his everyday life, but fierce when it came to his political commitments. He was smart, but not egotistical; unlike a lot of Afghan men who had connections, he didn't seem to think it was his right to be close to power, or to possess it himself. As an Afghan nationalist, he was accustomed to rebelling in order to be heard, and because of his education, and proficiency in Dari, Pashto, English, and French, as well as his unwillingness to toe the party line, he quickly gained respect, even if begrudging, among the political elite. We became friendly, and it was at my house during one of my usual evening gatherings that a guest, who was close to Karzai, asked if Bashardost would be willing to leave the national security council, where he was not in a senior position, and join the cabinet. The minister of planning at the time was a Hazara too, but there was a movement afoot to unseat him. "There needs to be another Hazara in the role," someone said. "Why not you, Ramazan?" He looked sheepish, and everyone laughed, but the next day, the guest suggested his name to Karzai, and soon Bashardost was appointed minister of planning.

As minister—a post he held for nine months before being forced to resign over public statements that the majority of international aid money had been improperly dispensed and calling for an overhaul of the entire system—and later too, Bashardost became known for speaking out against corruption, a lot of which he did behind the Arman microphones or on TOLO. He said what Afghan people were feeling, challenging the mechanisms that fueled corruption; calling out crooked politicians, including colleagues; bemoaning the ethnic-divisions-based politics in parliament, naming ministers who had bought power through tribal leaders and were now in their pockets. Even the fact that he had been chosen to replace a Hazara minister because he was also Hazara didn't sit right with him, and he said so on air. "Corruption comes in different forms," he was known to say. "But Afghanistan is the only country in the world where it is legal."

A few months before his resignation, Bashardost came on Arman to debate Amin Farhang, then minister of the economy, a royalist who happened to be a close family friend of my mother's. Farhang was a Germany-educated technocrat, generally a gentleman, but pretty hopeless at his job, inept, afraid to rock the boat, and, worst of all, utterly detached from his country. "All you know is the five-minute drive between your house, the Arg, and the ministry," I would tell him. "You might as well be in Washington, you are so removed from ordinary Afghans." I had little respect for him as a minister, although I found him likeable enough as a person and tried to keep the peace for the sake of my mother. Bashardost had strong opinions about Farhang's work ethic, and didn't mind coming across as the shouting populist.

A few minutes after we went live, a producer ran into my office, breathless. "Saad jan, you have to come to the studio," he said. "They are about to start fighting!"

Usually, Afghans are very measured, even when arguing. It is culturally unacceptable to lose your cool, and we try very hard not to. But by the time I arrived in the radio studio both men were hurling insults at each other, Farhang calling Bashardost "naïve" and Bashardost saying the finance minister was an "egoist," about as abusive as it got in the studio. They did seem poised to throw punches, and after I calmed them down, we had to walk them out separately. Bashardost was on the radio again the next day.

We tried to investigate and cover corruption as well as we could. Weekly, it seemed, we ran stories about government contracts that amounted to nothing concrete in the provinces; businesses and institutions left to crumble while politicians got rich; foreigners profiting off shady businesses. We reported on people close to Karzai, including the underhanded dealings of one of his brothers and several of his ministers and advisors, provincial leaders, governors, parliamentarians. Later, we did the same with the Ashraf Ghani administration; corruption was so blatant, so pervasive, it usually felt like we were screaming into a void. In 2012, when we ran a damning exposé on Omar Zakhilwal, then the minister of finance, with bank statements proving that the minister had amassed a great deal of money, it was reported that Zakhilwal broke down crying during a meeting with some foreign diplomats. "You're not going to believe what happened," one of the diplomats said when they called me the next day. "It was so odd, he just burst into tears, complaining about being unfairly targeted and accusing everyone around him of corruption."

Another TOLO report exposed the scheme of Nematullah Shahrani, the acting minister of Hajj and religious affairs, to swindle pilgrims by charging them for flights from Kabul to Mecca on behalf of a nonexistent company and then pocketing the money. Our report was ironclad—a paper trail linking the minister to the company coupled with evidence that the company itself was a shell—but the minister needn't have worried. Neither he, nor the weeping Zakhilwal, lost their jobs. Even Karzai, who had campaigned so convincingly on his patriotic duty to Afghans and Afghanistan, didn't want to engage with the media on the topic of corruption. When I mentioned the Hajj minister's exploits to the president, he was annoyed about being confronted, and responded facetiously. "Good," he said. "Everyone else is doing it, why shouldn't he?"

"We have no well. We have no road," villagers would tell our TOLO reporters. "We don't want this guy in parliament; he's stealing." You could see the anger manifest on the streets, the shopkeeper shaking his fist at the warlord speeding by in a black SUV, the road rage that radiated from traffic jams. It was disturbing how quickly it all fell apart. But what good did complaining to reporters do even if we aired these complaints? I began bringing up corruption at every meeting I went to with American and Afghan officials. Through three US administrations, I have visited the White House, the NSA officials working on Afghanistan, the State Department, and the Department of Defense, telling anyone who would listen about the corruption proliferating in Afghanistan. "These are your people," I have said. The corrupt advisors and ministers, many of whom had been championed by the Americans, were destroying the country. "Surely you have some leverage?" I would ask. They listened, but they seemed to think there was nothing they could do. "The country is too big; it's too chaotic," they would tell me. "There is no corralling this type of corruption you're talking about."

When some representatives from the Institute for Liberty and Democracy came to Kabul and pointed to absence of land rights as a fundamentally corrupting issue that had prevented Afghanistan from truly developing, I brought their findings into my meetings with the Americans. "The problem is the titles are too often in dispute because Afghanistan has seen so many regime changes and nothing was formalized," I explained during a meeting with some government officials. "A piece of land will be developed and then three different people come forward claiming to own it, and no one feels comfortable buying or selling land. We need a central fund that can compensate people if their land is used for national development projects, and we need to electronically register land titles. Otherwise, the economy will just stall." The beleaguered-looking Americans shook their heads. "It's too long term," they told me. They threw fistfuls of money from Washington across the ocean, and if it landed somewhere in Afghanistan, that's good enough, appeared to be their attitude. Any project seen as longer term gained zero traction among the Americans, who, when it came to Afghanistan, seemed only to be able to think in terms of one or two years. "It won't be perfect; we've always known that," they said.

"Why isn't TOLO hitting the government harder on corruption?" people would constantly ask me. And I would say, "We are hitting them so hard our fists hurt." We hit them as hard as we could, and we continued hitting long after our fists were broken. We never stopped running stories on the people who continued to steal from Afghans, throughout the twenty years of war. And yet we watched, along with all Afghans, as that corruption destroyed our country. In Kabul, an untrustworthy Afghan government, under two different presidents, grew more protective of its ill-gotten gains. There were elections, but there was no accountability. And in the provinces, among the ghost schools and ghost roads and ghost wells, and the very real presence of American soldiers and drones and night raids and extrajudicial killings, the Taliban only grew stronger.

My father, Yassin Mohseni, though, was a determined man, and he showed up week after week in Kabul courts with piles of paperwork, mountains of evidence, and a lawyer who not-so-secretly wished his client would just lean on his government connections already. My father wanted nothing to do with even the minuscule amount of corruption it took to call in a favor for a friend. And after years of patience and fortitude, gathering together all the right documents, proving that he had continued to pay the mortgage even when we were outside of the country, and showing the thug that it was better to take his offer than lose in court and embark on what could be generations of bad blood with such a tenacious family, my father won back our childhood home.

PART III

CHAPTER 13

A NEWSROOM

KABUL, 2023

Every morning, reporters, producers, and editors at TOLO—those who stayed after the US withdrawal and those new employees brave enough to apply for new openings—meet to discuss what stories will run that day, online and on television. It's a routine that we instated from the beginning at Arman, and no different from the morning editorial meetings that journalists and editors have at the *New York Times* or the BBC to start their day. Reporters outline their stories and pitch ideas, editors okay or kill stories, producers begin to line up sources and arrange transportation, cameramen are dispatched, a van is outfitted with sound equipment, new hires reluctantly agree to take on a few hours of copyediting on the website. For the hour the editorial meeting lasts, things at TOLO can seem fairly normal.

In a matter of weeks in 2021, Moby lost the majority of our star journalists and producers, the people who would be recognized and worried they would be Taliban targets; Jahid and Shafic Gawhari, Moby's managing director, took over the responsibility of arranging buses to the airport, securing seats on humanitarian flights, and starting paperwork for asylum status in the US or apartment rentals in Pakistan, while I also did what I could from afar, calling well-connected people I knew, like the Afghan-Australian BBC News journalist Yalda Hakim or the Afghan American diplomat Zalmay Khalilzad, who were already working feverishly to get people out. That we were assisting in the gutting of our company's personnel didn't seem ironic, or even particularly remarkable. We were ourselves out of the country already—Jahid and Zaid with their families in Portugal and Australia, respectively, our father in Dubai and our mother in Australia, and me by coincidence on a business trip in Europe. If the last thing we did for Moby was help our staff get to safety, it would be a worthy thing to do. We tried not to think about the possibility that the Moby offices might need to shutter, with our papers and books where we left them in our offices, the screens silent and dark, the whole place already a museum to another Afghan era.

But an interesting thing started to happen. As soon as we knew that someone had managed to leave, we would post the job opening—needed, a reporter fluent in Pashto, an actor with a comedy background to host a late-night show, a producer with some knowledge of online editing, a copy editor, a driver, a cook, a presenter; eventually, the head of human resources himself—and almost immediately, we would begin receiving applications. Some were employees from other local media companies that had shut down. Others were stringers who had worked for international news organizations and chosen to stay in the country. Recent college graduates, with no work experience, showed up at our door. On a few occasions, young reporters who had been cutting their teeth at other organizations quit those jobs to come work for Moby, which they told us had always been their dream. Positions were filled almost as quickly as they were listed. Months after the Taliban took over, TOLO was one of the few remaining Afghan news agencies still open in Kabul. Owing mostly to the doggedness of our staff, new and old, we were still reporting. And to this day, every day at 8:00 a.m., the TOLO team still meets to talk about the news programming for the day.

One morning, the meeting focused on women's and girls' education. TOLO reports on this issue nearly every day in some

capacity, interviewing critics of the Taliban policy, sending female reporters to interview girls at home. Another morning, they
figured out how best to report on protests against the Taliban's
latest suppressive measure, a delicate topic that our journalists
remain determined to cover. During another meeting journalists
might share tips on how best to conduct interviews with Taliban officials. You can ask the minister of education about when
schools are reopening, but not directly about girls' education.
When possible, have a male colleague call a source, or schedule
an interview. It's just easier, and we have to be pragmatic; our first
priority is to get the story out. Choose the words for your questions and for the on-air report carefully; the Taliban remain angry about all those years when they felt villainized by the media.
Be certain to refer to Afghanistan as the Islamic Emirate in your
interviews, news presentations, and writing. Women journalists,
of course, should cover their hair and, ideally, wear a mask over
their nose and mouth.

"Journalists should be fearless," a reporter, a Hazara woman
with years of experience, said. "When we're scared, that's when
the self-censorship comes in. We stop being able to do our jobs."
She sat on what served as the women's side of the room that
morning, even though the curtain between the two sides was only
pulled closed if outsiders were visiting, or if we got word of an
impending raid. Behind her, a wall of televisions played BBC,
CNN, and TOLO's morning news, a young anchor with stiffly
gelled black hair talking on mute in front of a photo of a minister delivering a press conference; a large window in the room
overlooked the studio where he was being filmed. Computers
lined the walls, showing stories and photos in various stages of
editing.

Afghan reporters continue to cover the big stories, even the
ones they assume would invite the Taliban's scrutiny but, somehow, don't always, at least not at TOLO. In 2023, we ran a one-

hour special on violence perpetrated by IS-KP that was aided by footage supplied by the Taliban, even though during the early days of the new Taliban regime we covered IS-KP violence only in headlines, rightly assuming we wouldn't yet have the cooperation of the government; the Taliban see ISIS as a threat to their own authority and are sensitive regarding any portrayal of ISIS's presence in Afghanistan. We cover the relentless, depressing Afghan brain drain, the professors, engineers, and scientists who have fled Kabul, making sure there's no suggestion of blame on the people who choose to leave. Every day we run stories on the astonishing challenges faced by Afghan women and girls. One day, it's a story about young female medical students not being allowed to finish their degrees, another day a story about women doctors leaving the country out of fear or inability to work, and the next day a story about women who can't be treated for pregnancy-related issues because of the lack of female doctors. The Afghan public has a right to know what's going on in their country. While we are careful about how we report these issues—often quoting the UN or statements by leaders of other nations, including a response from the Taliban spokesman, and avoiding anything resembling editorializing—these types of stories do not require commentary.

Uplifting stories, about the astonishing resilience displayed again and again by ordinary people, must also be done. Some women, having lost their jobs because of a Taliban restriction, set up small businesses in their garages, selling treats and clothing, and our journalists report on their newfound entrepreneurship. There have been stories about family members helping one another, including sometimes to leave Afghanistan; about girls finding a way to get some kind of schooling. TOLO TV producers have even adapted these clandestine lessons into a short series, which has aired without pushback from the Taliban, at least not yet.

In June 2022, a magnitude 6.2 earthquake struck southeastern Afghanistan, killing over a thousand and injuring over fifteen hundred people. Along the border with Pakistan, it is one of the poorest parts of the country. Our reporters were among the first to arrive at the scene, interviewing panicked, injured people and their families, who were trying to find a way to transport them hours away to the nearest hospitals. Even before the earthquake, the people of that region, harassed by years of air strikes and night raids—what the Americans called counterinsurgency— likely felt relieved about the Taliban's return to power. By the time TOLO reporters arrived, Taliban officials had already visited the affected areas and begun the process of arranging aid. Under Ghani or Karzai, the villagers were sure, it would have taken officials days to show up in person to inquire about such tragedies in the far reaches of the country.

TOLO ran stories about the victims' demolished homes, built by hand with mud and brick, which couldn't withstand the tremors. There were only dirt roads in and out of many of the villages, in these remote mountainous areas, and access was further limited because of the rains and mudslides that followed the earthquake; with the main paved roads damaged too, thousands of vulnerable people were left trapped where they were. When one of our vans broke down along a paved road up the mountains, reporters had to wait a long time for help to arrive. Local clinics struggled to cope with the injured, and it was feared that hundreds of people might still be buried under rubble.

Before the withdrawal and the sanctions that followed, international aid would have rushed in sooner and international media outlets would have picked apart every element of the disaster, analyzing it for what it said about the American war or the Afghan government's capabilities. Now their coverage was much more limited. They relied on local stringers, used footage produced by state media and first responders for their broadcasts. Although the Taliban asked for international help, no one seemed inclined to stay for a significant amount of time. There are a million reasons why foreign journalists have mostly moved on from Afghanistan. We can't dwell on why. Many of those outlets, as well as the United Nations, relied on TOLO's coverage of the earthquake.

Before the withdrawal, Afghan military helicopters and transport planes would have been used to deliver aid and services, but now many of those planes are parked in airports in Uzbekistan and Tajikistan, where Afghan Air Force pilots, fleeing with their own families, and high-ranking government officials and their families, had flown them in August 2021. There would have been more aid workers able to reach the region; now many told us they couldn't come, or their organizations wouldn't send them.

It was even more important, therefore, that TOLO reporters stay on in the region and report on the aftermath of the quake too, if for no other reason than to create a historical record. "When a major tragedy happens, you don't want to immediately start blaming the people in charge anyway," a producer said during the morning meeting. "You can highlight the lack of care for women in a subtle way. Give voice to the victim who says that by the time she was able to reach a clinic she couldn't get treated because there are no female doctors. People are smart enough to understand what that means."

ONE MORNING IN April 2023, the top story discussed at the meeting was the Taliban's recent announcement that Afghan women would no longer be permitted to work for the United Nations in Afghanistan. A huge blow to the hundreds of working women and the families that depended on their income, it seemed another step in the elimination of women from the workforce. In December 2022, a ban had been issued on women working for both local and international NGOs. The UN had been excluded, however, and several of the NGOs had managed to negotiate assurances from local leaders, so that their women staff kept on working. The fear now was that those exemptions would no longer hold. Thoughts about assignments and headlines quickly turned into a discussion about the particular challenges facing female journalists in the newsroom. "I'd like to interview a woman about losing her job," a reporter volunteered. Both the women's and men's sides of the room were so packed she shouted a bit to be heard. "Maybe a woman who is the only person in her family who is still employed. These UN jobs mean a lot to families now."

"It's a big story," her editor conceded. He looked distressed. "I'm not sure that we can air this story with a female reporter presenting it right now, though," he told her, holding up his hands in despair. The Taliban government had allowed Moby to stay open, with its officials regularly participating in panels and being interviewed for stories on TOLO. But we knew they watched us closely to make sure we didn't violate their red lines, which changed regularly, sometimes unexpectedly. Women still worked at Moby. In fact, in an effort to counterbalance some of the closures of other workplaces in the city, we had more women working for us now than prior to the withdrawal. But would sending a woman to report this story be seen as a provocation? Would it move the Taliban to ban women from working in media too? These were the types of questions we were forced to ask ourselves during these editorial meetings, and if we wanted to keep reporting the news, we had to be strategic.

The reporter tried not to show her frustration. She had been following the rules. Even at home, she watched what she said and how she acted. She pulled her scarf over her mouth when passing through the Taliban checkpoints, and she had not traveled outside Kabul without a male relative. But her ability to do her job was growing more difficult by the hour. One day, interviewing people on the street, she was harassed by members of Taliban security and told that if she didn't leave, she would be arrested. Pressure on reporters was hardly a Taliban invention; TOLO staff had encountered plenty of intimidation, including detentions and arrests, under both Karzai's and Ghani's administrations. But when the reporter called her ministry sources to press them on such treatment of reporters, they asked to speak to her male supervisor. "They said they didn't have to talk to me anymore," she said.

After that, her supervisor had suggested she work from the office for a few days, editing online stories, instead of street reporting. "It's safer," he told her. "Just until they forget your face." She complied, but inside, she felt furious, all the time. "We can't send a female reporter, and the story is about women," she complained, slouching down in her chair in frustration. "And we can ask the women, 'How do you feel about losing your job?' but if they dare to point fingers at the government, we can't air what they say. It's impossible to be a journalist in Afghanistan."

"We have to be careful," another female reporter said. "Even if right now we don't face a direct threat, even if women are still allowed to work in media in Afghanistan, no one knows what could happen next week, or tomorrow."

From the women's side of the room came yet another pitch. "I've been on the streets talking to people who have lost their jobs," the reporter told the room. "It's been two weeks. I've spoken to men and women. I asked their children to tell me how life had changed for them now that the Americans were gone."

Journalism ran in the blood of the reporter whose editor was protectively asking her to stay off the beat for a while; her favorite aunt, a TV reporter, had often taken her to work when she was little, and she'd studied journalism at Kabul University. She was one of the newer staffers who filled the place of a reporter who'd fled, and before coming to us, she had worked for a smaller Afghan news outlet. Working for TOLO had been her dream job, which the withdrawal made happen much faster than she'd ever imagined. Now, she was the only person in her household, which includes her parents and five siblings, with a steady income.

"The last step for this story on the UN ban was to talk to someone at the ministry," she went on. "I called the office and was told that I could come to meet the deputy minister." She compiled her questions, pinned on her headscarf, and went.

When she arrived for the meeting, though, she said she was greeted with contempt. "They kept me waiting with no explanation," she said. "After a while, his spokesperson came out of his office. The deputy minister doesn't want to talk to women, he told me."

"What did you do?" a colleague asked.

"What could I do?" The reporter sighed. "I had to leave, so I left." Because running the story without the government response could be seen as combative, and the reporter did not want to hand her hard work over to another colleague, they put the story on hold while they figured out what to do.

"That's not the only time something like this has happened," she continued. "A few weeks before schools were to reopen last month, officials from the Ministry of Education were still insisting that they were planning to allow teenage girls to return during the new school year." The Taliban had said that girls were only temporarily prohibited from attending secondary school while they figured out how to "make the environment safer."

"I got a tip from someone at a clothing factory that they had not received an order from the ministry for girls' uniforms," she said. "How could these girls possibly return to school if they didn't have the appropriate uniforms to wear?"

When our reporter showed up at a school to ask that school's principal about the uniforms, and whether they were preparing to enroll girls above sixth grade that year, he looked visibly unhappy. "It's not our job to get them clothes," he told her.

"I told him, you haven't answered my question," our reporter said. She pushed him, telling him that she knew that the factory she'd visited hadn't received any orders for girls' uniforms. "He got angry," she said. "He told me to leave. Your face isn't covered, he said, I'm not going to talk to you. Go home and cover your face."

Another reporter spoke about a middle-aged woman whom she had seen at every protest she'd covered. She spoke to the woman and found out that she was a wife and mother, someone who'd never taken part in a protest, until the Taliban took over. "I asked her if I could write a profile of her," the reporter said. "She agreed, so I started to shadow her." When the woman marched with other women through the busy main road alongside the ministry buildings, the reporter followed. When the protesters were confronted by security forces, the reporter was there. One day she saw the woman being led away by a police officer. "Where are you taking her?" she asked the officers, but they didn't answer. Months later, the woman's family told the reporter that she still hadn't returned home, and the reporter couldn't get anyone in the government to answer her questions.

When the Taliban first took over Kabul, and Afghans gathered in the streets, determined to voice their anguish and dissent, we sent our news crews to cover them. Taliban security forces would confront anyone they saw holding a camera, both men and women. "They acted like they couldn't stand us," a reporter said, referring to the Taliban police, many of them rank and file fighters who found themselves in Kabul for the first time, having fought in the far reaches of the country during the past two decades. "They think that it's because of us their relatives were killed, their young men went to fight, the Americans dropped bombs on their villages. That's what they think about journalists. They see us as the enemy."

TWO FORCES UNDERLIE every editorial meeting at TOLO since the Taliban regained power. One is the resolve of the journalists and producers, men and women, to do their best to get the news to the Afghan public. They have taken jobs they know might put them in the spotlight and could make them more vulnerable to scrutiny by the new government. Yet morning after morning they arrive with notebooks of leads, contacts to call, sources to share. Even the airing of grievances, particularly among women, is part of this resolve; the editorial meeting is a safe place, the newsroom a family.

The second force is something closer to pure necessity. It's the necessity to keep moving and working, to keep your head above water in an uncertain time in a changing place. Reporters, like everyone in Kabul these days, feel some relief at getting into a car in the morning, heading to the office, working, eating lunch, talking to colleagues, getting paid. At our various outlets—the predominantly Dari Arman and TOLO; our Pashto channels, Lemar and Arakozia FM; and of course our twenty-four-hour TOLOnews—they go into a machine that never turned off, working alongside the few colleagues who never left, and the new ones who joined when others did. Reporting stories, they connect to other Afghans, which feels good and meaningful even if the conversations happen over the phone and not in person. While some ministers might refuse to take the call of a female reporter, that same reporter is best positioned to interview other Afghan women, in part because of access, in part because they understand each other's challenges even better now than before.

When the Taliban took over Kabul in August 2021, we didn't let it occur to us that we might have to close our doors. But today we do sometimes wonder, although we try not to, why they let us stay open at all. The Taliban clearly understand that they need an independent Afghan media alongside state media. But what do they imagine that media to be in the years to come? Often, TOLO staff ask themselves the same question during the morning editorial meeting.

"It's because we're still the most watched channels in Afghanistan," one speculates. "They understand that it'd be a big deal to shut us down." More than fifteen million people still watch Moby products, and the Taliban understand there would be backlash if we suddenly went dark. We had been on the ground reporting from Kabul while most other stations had closed or left the country. We had the resources to cover the earthquake, and we have connections to international officials and legitimacy around the world. This isn't the Taliban of the 1990s; the men in power understand the power of a functioning, compelling media outlet. "It's simple," the reporter continued. "When they have a press conference, they want as many people to watch it as possible."

From the other side of the room, another theory, at once both hopeful and troubled. "When we are on TV, we demonstrate to the world that there are still women in public places in Afghanistan," the reporter said. "That's good for everyone."

CHAPTER 14

TOM

When Sarah first met Tom Freston, she had no idea who he was, never mind that the man her friend had invited along to have breakfast with them at Balthazar in New York was the COO of Viacom and the cofounder of MTV. She didn't know that Tom had lived in Kabul in the 1970s—a relentlessly inquisitive traveler who instantly fell in love with the place—or that he had once headed a successful company there, exporting clothing and textiles, and that, like Sarah, he had a passion for the country and its striking, singular aesthetics. All she knew was that, on a business trip to New York for her Afghan textile factory, she had met a woman at a party who, upon hearing that Sarah was based in Kabul, had teared up relating her own stories of 1970s Afghanistan and said, "You have to meet my friend Tom," and who, before they all walked into Balthazar for breakfast, had offered to share her joint, "a throwback to her hash-filled memories of Kabul," Sarah says. As it was ten in the morning, both Sarah and Tom declined, but breakfast was great, a meeting of minds that became a friendship.

At that point, Tom was already a legend in media. In the 1980s he had been instrumental in building MTV into a global phenomenon, spearheading the groundbreaking "I Want My MTV" marketing campaign and transforming a channel of music videos into a lifestyle for young people across the globe. He also had a colorful, adventurous background, having catapulted himself as a young adult from the dregs of Vietnam War–era America and then an unsatisfying career in advertising, to countries that, to him, seemed most fascinating, most exotic, most rich for exploration, and that would open up his American mind as quickly and fully as possible. Sometimes, he describes the choice as simple; either he explored the world or he stayed put in America and was put on the Charmin toilet paper account.

What others found daunting, Tom found exciting. Following a stream of Western travelers to Afghanistan, he was one of the few who stayed on out of a genuine reverence for the country and the people, and with a businessman's eye for profit. His clothing company was doing tremendously well when the April 1978 coup that forced my family out of Kabul happened. It was no longer safe for him to stay, and he moved to India for a while; by the time Sarah met him, Tom hadn't been back to Afghanistan in close to three decades. Still, even when ascending the ranks at MTV and then Viacom, he could never get Afghanistan out of his head.

Tom and I have been close friends now for nearly two decades, and his life has taken many turns during that time. But if I had to describe him in one word, it would be "curious." There are few new experiences Tom will turn down or interesting strangers he will refuse to meet. At that first meeting, Tom and Sarah talked like old friends, bound by their mutual obsession with a country where neither had family ties, and to which both nevertheless felt deeply connected. Tom is a natural storyteller, and Sarah would call the feeling she got hearing his memories of Afghanistan a "borrowed nostalgia."

"I listened to him, and I looked at his photos from the '70s, and I thought, this is the most beautiful place I've ever seen," Sarah would tell me later, as we discussed what had remained constant and what had changed about Kabul over the years. "Tom's Afghanistan became almost like a drug I was chasing," Sarah said.

Tom found Sarah equally fascinating. Being Iranian-American, she spoke fluent Farsi and was more clued in to the part of the world he so missed. She was adventurous and incisive and similarly fascinated with Kabul. And she was funny, joking about how, in her early twenties, she was so desperate to see Afghanistan that she would have considered marrying a Talib in order to relocate to Kabul. They both had a lightness and tenderness when they talked about the country, which was neither's homeland, which was rare at a time when the place was either misconstrued or maligned, and that had felt good to share. Tom had been following the news out of Afghanistan as best he could over the years, but it was painful to first try to make sense of a void of information and then to pick through a glut of war reporting. He'd tried to put it all out of his mind; almost everyone he had met during those years in Afghanistan was either dead, in exile, or missing.

Kabul today is different, Sarah told him, it is shockingly cosmopolitan and exciting and, as long as you are careful, you can travel outside the capital too. When they had finished eating, she said, in a classic Sarah way that made me cringe then and makes me cringe now, "You have to meet my boyfriend. He's the Rupert Murdoch of Afghanistan."

A few weeks later, I was looking for Tom in the lobby of the Four Seasons Hotel in New York. He'd brought along one of his two sons, who had heard about his father's adventures but hardly believed them; what teenager is going to be able to imagine his business executive father riding horses through rural Afghanistan? We sat near one another for forty minutes before realizing who the other person was. "I think I was expecting a warlord or something," he joked. "That's okay," I replied. "I was looking for the Marlboro man."

Tom and I hit it off instantly. After only a few minutes of talking, I was confessing to all the challenges of running Moby, but also all my ambitions for the company. I described the format of *Afghan Star*, an *American Idol*–inspired show, which had recently launched, and Tom gave me notes on it and correctly predicted that it would become TOLO's most beloved program. As different as our lives were—Tom, a senior executive at a multibillion-dollar corporation, me trying with my siblings to make sure that our media company in Afghanistan was sustainable and profitable; Tom, two decades older than me and shaped by 1960s America, me the child of an Afghan diplomat-turned-asylee—we actually had a lot in common. I gifted him a traditional Afghan coat called a chapan; it had been given to me the week before by Rashid Dostum, the Northern Alliance leader whose forces had been linked to the mass death of Taliban prisoners early in the war. Dostum had served in the Karzai administration, and I'd met him as I met everyone who was an important part of the government, no matter the controversy attached to them.

That chapan was a ridiculous garment, thick and heavy with a lining made entirely from fox skin, and I thought Tom would get a kick out of receiving such an item from so notorious a person. He did, sharing my sometimes darkly absurd sense of humor. His wife at the time, though, a vegan, did not find the coat very funny, and at our next meeting Tom admitted to me that she'd thrown it out.

"You know, the backlash you're facing is not that different from what we went through in the Deep South with MTV," he told me. Conservative Americans hated MTV and everything it represented about godless liberal America. Tom was told constantly that it would never be embraced in places like Alabama and that its international expansion would fail, whether in post-Communist East Germany or parts of the developing world, all of which turned out to be completely wrongheaded. "Kids everywhere sing in the shower," he said. "Or, you know, pretend their hairbrush is a microphone."

My family had largely spoken disparagingly of the Westerners who flocked to Afghanistan in the 1960s and '70s, seeing them all as hippies, aimless people with their messy hair and unwashed clothes. We didn't know what they wanted from Afghanistan, and some of the stories they later told us—about the prevalence of drugs, or meeting girls in hostels—seemed so foreign as to be from an alternate universe. When I once asked my most adventurous cousin if he had ever dated one of the young tourists who came to Kabul, he only laughed, saying they smelled too much of pot and sweat, although I was certain he had never been close enough to them to confirm that.

Tom was not really a hippie, or at least he wouldn't consider himself part of that crowd. His recollections of Kabul felt more familiar. Some of the places Tom had visited I knew from my childhood. I recognized the guesthouses he described, barebones but clean, nestled in the still-small city, run by friendly open-minded locals. He described navigating the courtesies specific to different Afghan tribes in order to get the best fabric, hire the most skilled seamstresses. "At the time, when you entered the country from the west via Herat, the police would make you buy a joint of hashish," he once told me. "Like a tax for crossing the border." I had no idea if that was exaggerated for a good story, but I felt some of Sarah's borrowed nostalgia when Tom talked about Kabul. "The 1970s were a great time to be in Afghanistan," I said to him, "but you know, 2006 isn't that bad either."

Not long after we first met, Tom was fired as CEO of Viacom for failing to buy the social media website MySpace before its competitor News Corp. The decision would turn out to be prescient after the social networking site, within just a few years, was overwhelmed by Facebook's growth. Still, in the immediate wake of his firing, Tom felt unmoored and yearned for an adventure. "Come to Kabul," I told him. "Clear your head."

I MET UP with Tom in Dubai, from where he was planning to fly into Kabul with a couple of friends. In late spring 2007, Tom's itin-

erary for his Afghanistan trip wasn't particularly adventurous—
some days in Kabul, a trip to Bamiyan, meetings with interesting
people in politics and culture and business—but I knew the logistics could be a hassle, and I wanted to make sure everything went
smoothly. I was hoping that Tom would join Moby's board once
he saw the energy in our offices and got a sense of how eager,
smart, and imaginative our staff were, in spite of their relative
lack of experience.

As we were boarding, I received a call from Amrullah Saleh,
then head of Afghanistan's intelligence agency. "Sabet is furious,"
Saleh told me. "He says he's reached the end of his rope." In mid-
April 2007, Abdul Jabbar Sabet, Karzai's mercurial attorney general, had expressed his fury at TOLO for airing a quote of his on
the evening news, which he insisted was taken out of context; on
his orders, police raided our offices and detained three of our staff
members for several hours. Now, weeks later, he was still insisting
that we retract the quote, and was also threatening to arrest me.

A lawyer with a bushy grey beard, Sabet had worked in Washington, DC, for *Voice of America Pashto* during the '80s and
emigrated to Montreal in the late '90s before returning to Afghanistan in 2003. Prior to his appointment as attorney general
in September 2006, Sabet had been a special advisor at the interior ministry, where he headed a campaign against prostitution
and alcohol sales at foreign-owned bars in Kabul. As attorney
general, Sabet had the authority to ask the police force to investigate crimes and make arrests, and he soon became known for his
loose-cannon manner of prosecution. He'd been tasked by Karzai with cracking down on corruption, and he talked a big game,
declaring the work his personal jihad. "We have corruption because of temptation, poverty, and war," he told NPR. I happened
to agree with him—corruption was inevitable in a country where
inequality was extreme and pervasive—but the attorney general's
vindictive approach did little to counter the root causes.

Sabet craved the spotlight and had tried to use TOLO to get attention even before he became attorney general. "Send your reporters tonight," someone from his office would call to tell us. "There will be a big raid on a human trafficking ring." Our reporters would return later, shaking their heads. "They just went into another Chinese restaurant," they said. "Arrested a few waitresses." Sabet's work may have saved those waitresses from being trafficked, or breaking the law by participating in sex work, but regardless of the outcome, Sabet's focus seemed always to be on painting himself the hero.

The Americans had supported his appointment, it was said, because he had spoken positively, in his capacity as an Afghan official, about the conditions at the Guantánamo detention camp. He was fluent in English and would give an impression of being honest and upstanding. Americans were always looking for a silver bullet in Afghanistan. "Is he a good guy or a bad guy?" they were fond of asking me, as though anyone's character could be reduced to that simple binary. When it came to Sabet, I couldn't tell the Americans what to think. But among Afghans he became known mostly for being thin-skinned and quick to retaliate. When Moby became the target, I could usually smooth things over with a conciliatory phone call or visit, but not always.

With pressure on him to do the impossible task of ridding a country fueled by bribes and corruption, and possessing an unforgiving ego that made Moby's independent viewpoint particularly challenging to him, Sabet decided to scapegoat the media. Karzai's administration had been putting pressure on us for at least a year, and Moby was the target of a string of hollow cases, busywork meant to distract us or strain our resources, something Sabet supported in his capacity. None of the allegations were strong enough to go to trial, but each kept our legal counsel and TOLO executives tied up at the information and culture ministry, answering inane questions about whether the soaps we aired were anti-Afghan, or if a character on one of our comedy sketch shows was actually a caricature of the minister of interior. (That dimwitted character very plainly was, but this was not, our lawyers reminded the interrogators, illegal under the media laws that had been ratified by Karzai himself.) Zaid and I also expended a whole lot of time presenting our case to Afghan and international allies; at one point we filed a complaint with the Supreme Court, and I visited the chief justice myself just to ask him, "How can we get these guys off our backs?"

Sabet's first move against Moby was to open a case, at the behest of the minister of information and culture, Abdul Karim Khurram, for, according to them, illegally giving Al Jazeera English a platform on our Pashto-language station, Lemar TV. "Al Jazeera is operating on the Afghan airwaves without a license," the complaint read. "They are being illegally hosted by Lemar." The minister had accused Al Jazeera of challenging the "cultural and the legal authority of the government."

It was a case so straightforward, so clear cut, that it was almost comical. No one wanted to spend any time arguing against it, but of course we had to take it seriously. "We have a commercial arrangement," Zaid said, showing them the contract. Al Jazeera English had launched only a few months prior and was clearly going to be a very strong outlet, and we thought that airing some of their content every night on Lemar would help bolster trust and interest in our equally new station. "We buy one hour of programming and air it," I said, more times than I cared to count, over the course of so many meetings with the ministry my head spun at the wasted time. "They do not need a license in order to be syndicated by us."

We went back and forth for weeks, Moby's lawyers spending so much time at the ministry arguing the same points, producing the same evidence, that it started to feel like an absurdist drama, one in which a critic might roll their eyes at the cliché of a playwright once again equating bureaucracy with hell. Eventually, out of pure frustration and just to try to reclaim some of those wasted hours, we got rid of the Al Jazeera segment in April 2007. After several more months of arguments and meetings, the case was eventually dropped.

I was en route from Kabul to Dubai on April 17, 2007, when the evening news at TOLO ran a story about prisons and capital punishment in Afghanistan. It included a clip of Sabet at a press conference criticizing the "system" for having one set of rules for locals and a different one for foreign soldiers who committed crimes in Afghanistan. We aired the quote, which Sabet had spoken, on the record, with full knowledge that he was being recorded by news cameras, but Sabet, no doubt after receiving criticism from his colleagues at the interior ministry, was furious. He called the reporter, saying that his remarks had been presented out of context, ordering him to come to his office and apologize. The reporter, with full support of the Moby team, refused. While my phone was on airplane mode, Sabet filled my voicemail with his rantings about how the story made it seem as if he'd been criticizing the Karzai government.

That same evening, Sabet ordered a raid on TOLO. Fifty armed policemen arrived at our offices and arrested three of our staffers; four AP employees who were observing the raid were also arrested, and other TOLO employees were shoved to the ground, kicked, and punched. These scenes were captured on TOLO security cameras, and, of course, we aired them on the news later that night. By then the TOLO and AP staff had been released, and I had flown back from Dubai. Over the coming weeks, as journalists and politicians and civil society figures rallied to our support, TOLO's news team aired interviews with people criticizing Sabet's dismal record of fighting corruption and his use of the Afghan police and judiciary to fight his own vendettas. We did stories about his past alignment with Gulbuddin Hekmatyar, whom the Americans had recently declared a terrorist and made public a shady deal he'd made to secure his house. We filed complaints against Sabet for at least eleven breaches of the law, asking that he be suspended from his position, and I called my contacts in the international community and the Arg to protest his aggression. TOLO's comedians mocked him on the late-night shows, and each day our news team went through his press conferences and media appearances to pick the most incendiary quotes to put on air; there were plenty to choose from.

Sabet, of course, fought back. He appealed to the media commission, which ruled against us. Some of his supporters alleged that we ourselves were taking an ethnically partisan position. He called people who knew us and those who used to work for us, trying to build a case but getting nowhere. Inarguably one of the most powerful figures in Afghanistan at the time, Sabet was also one of the most disliked. I have never heard of a single person who agreed to contribute to his case against Moby, and no one came forward on their own to be beside him. One day I pushed my way through a crowd of protesters in front of our offices, chanting against TOLO. I recognized Haji Abdul Rahman Mohammadi, a well-known former strongman who had been paralyzed in a fight and gone on to lead the Afghan paralympic team. Like Sabet, Mohammadi was a bit of a loose cannon, once shooting himself in the foot to show his displeasure with a government measure. He now led a gang of former fighters and paralympic athletes, all in wheelchairs or on crutches, who would, for a small fee or political favor, pose as protesters outside of government offices or businesses, or do some interviews for the state media to show how much support there was for Sabet. "What are you doing?" I asked, annoyed.

He shrugged. "Someone told me to be here," he replied.

"I know who it is," I told him, heading toward Moby's gates.

In the office, I and a few others rang Mohammadi to try to

get him to leave. We explained what Sabet had been doing. We wouldn't offer money, of course, but sometimes men like Mohammadi just crave acknowledgment, to be reasoned with rather than bribed. When I left that evening, the protesters were still there, but this time they were holding signs in support of Moby. "Down with the attorney general," they shouted, clapping. Approached by a reporter and his cameraman, Mohammadi spoke passionately into the microphone. "It's good TV," he said. "They defend the rights of the people."

"SABET HAS HAD enough," Saleh warned me. "He has ordered you to be arrested at the airport." I called Vice President Ahmad Zia Massoud, a friendly acquaintance, with the news. Massoud said he would help if he could, but I boarded the plane without any idea of what might happen when we landed. "Listen," I said to Tom. "Just a heads-up, when we get to Kabul, I may be arrested." I was worried the scene might ruin Tom's trip to Kabul, his first time back since 1978, or that it might discourage him from joining the Moby board. But Tom was game for anything. Later, he would confess to me that, in his excitement, he had found the possibility a little exhilarating: an authentic Afghan experience.

I managed to evade arrest at the airport that day. Massoud had sent twenty of his bodyguards to the airport, and after a standoff on the tarmac between them and the police, I was driven to his office. Tom and his friends made it through customs and to their hotel without incident. My relief was short-lived, though; what had been a game of cat and mouse between Moby and Sabet had become an all-out war. Rather than going to my family's home, I went to Sarah's. She had rented a large house within the UN compound, and although there wasn't much security, it felt like the safer option. The raid had gotten a lot of coverage in the international media, adding, I was told by my contacts, to the attorney general's unhappiness. "He still thinks he's the hero in this," I said to Zaid. "How can he not realize he's the villain?"

Just to be safe, I left even earlier than usual for the Moby office the next morning. I met Tom and his friends when I could and reveled in their stories of travels, although I couldn't be with them as much as I would have liked. When it was time for them to leave, I helped them through the airport, looking over my shoulder, succumbing to this new normal.

A new year came, and the harassment continued. In April 2008, a complaint claimed that because one of the beloved lead characters in one of our Indian soap operas was often shown praying to her favorite god, the show, and by extension Moby, was proselytizing idol worship and Hinduism. We consented to pixelate the gods whenever they appeared on-screen, even though we thought it was ridiculous. "Afghans aren't so dumb that they will get carried away and change religions midstream because they saw it in a soap opera," I would fume to the officials I met.

The Americans, no matter how much I appealed and argued, didn't get their "friend" off our backs throughout this ordeal. That was a lesson for us; there's only so much they could, or were willing to, do. For the hundredth time, I heard the argument made, "Afghanistan is a sovereign country; we can't just go into the president's office and tell him what to do." It would be far from the last time an American official would say that to me in order to explain their inaction. Karzai, meanwhile, passed the buck back to the Americans. "They brought him in; they can deal with the fool themselves," he said to his chief of staff, who relayed it to me. This line of reasoning, blaming external forces and not taking responsibility and ownership for what was happening in the country, for what Afghans were doing to other Afghans, would become more familiar and entrenched as the years wore on.

Many months had passed since the raid, when Chris Alexander, the second-in-command at the UN's assistance mission to

Afghanistan, intervened. "Saad," he said. "If you just come in, by yourself, no security, and meet with Sabet, this will all be over."

I had grown weary of the fighting—and of the long, circuitous rides to the office, the hiding out at Sarah's house, the worries about getting arrested at the airport—and I was inclined to say yes. Our fight was existential; Sabet had made no secret of wanting to shut us down. If he managed to arrest me, even for twenty-four hours, he would use it as an opportunity to humiliate the company, with the cameras now on me instead of him. I was willing to meet with him, hoping that my personal apology would be sufficient to put an end to the madness. "You can stop worrying," I told Chris. "I'll talk to him."

We sat down with our chosen mediators, including an aging parliamentarian from Kandahar who swore like a sailor and the regal deputy culture minister, a friend of my father. I was calm, while, to add to the drama, Sabet pretended to storm off a couple of times. When it became clear that Sabet wouldn't stop antagonizing Moby without an apology about the quote he had found offensive, I reached my hand across the table. "I am sorry I caused you hurt," I said as earnestly as I could.

Sabet enlisted the RTA to run stories about the meeting, which infuriated Zaid, who had opposed me trying to placate the attorney general. "When you apologize," he told me, "it's the institution apologizing."

"The news team is down because of it," he said. "They were willing to keep pushing. I don't want them to think that we have caved."

My brother and I had plenty of disagreements over the years. On this issue, we resigned ourselves to not seeing eye to eye. "It's the best thing for us," I told him. "I don't know what he'll do in the future," I said. "But I don't think people will want to tune in forever to watch us fight with this guy."

The apology took some of the pressure off. And, after all the worry, it turned out that Tom had loved that first trip, even the commotion on the tarmac when we landed. He and his friends visited the tall caves that once housed the Bamiyan Buddhas, every corner of Kabul, and the countryside on its outskirts, and shortly after had agreed to join Moby's board; his partnership signaled the beginning of our real growth, first into the Iranian market with the help of James and Rupert Murdoch and then expanding across the region into places like Pakistan, Iraq, Ethiopia, and India.

By mid-July 2008, Karzai had sacked Sabet for his own reasons, and Sabet's replacement did not create as much trouble for us. A few years later Sabet was kidnapped by gunmen, and it was TOLO far more than other outlets that pushed the government for information about his fate and what actions they planned to take. "Why do you care? We thought he hated you," government officials would say, and we would remind them, again, that we were a news organization. Everyone could see that the kidnapping of a former attorney general, no matter how disliked he might have been, and no matter the headache he put us through, was a good story.

CHAPTER 15

COVERING THE TALIBAN

As Moby grew, adding more programs to TOLO TV and Arman, launching TOLOnews in 2010, expanding outside of the country into Pakistan, the Middle East, India, and east Africa, growing Lemar and a pan-regional Persian-language station, the war also grew deadlier and conflicts more entrenched, the Americans in the thick of training local forces. Our reporters had to learn on the job how to balance coverage of all the competing forces in the country, to stay out of the crosshairs of angry officials, to tell stories as faithfully as possible, and to try to get home safely after they'd done so.

In 2006, a year after TOLO was awarded the Reporters Without Borders Press Freedom Prize, and by which time it was being broadcast to fourteen cities, we heard through Amrullah Saleh that President Hamid Karzai had accused us of being Taliban sympathizers and approved of authorities putting pressure on us. This was a very different president from the one who had encouraged us to return to Afghanistan just a handful of years back.

Karzai may disagree with this assessment, but Zaid and I trace the president's anger to a single story, a straightforward one that is frankly simple to defend and that, to be honest, should not have been particularly controversial. But one would be hard-pressed, I suppose, to find a government anywhere in the world that would celebrate the media giving voice to those it considers the enemy.

The story took Nawab Momand, one of the senior reporters who had interviewed Karzai at his palace the previous year, to

Helmand province, where the American-led security presence had been negligible and the Taliban forces were resurgent. Momand had received tips that warlords, who had been profiting from the opium trade, had been brutalizing locals who they believed were sympathetic to the Taliban.

When he got there, Momand discovered that what his sources had been telling him was correct. The men in power were notorious war criminals from the early 1990s, part of a cast of strongmen splintered across the country who had been responsible for tens of thousands of deaths during the civil war, the reason that so many Afghans appreciated the relative stability of the Taliban years, as strange as that might seem to outsiders. Now some of the men who had killed and rampaged during the civil war years occupied positions of power in the Karzai government.

Momand followed the story, interviewing the families of the victims and people on the streets whose lives had been shaken for generations by this brutality. His sources had described themselves as Taliban on the phone, although when he met them in Helmand, they confessed that they had no formal affiliation with the group. "We just call ourselves that because we are also religious," they told him. They didn't reject the association, though. As far as they were concerned, the real threat to their lives as Afghans came from the Americans and from the corruption in Kabul, and the Taliban were their best bet to push back against these forces. "All we know is we have to resist this government," they told Momand.

When the story aired, complete with on-air interviews with the "Taliban" sources, we heard that several in the Karzai government thought we had gone too far. Dostum and Karim Khalili, whom our sources named in the interview as examples of these brutal leaders whose behavior, they suggested, had set the country on course for this violence, had been powerful members of the government. Both men, our sources said, were criminals who had violated the human rights of Afghans. Why, instead of being held accountable, were they promoted in the Arg? Karzai's officials, we'd later learn, were furious that men who claimed even a casual appreciation for the Taliban would be given a chance to tell their side of the story on TOLO. The next day, Zaid, along with a few others the administration were blaming for the story, was summoned to the intelligence agency, where they were held.

Our mission from the beginning was to give a voice to all Afghans. Remembering that early story of the Taliban fighters suffocating in shipping containers, I was determined that our journalists try to understand why and in what context the group had emerged, and, if it was impossible to empathize with them, then at least to give some airtime to our countrymen who would join its ranks or consider them the "good guys" when compared to the Afghan government.

Our reporters were sent regularly to interview Taliban recruits, occasionally after they had been arrested or imprisoned. We wanted to know why they had decided to join. Their answers varied but had a common element, usually some form of unimaginable desperation. Some felt compelled to avenge the death of a sibling or a father. Some recognized that they had been brainwashed in madrassas, schools devoted mainly to religious indoctrination where it was common knowledge that they had suffered abuse and abject cruelty by those in charge. Their families, pious and poor, often had no choice but to send their young boys away to those madrassas in Pakistan; in so many parts of Afghanistan there were no jobs, there was no food, and the families made the decision knowing that their sons or nephews could end up on the front lines, or in jail, where they could suffer more abuse.

Afghanistan is a country of distinct groups separated by ethnicity and language, religious practice, and appearance. Each group, no matter who you are, has some kind of grievance to work through, with other groups, with the state, with the international community, with neighbors and families, grievances that go back days or weeks or generations. Over the past forty or fifty years, everyone has suffered in some way. My extended family of both Dari-speaking Tajiks and Pashto-speaking Pashtuns is squarely in both dominant cultural groups, rich with connections and a tribal legacy we could trace, when it was helpful, to Afghan royalty. Our privilege is clear, and immense. Yet like so many other Afghans, we also suffered the indignity of displacement, the stress of political exile. My parents still had to remake their lives outside of their homeland. Others had to do so with nothing.

Those in power, whether Afghan or foreigners, have exploited this diversity as a way to maintain control over the population. They have inflamed tensions and distrust between communities, highlighted the differences, and then nurtured those differences with their policies or acts of violence. Through war and hardship, it becomes easier and safer to live in the bubble of your family and neighbors, all speaking the same language, remembering history the same way, nursing the same grievances. When the leaders avoided transparency and it became clear that they were motivated by their own group's interests, it only exacerbated a lack of trust in the political establishment. Afghans became prone to conspiracy theories. As is, we've also somewhat been in awe of foreign powers—the British colonizers, the Soviets, and then the Americans and their allies—who invested so many of their resources into trying to get something from our country. After a certain point, it can be hard for many Afghans to believe that not everything, from elections to coups to natural disasters, happens by foreign design.

And so, in order to live in Afghanistan without following one's partisan grievances into a bottomless pit of anger, you have to be empathetic. You have to try to see pain from all sides. This is particularly true and essential for the Afghan media. But it is that pursuit of empathy that got us into the most trouble.

AS THE TALIBAN fighters began to win on the battlefield, they amped up their propaganda too, detailing civilian casualties and the suffering of the people under regional warlords and the central government installed by the Americans, bragging about how they were welcomed in villages ravaged by aerial bombings and arbitrary detentions. The Taliban leadership, regrouping during these years in the border regions with Pakistan, and receiving critical help, both military and financial, from the Pakistani intelligence agency, issued communiqués, released DVDs and audiocassettes, and gave media interviews presenting themselves as the legitimate voice for Afghans marginalized by war and a corrupt government. Afghans were familiar with such messaging from the mid-1990s, when the Taliban first took power, offering piety and stability, only to grow more brutal and disconnected by the day.

"If you're so confident in your own popularity, why don't you participate in an election?" Momand had asked a local Taliban leader in the segment from Helmand.

The leader, whose face was partly hidden with a scarf, shook his head furiously. "This government has committed war crimes," he said. "Innocent people have been massacred because of them." Dostum, whose forces were accused of committing the shipping container massacre and who had been a minister in the interim government, was the main focus of his anger. The other was Karzai's vice president, Karim Khalili, a former mujahideen leader whose followers had been accused of committing war crimes during the 1990s. "Why would Karzai surround himself with the likes of Dostum and Khalili?" he asked. "They brutalized people; they cut off women's breasts."

"We don't trust this government," the Taliban leader added. "So why would we want to legitimize it?"

The day after we aired Momand's interview with the Taliban leader, Zaid, Momand, the head of TOLO, the station's lawyer, and our head of admin were ordered to go to the intelligence agency, where they were detained. For two hours they argued with their interrogator, who insisted that the interview broke an obscure Afghan law, which he could not, or would not, explain when asked. Meanwhile, Saleh, the intelligence chief, was dealing with me over the phone. Saleh and I had a working relationship, although because of his background in intelligence he held his cards close to his chest and was often difficult to read, and sometimes difficult to trust.

Our head of legal, though, had come prepared. "I have the Afghan penal code right here," he said, retrieving a sheath of documents from his briefcase. At the time, it was very hard to get copies of legislation and, as Zaid would tell me later, the intelligence official was clearly betting on our being unable to challenge his citation. The law he mentioned had nothing to do with media. "They were trying to bluff us," Zaid said.

Outsmarted, the official got angry. "You need to tell us how you got this interview," he said. "Who arranged it, what is the exact location where you met. Give us the names of the people involved."

"We can't give you our sources," Zaid responded. That, he knew, was protected by Afghan law. "But as for the identity of the Taliban leader, you have the interview itself," he continued. "No one is trying to conceal his identity; he names himself on air." It was so absurd, these clumsy attempts to catch us in a wrongdoing that not even the government could define.

Finally, the intelligence official ordered Zaid and the others out of the room. After a long wait, he came out into the hallway. "You will be our guests until further notice," he said. The men who escorted them were polite, even apologetic. They collected everyone's mobile phones and led them into a small room with a few beds and chairs, which Zaid later found out was normally used as a guard breakroom. They stayed there all night, drinking tea and sleeping. Every once in a while, a guard would poke his head in to ask if they needed anything. "They left the door open, but we didn't test them," Zaid said. "Not even to use the bathroom."

That evening, when I called Saleh, to find out when my brother and our employees would be released, he'd said it was on Karzai's insistence that he had done all this, and when I arrived at the Arg to negotiate my brother's release the following morning, I found the president looking furious. Whatever camaraderie had existed between us some years ago seemed dead. Before I even had a chance to sit down, he began screaming at me. "How could you air this story?" he shouted. "You are making the Taliban seem like the victims. They are not the victims. They are criminals."

I was at the Arg for two hours. The first hour he spent berating me, and, with not really any other option—and at the advice of a mutual confidant—I let the president scream. He was jumping from topic to topic. Every few minutes he would dial a number and shout into his mobile phone. "Tell Saad what's really happening in Helmand," he would say, and I would listen to the voice on the other end list violent acts carried out by the Taliban.

As president, Karzai listened to everyone. It was certainly one of his greatest qualities as a leader. He had been keenly aware of the continuing threat of extremism in Afghanistan, even when the Americans insisted the Taliban had been vanquished, because he paid attention to what the religious leaders across the country said in their Friday sermons. Our very first meeting at the Arg in September 2002 had ended with him advising me to pay attention to the conservative forces in the provinces. "Be careful of the mullahs," he said. They had been telling him even back then that certain factions in Afghanistan, those as religious but more extreme than them, would not be happy with the rise of an independent Afghan media.

I knew that Karzai watched TOLO. "But our story is not about that," I said. "We have to listen to people; we have to understand why they take up arms against the government." It was important in these early years of the insurgency that we at least try to get to the bottom of why the Taliban were fighting. I did not admit to him that I knew that the Taliban used TOLO's news coverage in its propaganda to say that the Afghan government had fully capitulated to the Americans, that the Taliban cited our dramas and musical shows in their recruitment materials. "We are hardly easy on them," I rather insisted. "We have covered their violence from the beginning."

"These people are cruel," Karzai said. "They prey on others." He seemed desperate to prove to me his government had the best interests of the Afghan people in mind, even if some of the characters had unsavory backgrounds. By the second hour, the president had cooled down a bit, and we were arguing more or less like we'd done so before. Karzai was adamant that, even if TOLO hadn't violated any law, we were in the wrong. "What for?" I asked. "Interviewing someone? That's our job."

"The Taliban are stronger now because the people feel like they have no alternative," I told him. "If you governed well, and looked after these people, the Taliban wouldn't be able to prey on them."

"You better fix your TV station," Karzai said.

"When you fix your cabinet, I'll fix my TV station," I replied. For the first time during the meeting, we both smiled.

After that, I was told that Zaid and the TOLO staffers would be momentarily released. I'd made one begrudging concession at the Arg, though, agreeing that in any future segment featuring a Taliban fighter, their faces wouldn't be shown, nor their voices heard. We could quote them, but not play the audio or video of interviews. I thought it was resolved, but apparently Karzai and his cabinet held a grudge. About two years later, when Tom was about to introduce Karzai at an event in New York, I came up in a conversation, and Karzai suggested that I was a Taliban sympathizer because I put them on television. "What the hell did you do, Saad?" Tom asked me later on the phone. "Karzai really hates you."

ABDUL KARIM KHURRAM, the minister of information and culture who in 2006 replaced my friend, the flamboyantly dressed, poetry-reciting Sayed Makhdoom Raheen, turned out to be particularly difficult, constantly calling me about shows he considered offensive, presenters who had crossed the line, women whose very presence on TV violated traditional Afghan values. The Taliban certainly didn't originate the panic about a woman being too independent outside of the home.

Khurram, I thought, was a bit of a fool, and he hated us, announcing once during a press conference that TOLO was funded by foreign money, citing our recent venture into Iran with our channel Farsi 1, a collaboration with the Murdochs, which he considered to be a direct attack on Iranian clerics. "Media is more effective than guns or tanks," he would say. On that point, I agreed, although I saw it as a positive thing, whereas he saw Moby as a Trojan horse for America's interests.

Khurram's accusations were nothing new. Because of the small USAID grant with which it was launched, Arman had been accused of being an American mouthpiece. Because we hired many Hazara presenters in the early days of TOLO—they were comfortable being on camera—we were rumored to be close to Iran and therefore Shias. Our ventures outside of the country made us suspicious, but when we focused on our internal products, we were called part of the occupation. I wasn't truly worried that Khurram would shut us down; he knew that would reflect poorly on him and there would be backlash in the international media. But a minister of culture suggesting that we were not independent, and were instead puppets of a foreign government, was potentially very damaging. "Afghanistan is like a pressure cooker,"

I would tell him at one of the many meetings in which I was expected to defend one show or another, beg him to be allowed to stay open. "You have to let off a little steam or it will explode, and that's what these television shows allow people to do," I'd say. Later, to the delight of our late-night comedy hosts, he butchered the image in a speech. On TOLO TV, we made fun of everyone, although we tiptoed slightly around Karzai, cloaking our satire against him in metaphor or depicting the president with puppets or as an ancient Persian king, just to be on the safe side. Khurram, though, didn't see the humor in it.

Ministers, parliamentarians, mayors—everyone gave Afghan media a hard time. At the beginning, for a while, we were a lot more combative. When Sabet or Khurram targeted us during a press conference, we would record a segment digging at their shortcomings and play it dozens of times over twenty-four hours, just to get under their skin. It was about more than settling personal grievances, although we weren't always above using TOLO to do that, at least in the early years; they had real power, if only temporarily, and the power we had was in the media we controlled. Plus, the audience loved the teasing, feeling that we were holding these men accountable. For a time, they would tune in just to see it.

But soon enough, we became savvier in how to respond to such criticisms. We had people on staff whose job it was to reach out to officials and forge relationships with them, in the hopes they would stop putting pressure on us to censor shows or to change our coverage of certain topics like the Taliban. I kept a list of parliamentarians, and every week we invited a group of them to come tour the office, chat with me and sometimes my brothers and sister over tea, if they wanted to, come on TOLO for an interview. Occasionally, they were impressed; more often, they seemed surprised by how threadbare the offices were, telling us that the studio looked better on air. "I was going to ask you for financial support for a future campaign," one official joked. "But after seeing your office, I think I need to give you money!" It helped, though, for these would-be adversaries or supporters to see the offices for themselves. Whatever worked. Those years during the Karzai era were difficult, but we survived. Even after Khurram was dismissed in December 2009, and Raheen reappointed, we still needed to push back against the system.

One afternoon, after a particularly difficult meeting with Minister Khurram, the details of which are too mundane to recall—another chat about another show, another reprimand and argument, another empty threat—I called an all-staff meeting. Although I shrugged off the tension with officials, to the staff things could appear more dire, a harbinger of raids or arrests or losing their jobs. Over the years, we had a series of indictments against us, arrests, and arrest warrants, and I knew that some of them felt under siege, while others felt simply deflated.

The weather was nice that day, so we met in a courtyard, some dragging chairs outside, others standing against the walls, some sitting in the grass. Momand was there, as were Massood, Sima, Humayoon, and my brothers. I stood up on the grass, the crowd milling around me, and gave an uncharacteristically rousing speech.

"I know you feel that between Karzai and Khurram we have an administration intent on weakening us," I said. "But I want you to know, we will outlast Khurram. We will be here when Khurram is gone, and we'll be here when the minister after him is gone, and the minister after that and the minister after that. Minister after minister, it doesn't matter. We will outlast them all."

CHAPTER 16

GHANI

I have never lost hope in Afghanistan or in the potential for Afghans to change our country for the better. My parents set a good example; even as political asylees, living somewhat in the dark in Australia during the first Taliban era, they were certain that Afghanistan would survive and one day open back up to all those who had been forced to leave. My father didn't resign from the foreign service because he was giving up on Afghanistan. On the contrary, he resigned after the Soviet Union invaded Afghanistan to protest the government it installed, which he thought would lead the country to ruin; his protest was his sacrifice for the home that he loved.

His four children have maintained a similar faith in Afghanistan, maybe beyond reason, occasionally obsessively, often in ways worth teasing each other about. But if anything gets buried in the heaps of news coverage of our country over the years, it most often tends to be this: we would all prefer to live in Kabul than anywhere else. Tens of millions of Afghans would live in Afghanistan if they could, and we all will tell you that there is no place in the world like it. We easily remember the good, in spite of everything, because there is so much good that happened, and so many good people who gave up so much to try to rebuild Afghanistan and who are still trying.

I have never lost hope in my country, or in the Afghan people, but I had given up on the US-led war, and the Afghan governments that arose from it, many years before President Trump and then President Biden announced the US withdrawal of troops from Afghanistan. This disillusionment happened slowly at first, a small leak getting bigger with every story of corruption, every report of violence, with every Afghan who confessed off the record or on air in a TOLO studio that they no longer believed that Afghanistan would be the place where they wanted to raise their children. In 2010, TOLO expanded into a twenty-four-hour TV channel dedicated to covering the news. Each time its reporters returned from rural Afghanistan with a story about the terror of American drone strikes, the night raids and the frequency of arbitrary arrests, and the growing fury at the occupation, it was a blow to the promises of the years that followed the toppling of the Taliban regime. During every election there were allegations of fraud. But it wasn't until 2014, when Ashraf Ghani was elected president in what appeared to be a brazenly fraudulent election, that I really started to worry that, unless something changed and quickly, we were careening toward something terrible.

When Ghani first came onto the political scene, as advisor, then finance minister in Karzai's administration, he had support across generations of Afghans. Ghani was smart; he had the right ideas. My father had been at the Ministry of Foreign Affairs when a twenty-seven-year-old Ghani applied for a ministry scholarship, and impressed the people who interviewed him. He already had a bachelor's from the American University of Beirut, and the scholarship was for a two-year master's degree in cultural anthropology at Columbia University. Because of the unrest that followed the 1978 coup, during which many of his male family members were imprisoned, he decided to stay on in New York, getting a PhD from Columbia. He then taught at Berkeley and Johns Hopkins and worked at the World Bank for a decade. His scholarly achievements and his impressive career seemed evidence of discipline and an open mind, and we thought the fact that he returned to his country so soon after the fall of the Taliban spoke volumes about his character and patriotism.

Before Ghani was appointed finance minister by Karzai in June 2002, Jahid had happily worked for him, feeling that through Ghani the vision of younger Afghans could be realized. After Ghani became finance minister, Zaid provided the ministry with pro bono legal advice, and I made a point of visiting with him whenever I could. He was always an interesting person to talk to. I recall that our first meeting was scheduled for thirty minutes and extended well past two hours. Over the coming years, although I was not interested in working for the new political structure, I understood that there had to be a symbiotic relationship between the Arg and Moby, and I liked these meetings too, for the feeling, however superficial, they gave me that any Afghan could have an impact.

Intellectually, Ghani understood the economic challenges Afghanistan faced. His experience at the World Bank gave him a global perspective on how to shape the Afghan economy. But I found that his policies, particularly regarding taxation, were not tethered to reason. He had an academic bent, and although he acquired the data and had the ability to analyze the structural problems that beset Afghanistan, I was never convinced that he ever cared to truly understand other Afghans, particularly those different from him, and that this distance became worse after he was elected president.

Like Karzai, or probably any leader, Ghani could not handle any kind of criticism. But when it came to taking things personally, Ghani was in a class by himself. He was notoriously thin-skinned, famously mercurial, absolutely unhinged when he felt he was being challenged, particularly by anyone who he thought lacked the authority to do so. While we had disagreed before, we had a falling-out only after TOLO ran a story critical of one of his proposals as finance minister.

The story challenged the hypothesis behind his proposal that in order for the Afghan economy to grow, all Afghan income earners and businesses earning above a certain amount needed to pay a 20 percent flat tax rate. After the story ran, I visited him in his office at the ministry. Foolishly, I expected a rational conversation about sliding tax rates and what a taxpaying citizen and corporation might expect in return from the state. Our reporting was based on interviews we had conducted; Ghani's 20 percent tax rate was deeply unpopular among most Afghans. The minister would want to consider that, I thought. Instead, I found Ghani in his small office, fuming.

"Look," I said, sitting down and accepting an offer of tea. There was always tea; as angry as he was, Ghani was still Afghan, eternally hospitable. "This can't work here. We're competing with places like Dubai, where the corporate taxes are much lower."

"No, no," he said. "We aren't like Dubai; we are more like our neighbors, Pakistan, or Iran."

"Due respect, Minister," I said. "We have to think about what makes Afghanistan unique. We have to think toward our future and not only compare ourselves to our neighbors." Such a statement might have suggested that his policies, therefore, were not ambitious enough. I could be a bit of a smart-ass, particularly when I was sure I was right. I didn't want to bring up Moby and give the impression that I was pressuring Ghani based on self-interest, but at that moment we were struggling to find ways we could make Afghanistan our corporate hub, as we had always intended, and cope with the minister's tax policies.

Ghani refused to listen, dismissing me with a haughty shake of his head. He took my questioning personally; I suppose I also saw these interactions as personal. After that exchange, for a while, Ghani refused to take my calls. At one point, he threatened to kick me out of the country. The next time he saw me in public, at some government function, he hurled something along the lines of "Watch yourself. Or I'll tell the Americans to cut your funding." Ghani, from his experience as director of the AACA, had a disdain for foreign aid. He rightly predicted that the influx of foreign money would lead to massive corruption. By tying Moby to foreign money, he was telling us that we were part of the system he hated, even though he was aware that aside from the small USAID grants we had received no aid money and even though, as finance minister, he had no power to shut us down.

The next occasion I had to witness Ghani's by then infamous temper was a few years later when he was serving as chancellor of Kabul University. By then we had repaired our relationship and, since we were both in Washington, DC, he had agreed—graciously, I thought—to have breakfast with me in the dining room of the hotel where I was staying. Breakfast was pleasant; with his wife there, Ghani was cordial. I felt that I could be honest with him. "Mr. Ghani," I said. "You have so much to offer the country. But I worry that you lose your temper too often."

He immediately stiffened. "I don't," he said. "That's not true."

"It is true," I pushed back. "You have a short temper. Everyone knows it. And that's fine, but you should acknowledge that you get very emotional. You go from zero to a hundred in three seconds, and, to be frank, it alienates a lot of people, people whose support you could use." Ghani had long wanted to run for political office.

I could tell that I was getting under his skin. "No," he insisted. His anger was cartoonish. Steam practically rose out of his shirt collar. "I don't lose my temper. That's a lie."

I shrugged. "I've seen it," I said. "My brothers have seen it. Our reporters have seen it. It's something you need to control."

Then, right there by the wilting pancakes of the American hotel breakfast buffet, Ashraf Ghani truly lost it. Raising his fist, he slammed it down on the table so hard a boiled egg flew up off of his plate, landing with a loud crack on the table. His wife, who was sitting with us, remained silent, while he stood over us, fuming.

"Hey," I said. "See, this is what I mean."

Ghani paused for a second. He looked at his wife. "I know what I'm doing," our future president said, the perfectly cracked hard-boiled egg resting on the tablecloth. "When the situation calls for it, I get angry."

ASHRAF GHANI WAS hardly the first politician with a temper. Bill Clinton famously had "purple rages" during his time in the White House; the less said about Donald Trump, the better. But it became very obvious during his first presidential campaign in 2009 that Ghani's temper was not only recurrent outbursts of rage. Ghani's anger was evidence of how disconnected he was from the people who tried to engage with him, how tone-deaf, how arrogant, how uninterested. Ghani had other qualities, many of them good. But in rehashing his career and influence, it is his temper that stands out.

Everyone had a story to share about Ashraf Ghani's thin skin, his inability to accept dissenting opinions or admit his own shortcomings. Foreign leaders would complain he always felt he was the smartest person in the room and never let anyone else talk. Once, the palace lore goes, Ghani hurt his leg after insisting that he get to race some visiting athletes (who, the story continues, were so terrified they would be blamed for the president's injury that they stood frozen above him while he cried out in pain, unwilling to touch him). "You have ten minutes," Ghani was fond of telling visitors, Afghans who were eager for the president's ear. "You're not important to me" was what he was saying. "You're not worth my time." In Afghanistan, he seemed to forget, a personal slight could turn into animosity that lasted generations.

In 2014, when he again became a presidential candidate, and

was one of the two front-runners, along with Abdullah Abdullah, a well-known former member of the mujahideen turned public servant who had come in second to Karzai in 2009, we started to panic that something corrupt was going on behind the scenes to get him elected. In 2009, Ghani had gotten only 3 percent of the votes, but many were now predicting his victory. Just before voting began in April, I visited President Karzai in the Arg; because of term limits he was barred from running in these elections himself. Our relationship had cooled long ago over his objections to our coverage of the Taliban and his accusations that TOLO was too ideologically in line with the Americans. After the 2009 elections, he grew more sequestered and distrustful of the Americans' commitment to Afghanistan's future. We had never really reconciled, but that didn't bother me terribly. Even at the height of his anger toward TOLO, Karzai remained committed to free media and hadn't tried to cut off our news reporters' access to the Arg. In any case, it's not the job of the media to be well-liked by the president.

I can't be entirely sure why Karzai decided to call me in for a meeting that day. He met with people from all walks of life all the time and, in spite of our history of arguing, my family and I did still own the country's largest media outfit. He likely saw value in my take. In any case, I was interested in his. He looked tidy and put together, but he wore the job on his face, which had aged him many years beyond the length of his two terms. He had become conspiratorial in a way that seemed desperate, which was all I could think of to explain his reluctance to publicly critique Ghani, a man who, despite his intellect and experience, clearly did not have the temperament to lead the country. It seemed to me that Karzai was reconciled to Ghani's victory.

On that visit I hoped, perhaps in my hubris, to get to the bottom of Karzai's feelings about Ghani. In my own conspiratorial way, I was convinced that Karzai thought Ghani's presidency would teach the world a lesson. "This is the man you want?" he seemed to be saying. "See what he does and then compare him to me."

The Karzai I know is not a petty man by any stretch, but the job had driven him to become spiteful. His years in office had brought plenty of scrutiny to members of his family, many of whom had grown rich, with media allegations, including from TOLO, of corruption particularly aimed at one of his brothers. He was now extremely critical of how the Americans had conducted the war, and increasingly concerned about the insurgency. And in the lead-up to the 2014 election, as it became clear that Ghani, as popular among the urban youth and qualified as he might have been, could win the election only by cheating, Karzai appeared to become even more bitter. It might have seemed to him that if a fraudulent election put Ashraf Ghani in the Arg, chaos would ensue, and that would be a wake-up call to the complacent, checked-out, cynical arms of the occupation. "I let the Americans know," he told me, his face angrier than I had ever seen it (and I had plenty of shouting matches with the man over the years). "If they want Ashraf Ghani, let them have him and see what he does to the country."

I told Karzai the story about Ghani hitting the table so hard that the egg flew off the plate. But it didn't stir the president. Everyone had a story about Ghani's temper, including Karzai.

"I wasn't in the room at the time," he told me. "I left in the middle of one of his outbursts. When I came back, he was holding his hand in pain. He had smacked the table so hard in one of his fits that he broke his hand. They had to take him to the hospital to have it cast."

We sat there talking about the candidates. The former minister of foreign affairs Abdullah Abdullah was considered the only real challenge to Ghani. I was in favor, quietly of course, so as to not cast a shadow over TOLO's news coverage, of Zalmai Rassoul, also a former minister of foreign affairs. Rassoul had his flaws. He was known to be a bit work-shy, but he was old-school, a descendant of the royal family. With the right team, I felt he could do a good job. I had read in the international press that Karzai, too, preferred Rassoul, but during my meeting with the president I got no such confirmation. "At least he's not corrupted," I said to Karzai. "That counts for a lot."

Karzai, though, didn't want to weigh in and sway voters. "I can't see anyone else winning," he kept saying.

I was alarmed by his resignation. Hamid Karzai had been in power for thirteen years. For the thirteen years he had been at the wheel of this Afghan project, he had met nearly every person who wanted power in the country, those supported by and those rejected by the Americans, those corrupt and those resistant to corruption, those who spent years abroad and those who had never left. And he really couldn't think of a single person who would make a good president? Were we really that doomed?

"Mr. President," I told him. "Why does it seem that you are supporting this man? Why aren't you more critical of him?"

Years later, Karzai would admit to me that supporting Ghani had been a mistake, using a very vulgar Dari term that I won't repeat here, although he never came out and admitted that his election officials actively colluded with the Ghani team. "I could have tried to stop him," he told me. But that day, one of his last days in the palace, the president balked. "If the Americans want him, they can have him," he said.

THE 2014 ELECTION results were so disputed, with Abdullah accusing Karzai's government of orchestrating a massive-scale fraud to either help Ghani or create instability so that Karzai could extend his own stay in power, that after months of crisis and mutual recrimination, the United States had to step in and broker a power-sharing deal. Ghani would be president, and Abdullah, as runner-up, would serve in a newly created position of chief executive of Afghanistan. I felt utterly depressed, as did many of the Afghans I knew. A few days after the election, I had met a member of Obama's national security council at a Peet's Coffee in DC, close to the White House. Sitting there over a cup of some dark roast, I listed all the confirmed evidence of fraud we had collected at TOLO. "The whole election was corrupt," I said.

He sighed. "We've been hearing about it too," he told me. "But there's not much we can do beyond what we already have." Afghanistan is a sovereign nation, he told me. Never mind that the US had helped build it in its current misshapen form. They were content to wash their hands of the whole corrupted place. NATO combat mission in Afghanistan was coming to an end by the end of the year, and Obama had announced a deadline of two years for the withdrawal of the remaining ten thousand US troops from Afghanistan, many of whom had been put in place as part of a surge that tried, and failed, to defeat the Taliban. It was a disheartening meeting, one of many to come.

I wasn't the only one who felt deflated by the 2014 elections. With the dysfunction and constant squabbling between Ghani and Abdullah that followed, the parliamentary elections were delayed by two years; when they took place in 2018, they too were beset by fraud allegations. The disconnect between Afghan politicians and the Afghan people had become ever starker, particularly in the war-torn areas of the country. Politicians came to power through a lazy form of ethnic gerrymandering designed to marginalize minorities, although it didn't always work, and they never worried about being held accountable. Everyone knew that if you needed a parliamentarian to do anything, you had to bribe them.

People lost faith in their government, and they also lost faith in the international community to right the country's course.

With Ghani as president, the inevitable day when the Americans would finally leave for good seemed to come into sharper focus. Although Afghans had been trickling out of the country for some time, seeing this period of relative peace as a chance to apply for residency elsewhere, we now started getting word of people fleeing almost every day, many in secret. Some Afghans became so desperate to leave that they risked their lives to do so. We began to hear of migrants drowning in the Mediterranean in their desperate attempt to reach European soil.

Working for a media company strengthened an Afghan's case for asylum since they could demonstrate that, given the situation in Afghanistan, their work put their lives in peril. Staffers began disappearing on Moby-sponsored work trips to Europe or the US. Some, I think, might have even applied for the job simply because they saw it as an off-ramp out of the country. Others couldn't take the stress of working in media, which grew worse as the war became more violent, the president angrier and more disconnected, and the extremists more powerful.

Of more than a dozen reporters from various media organizations accompanying Massood Sanjer to a training in northern Europe, only a few returned to Kabul. A female producer who had won a scholarship arranged by Tom to attend a conference in Washington, DC, abandoned the trip the moment she was alone. Back in Kabul, our harried human resources director struggled to fill their jobs before their absence disrupted our schedule. We were angry, and we worried about the brain drain in a country that needed Afghans to rebuild it, but what can you say? I'm a man, and I have an Australian passport. The pressure on the staffers, and particularly the women, was a lot to bear. And what they must have felt after they left, being far from Afghanistan, leaving friends and family, and a job that had meaning—a feeling I was familiar with—was punishing enough. I worried about them in the new world they had fled to, and I understand the reasons they might have felt they had to leave so abruptly.

Ghani, who'd lead the country for the next seven years, though, could be blunt and cruel in his response to this exodus. He said outright that he had no sympathy for the Afghans who fled, that they were making a voluntary choice and impoverishing their families in the process. If his temper was the first real sign of his unsuitability for governance, those insults were the first indication of his malice. In 2016, he signed an agreement with the European Union to take back Afghan asylum seekers, most of them deported from Germany, but his government did little to help them find opportunities to work or study, or to keep them safe, when they were forcibly returned.

After 2014, I grew more anxious about the future of the company and of the country. I still believed that Afghanistan could succeed. Still, if our new president did little beyond insulting the people desperate enough to leave, what hope did we have of getting them to stay? The new Afghanistan was built on a weak foundation that was beginning to show large cracks. In some of the provinces, more and more people started to look for ways to resist the government and the security forces that the Americans still funded, but which had failed them. The cracks grew bigger and the foundation less stable, unable to hold up the institutions and businesses and schools that Afghans needed. The pillars of our democracy were crooked from the first stone that was laid. The Afghan media also wasn't perfect. But at least we were strong.

CHAPTER 17

FOOTBALL

Shafic Gawhari grew up playing football whenever and wherever he could—on the streets near his family home in Kabul; in the schoolyard, where he showed talent at a very young age; and eventually in stadiums throughout the country as part of the under-nineteen national league. Shafic was born in 1961, growing up during a period of relative stability, and as far back as he can remember, football was at the core of his identity. Even when the city eventually plunged into violence, he found solace and stability on the pitch, where he could block out everything else that was happening, where the rules were consistent and fair, where fighting was brief and controlled and stopped with a whistle, and where he and his teammates became a family.

No matter what was going on in Afghanistan, football was there to pull people together. Some of my best memories from my childhood in Kabul involve riding on the front of my cousin Humayoon's bicycle or in my father's car to the football stadium, where, every August, Afghans would celebrate our independence from the British for what felt like the entire month. Performers lit up the stadium—singers from Pakistan and Iran and across Afghanistan—and every government ministry would send representatives who would set up events nearby to host important employees and guests. Military parades and concerts were followed by fireworks and abundant food; I stayed up as late as I possibly could. And in the same month the stadium hosted the football championship.

Afghanistan, which had had a national team since 1922 and had joined FIFA in 1948, then had many football clubs and four or five regional teams, and its national team played against Iran and other teams from Central Asia. Because of his work at the foreign ministry, my father could get tickets to even such coveted games, and I never felt more powerful than I did as a ten-year-old holding tickets and walking with my school friends into the football stadium. When we didn't have tickets, I imagined scaling the fence, which was far too high. We cheered on the Afghan team but practically worshipped the Iranian goalie Nasser Hejazi, a superstar who would go on to play in the World Cup in 1978, matches whose recordings we watched on VHS at the Goethe-Institut in Kabul, a week after they were played.

Shafic is five years older than me. Our paths never crossed in that stadium, where he started as a ball boy and would later become a young star. He stayed in the country a bit longer than my family, leaving for West Germany in the early 1980s a couple years after the Soviets invaded. A refugee in his early twenties, his former life seemed to lie around him in pieces. He didn't speak German, he had left many of his friends behind, and his family seemed utterly lost without work or community, thinking about their Kabul home taken over by Afghans who now seemed like strangers. In Germany it was nearly impossible to access news about the football games being played in Afghanistan, which sputtered on for a few more years after Shafic was forced to leave.

After the Soviets invaded, several thousand Afghans fled to West Germany, where a tiny community of Afghan students and entrepreneurs already existed, in part because of the easy visas that had been provided to them in the heyday of Ariana Airlines. Most of the asylum seekers were well-educated professionals, Shafic's family and friends being among them. And so Shafic was soon playing football with some new Afghan friends on German pitches. In that way, he began to adjust. There, they were transported as if back to Kabul and, just as magically, feeling somewhat more at home in Germany. Just as I stayed connected to Afghanistan in my youth in Australia by eavesdropping on my parents' conversations about art and politics, Shafic maintained his connection to home through football.

And yet, like me and my family, the urge to return in some capacity never left Shafic. After getting a master's degree in chemical engineering in Germany, he started working for a German government agency that did humanitarian work in developing countries. As part of that agency, Shafic moved to Pakistan in the mid-1990s, after the Taliban came to power, to work on Afghanistan-related projects. Those were the years when I was in Uzbekistan, and like me, Shafic could practically smell our homeland across the border. Shafic still had close family in the country, and he would sometimes make the risky border crossing on foot from Pakistan. Using his German passport as ID and speaking only German and English at the Taliban checkpoints, he appeared sufficiently foreign to pass through without excessive interrogation. It was only when he reached Kabul and was safe inside a family home with people whom he trusted that he switched to Dari.

The first time Shafic made the trip in 1997, he had been shocked by what he saw. He'd seen the images of wartime Sarajevo on TV—buildings flattened, burned—and he saw little difference between that city, until recently under a four-year siege and bombardment, and his own. Much of what he remembered from his childhood and adolescence in Kabul was gone. His modest home, his school, the training pitch where he had spent so much time—all destroyed. Roads and buildings were pockmarked with shells, blackened husks of vehicles lay abandoned on the side of the roads, a depression hung over the city. The national football stadium was still there, but in a gloomy disarray, the gates padlocked, and the pitch caked in debris. The Taliban would soon use it to stage their executions.

Shafic crossed into Afghanistan once a year after that, each time using his German passport. The economic situation only worsened, and the people living in Kabul seemed more desperate, the city quieter in its sadness, the future not an open question but a cliff's edge, waiting for the whole country to fall off. Shafic worked on projects aimed at helping Afghan refugees in the direst need, the ones who were stuck in Pakistan, a country that never, not in the 1990s and not in the 2020s, truly accepted them. In the refugee camps at least, it was possible to see the relief brought by some well-allocated funds. It was harder to be hopeful in Kabul. There, relief seemed utterly impossible.

When the US invaded and expelled the Taliban, Shafic returned semipermanently to Kabul, still working for the same development agency for the German government. By then he had visited enough times that the shock at the state of the city had worn off. His previous visits had inoculated him against the signs of war and poverty, and so while many returnee Afghans spent the first few days absorbing the magnitude of everything that had happened since we left, Shafic's mind was fully open to the good things, the possibilities. "So many people returning from Pakistan, every corner of the city people laughing and celebrating and being hopeful," he would recall. "Everything was new." Shafic says to us now that of the last forty years of Afghan history, those first three or four years after the US invasion were the best.

Shafic can be a stickler for rules; we joke that he's spent too much time in Germany. As he would remind us of many times over the years, the first time he laid eyes on Zaid and me was when we were breaking a rule, skipping the interminable immigration line at the Kabul airport. "It was the first time I'd brought my family to Afghanistan," he tells us. "March 2003. You and your brothers were young then, nicely dressed, waiting in the same queue as us. I wondered, *Who are these young Afghan men?*" The line was long and moved slowly. People shifted and sighed; Shafic's children started to complain. Then, out of seeming nowhere, a man in a suit—which man in a suit, I cannot now recall—came to me and Zaid, took our passports, and ushered us to the front.

"I was so angry," Shafic recalls, laughing. "*These guys don't respect the rules*, I thought." But after we met the next day by co-incidence at the house of a mutual acquaintance, he let go of his irritation and we became friends, picnicking together, talking about politics and sports and the radio station we had launched, throwing around ideas for how the German government could better contribute to Afghanistan's future—those were the days when we were certain that foreign money could be harnessed for good. Shafic would work for another decade for the development agency, rising to the post of country director. But from the beginning, we all toyed with the idea of reviving Afghan football.

"I'm alive because of the sport," he would tell us. He recalled that his prowess at football meant he didn't have to express an opinion on the changing currents in Afghan politics. While some of his friends protested the Communists, and others professed their loyalty to them, Shafic focused on what was happening on the pitch. Security officials, realizing the teenage Shafic was a starter on the national youth team, didn't question him about his or his parents' political affiliations. And later, when he had felt so lonely in Germany, football gave him a community, a way to stabilize his life so that he could move on to the more ambitious pursuits that eventually led him back to Afghanistan. "I owe everything to football," he would tell us. Many of his friends from those years, those who had no clout or connections, had not fared as well.

After the American war began, the Afghanistan Football Federation was resurrected, and in February 2002 the first match at Ghazi stadium, between Kabul United and a team composed of ISAF soldiers, was played in front of an excited thirty-five-thousand-strong crowd. The Afghan national team also played its first international game—against South Korea—that year; it was its first international game since 1984. Over the coming decade, the Afghan team's performance was, fair to say, spotty, and it wasn't transparent how the team selection process worked; there were rumors regarding nepotism, favoritism, corruption. (When in 2019 the head of the Afghanistan Football Federation fled Kabul under allegations that he had sexually assaulted players on the national women's football team, the only surprise was that his crimes had been exposed at all.)

I first brought up the idea of starting a private football league as a Moby entity with Shafic around 2003, but there was no money, and the proposal was quickly dismissed by international donors. Indeed, our early idea did seem somewhat far-fetched—there was no point in getting funding for a football league without permission from Afghan football authorities, or a television station to broadcast games, or players, or any idea how to recruit them or who would watch once we did. Some potential donors worried that, even though there had already been football games in Ghazi stadium, Afghans would be too scared to show up in the numbers needed for a new league to make financial sense. I had regularly jogged there, along with others, since I arrived in Kabul, but as late as 2008, Reuters ran a story quoting some locals who said they could sense the spirits of executed people when they walked past the national stadium.

Years went by and the promises of the American occupation began to be overshadowed by the reality of an ongoing war. Our once-vibrant city started experiencing more frequent violent attacks and became more partitioned by the blast walls. The pursuit of bin Laden had turned into the project of nation building, but nation building was rotten with misspent money and greed. As much as Shafic, whenever we met, would wax poetic about the healing properties of sport, everyone we approached for money dismissed the idea of a private football league as impossible or, sometimes, frivolous. No matter my argument that no one deserves a break from the real world more than those living in the midst of a war, we just couldn't find the money.

Then, as so often happened during those twenty years, it took the open mind of one single person who listened to us and agreed to help. Eileen O'Connor at the American embassy in Kabul was in charge of overseeing $400 million in funding for "public diplomacy" programs, such as independent media and women's empowerment. Our relationship was affectionately combative. During the year she worked in Kabul, she had become something of a sparring partner; she hung up on me more than once when she felt I was pushing her too much. Yet I sensed that in Eileen I might have found someone who could see the vision behind a private football league. By the time I approached her, accompanied by Chris McDonald, an American entrepreneur who'd built a hugely successful sports TV network in India and whom I'd met in Dubai, about securing US funding, we had all but given up on the idea. Still, we extolled the uniting properties of the sport that generations of Afghans have held dear. "It would be a fair and open league," we said. "We would travel the country looking for players of all ethnicities to play together on the same team. Our players would come from Kabul, and from Kandahar." By the time we got to the part about setting up a companion women's league, Eileen was on board. After that, we approached Shafic to ask if he was still interested; he agreed to take a year off from his job working for the German government and run the new league.

BEING AN AFGHAN requires, on a good day, accepting that you live a fractured, at times contradictory, existence. When most of what the world knows about your country is violence, you might have to pause to remind yourself that the life you live each day in Afghanistan includes your friends and family beside you, that the joy of being home is real, that you do laugh and watch dumb television and get married and work hard at interesting jobs and that none of that is erased by the reports of bomb blasts. Those twenty years of US occupation were fundamentally surreal, when the promise of a new country seemed to lie within reach in spite of the indefinite expanse of a terrible war and when the very real progress made during that war—vastly improved education, increased life expectancy, lower infant mortality being just a few examples—cannot credibly be weighed against the horrors of the violence or the pain of abandonment. Every day, Afghans debate issues about our lives and our country that the international media has reported as settled.

Being the co-head of a thriving Afghan business during those years was at times similarly bewildering. On the one hand, corruption was on the rise, American drones buzzed over villages, and at Moby we regularly dispatched reporters to far corners of the country to cover natural disasters, the fallout from the occupation, and the Taliban's return. We fortified our offices until entry to them could take a half hour at multiple checkpoints. For a while the attorney general was on our back, and the president was expressing his displeasure, or an American was whispering to me at a meeting that, unfortunately, American voters just didn't want to hear about Afghanistan anymore, like he was telling me the restaurant was out of whatever I had ordered for dinner.

On the other hand, I was now regularly in touch with people like Rupert Murdoch, who in 2009 had partnered with me to bring uncensored and entertainment-oriented television programming via satellite from Dubai into Iran, and invested some money in Moby, which would help us expand into six countries, including India and Ethiopia; Jahid had taken over Afghan operations so that I could focus on our international expansion. In Afghanistan, we continued to grow, alongside plenty of other positive developments; more Afghans were going to school, including university, getting better jobs, running for government, reporting the news. TOLO was so popular that we often got calls from staffers telling us that they had passed another business in Kabul with the same name. "There's a Tolo restaurant," they reported. "A Tolo travel agency." We laughed. "We should sue them," my brothers and I joked back at the office. Three News Corps—later 21st Century Fox—executives now sat on the Moby board, and Tom had only become more invested, and a closer friend. I had been profiled in magazines and newspapers and was regularly visiting contacts in the White House to discuss the political future of Afghanistan. I was then, as I am now, a single-issue person; aside from the policies on Afghanistan, I am mostly agnostic about American politics, and I don't care very much who sits in the White House as long as they show some genuine interest in my country.

Against the backdrop of war, as incongruous as it may seem, we had so much *fun*—the parties and tapings of *Afghan Star*, the concerts, and trips to the countryside that had nothing to do with violence and everything to do with taking in the beauty of Afghanistan. We were constantly adding new shows, comedies, and dramas; some were runaway successes, and others fell flat, but the fun was in trying as many things as possible. By now we had five major radio and television platforms, as well as half a dozen digital ones, and were hoovering up all the local talent, and there was a lot, creating what we all felt was the next generation of Afghan journalists. And now, after so many years of talking about it—not during the early period of hope and peace and exhilaration, but during a time of great vulnerability, with devastating terrorist attacks happening around the country—we finally had some money to start a football league.

BEFORE OUR MEETING with Eileen, Shafic had been planning on leaving Afghanistan. He no longer felt confident sending his young children to school; the Taliban had shown they would not hesitate to target a place with kids. Still, when we asked him to commit to a year running the league, he didn't require much convincing. His wife and children moved to Holland, and he stayed. Working backward, we planned the championship, to be played in Kabul, first, and then gave ourselves six months to recruit and form teams, find referees and pitches, draw out a schedule, and play a first round of matches that would get us there.

We first had to convince the Karzai government and the Afghanistan Football Federation that it was a good idea to support this upstart of a private league, Afghanistan's first. Then there was the issue of security. We planned to not only send recruiters but also to film the tryouts, but to send cameras into the south and southwest, in summer 2012, where the fighting was the most intense and the presence of the Taliban most apparent. Once the recruiters and the cameramen got there, came the challenge of convincing the people who lived there—who loved football but despised the American occupation—that we were Afghan, regardless of where we got the initial funding, and that even though we were filming them for television and planned to hold the first championship in six months, it would be a professional league. "Dribble a little more when the cameras are around," Shafic would tell the players. "Shoot the ball a little bit more . . . dramatically." At first wary, it wasn't long before the players felt comfortable, showing off for the cameras they had initially considered emblems of the occupation.

At first, our crew were scared to go to Kandahar. "I'm worried the Taliban is going to target us," a cameraman confessed to Shafic before they entered the local stadium in the city, which was, and still is, a Taliban stronghold. But in every city they went, the promise of football eclipsed the fighting. "Don't worry," a local with Taliban connections, precisely the type of person our cameraman might have been scared of, said to Shafic. "They are my relatives. I can promise you that you'll be safe." He was right.

Once players had been selected from the other provinces, we brought them all to Kabul for a few nights, where we put them up in a midrange hotel in the city center. Many of them had never met Afghans from other parts of the country—they might have never met a Hazara, or a Tajik; it's helpful to remember that Afghanistan is a sizeable country, but with terrible roads made impassable by war.

We worried that because of this unfamiliarity, fighting between players could erupt on the pitch. We worried that the ethnic tensions would ruin the game, that it would turn out that the war was everywhere in Afghanistan, that not even football could be free of its stain. Remembering how much the sport had shaped his relationships with other Afghans—growing up, it mattered little who other players were and where they were from, only whether they could play—Shafic arranged seating at meals so that the players were forced to talk to other players who were from a different part of the country.

"In a few days, you will be on the pitch," Shafic said, delivering a short speech to the dining room. "Everyone will be watching— your mother, your father, aunts, uncles, sisters, brothers, classmates." He laid it on thick. "And it's not just the people in the stadium who will see you if you let your anger get the better of you," he said. "Remember that at the end of the tournament you will go home. Your neighbors and your families will remember how you represented your province on the pitch, so be respectful; think about what you're doing."

Initially, it was awkward, like the first day of school. But soon enough we realized that we'd worried for nothing. Players happily ate together, practiced together, switched between Dari and Pashto as fluently as Karzai and our Arman hosts. Their only gripes were about the city itself—for most of them it was their first time in Kabul, and the place seemed so unnecessarily hectic—and the hotel. "Was there something wrong with the beds?" the manager asked Shafic the morning after their first night. "They've taken the blankets off the mattresses and were sleeping on the floor." When some of the players complained about the bland food served in the hotel dining room, Shafic decided that each evening a different group of players would choose what food to bring in from a Kabul restaurant featuring their home cuisine.

During the day, the players trained or networked with members of parliament and business executives. When it came to featuring sponsored products, the goalie from Kandahar was a particularly quick learner, gracefully turning the front of an energy drink toward the camera, mentioning the name of a mobile phone company in an interview with the media. We placed Hazara players on the Kandahar team, and players from Herat to play on teams in the far eastern part of the country. It turned out that for a more favorable contract, and the prospect of more money to send home, players happily went anywhere, and as long as they were good at the game, they were welcomed.

The morning of the first match of the championship tournament, a dozen people were killed in a suicide attack on the highway leading to the Kabul airport. Suddenly, all of our progress seemed to be for nothing. "People will hear about this, and no one will come," Shafic worried. We had spent every penny of the money we had raised through donors and sponsorships, not just on the players but on a new stadium, smaller and more modern and just a short drive from the infamous national stadium, which we eventually outfitted with state-of-the-art lights and seating, a new turf, and an electronic scoreboard. Some of our referees had been trained with the help of the English Premier League. Along with the Kabul police, we had hired private security to guard the stadium and check people's belongings, control the crowd that seemed poised to come. "They'll see all the security and get scared," Shafic said.

For a moment we wondered if we should cancel the tournament. A crowded football game, particularly our league's inaugural championship, seemed like a worthy target for a suicide bomber. Thousands of people were set to come, along with ministers and parliamentarians. Jahid and I planned to watch from the sidelines, underneath a canopy in a long line of VIP seating. The league was linked to Moby, and TOLO reporters were preparing to walk through the crowd interviewing spectators. During the breaks we had arranged for music, and a performance by Qasim Ibrahimi, one of Kabul's most beloved comedians who was fond of making cheeky jokes about marriage and dating, not exactly Taliban humor. But what kind of a message would we be sending if we canceled? What kind of a reality would we be accepting?

The afternoon was cool, and people packed the stadium entrances as soon as we opened the gates. Men and women opened their bags, allowed themselves to be patted down, passed through metal detectors, and took their seats in the stands. At halftime the women's national team, which had won a game against Pakistan that past week, came onto the field to a standing ovation. "I never thought this would happen," a female spectator said, weeping into a TOLO microphone. "Just a decade ago, I couldn't even leave my home. And now I'm clapping for women in a new football stadium." War was all around us, but war stayed off the pitch.

My mother had insisted on coming, although she told me later that she had been panicking the entire time. "Saad, people are climbing over the walls to get in," she told me. "Men, who knows who they are?"

It was a concerning sight—boys and young men scaling the walls of a Kabul stadium, much lower than the ones surrounding Ghazi, breaking the rules and shirking the security, gathering along the perimeter and craning their necks for a view. But I felt a connection to them. In 1976, I thought, I had watched boys my age trying to climb over the walls of the national stadium. I might have joined them. "Don't worry," I told her. "They just want to watch the match."

CHAPTER 18

MILITARY TARGET

In April 2015, Taliban fighters began battling Afghan security forces for control of Kunduz, a provincial capital and strategically located city in the north of the country close to the border with Tajikistan. By late September, with hundreds of people having been killed and tens of thousands more displaced, the Taliban prevailed, raising their flag, for a moment at least, over the defeated Afghan city.

At TOLO, we covered both the fighting and the stalemate during the summer. After the Taliban had begun their attacks on key posts outside the city in April, we ran stories from those posts. When after the fall of Kunduz, thousands of government forces launched a counterattack, we sent more of our reporters to cover it—those who were familiar with the area because they had relatives there, producers who spoke flawless Pashto and could more easily get through Taliban checkpoints, fluent English speakers who could get a sense of what the US special forces might be planning.

When an American air strike hit a Médecins Sans Frontières hospital in Kunduz in early October, killing forty-two hospital staff, patients, and their caretakers, we went live with analysis. And two days after the bombing, when President Obama called it a "tragic incident," offering his "deepest condolences" to the families, and then two days after that, called the MSF president to apologize, we grumbled out loud in the newsroom about why the American apology came so late and sounded so hollow.

By then, with both the entertainment and news divisions running smoothly under Jahid and Shafic's care—Shafic had resigned from his German government job and joined Moby full-time as managing director—as well as the careful supervision of Sapai's predecessor, a talented young man named Lotfullah Najafizada, I was devoting my time to expanding Moby outside of Afghanistan, and to nurturing the networks of people—donors, sponsors, government officials—who made that possible. I was spending some time in India too. There was a nice symmetry in bringing Moby to the same country that had supplied us with some of our most popular soap operas, and the money we could make by taking a piece of such a huge market would fund our work in Afghanistan for years. The harder we worked to make Moby a solid company, the more assured we felt that no matter what the future held, we would survive.

It was January 20, 2016, and I was in our Mumbai office, already one of our most exciting new projects, when Husain Naikzad, then our head of dubbing, called. As soon as I picked up the phone, I sensed that something terrible had happened.

"There's been another explosion," he said. The Taliban had hit Kabul multiple times the previous year, incurring massive casualties, and this year had already claimed responsibility for two of three bombings in the city. That evening, around 5:30 p.m., there had been reports of an explosion on Darulaman Road near the Russian embassy, about half an hour drive away from the Moby offices. No one had specific information yet, but a minibus carrying thirty-three of our staff members home would have been on the road at that time, and now they weren't picking up their phones. "No one can reach them," Naikzad said. His voice was shaking. "Their families are really panicking, and I don't know what to say." He worried that the bus had been targeted.

In October 2015, working on a lead from Afghan intelligence, TOLO had run a story alleging that Taliban militants, after they'd taken over the city of Kunduz, raped young women at the Kunduz University hostel. Our reporters were trained to receive tips with skepticism, especially when someone from the Afghan intelligence agency rang them up. The tips were sometimes a clumsy attempt to use TOLO for government propaganda, and receiving, fact-checking, and discarding them became as much a part of our everyday routine as our morning editorial meeting. We knew that their attributing violent incidents to the Taliban could be to distract from the violence committed by the Afghan security forces themselves; their accusing TOLO of being Taliban apologists when we refused to run the unsubstantiated stories was also something we got used to.

Still, we listened when they called, just as we listened to all tips, and every once in a while, the stories they offered us actually checked out. In this case, the former military officer who corroborated the story about the rapes to our reporter had been high-ranking, and we felt it was worthy of a follow-up. "Our agents will take to you to the hostel," the intelligence sources had told our Kunduz reporter. "You can interview witnesses; you can see all the evidence." TOLO would be the first news station there, they said. If it was true, it was too brutal of a story to ignore.

When the reporter arrived, the hostel looked ransacked. Suitcases had been flung open and clothes thrown everywhere. None of the students were there, and it looked like they had fled something terrible.

There were also no witnesses there to talk to, even though the intelligence officer had promised there would be. But an army officer said on camera that some of the girls who'd been there before had confirmed that "such a thing had happened," and another officer said that they had been told that girls had been killed in the hostel, although he admitted that he'd seen no evidence of it himself. Our reporters began putting together the segment. It would hardly be the first story of sexual assault during the past fourteen years of war. Earlier that week, Amnesty International had published a report alleging that Taliban fighters had raped many women, including female relatives of Afghan police, in Kunduz; these allegations were then reported in the international press.

Some members of the news team in Kabul had reservations. Sapai strongly opposed running the story, which he felt was built on flimsy information. "We have a reporter down there," he argued. "Why not wait until he can confirm more details?" But the majority of the editorial team thought it was too important to hold, and that it was solid enough to air as part of the 6:00 p.m. news bulletin, with some hedging; rather than stating outright that the rapes had taken place, we reported that Afghan intelligence was investigating alleged rapes by Taliban fighters in a Kunduz hostel.

From the moment it aired, the story was explosive. It seemed to confirm everyone's worst fears about this stage in the war and insurgency, the brutality of the Taliban, and the vulnerability of Afghan girls. Just as quickly, however, it became clear that there were major factual problems with the story we had been told by the authorities. We could find no evidence of rape. In fact, there had not been any students at the hostel at the time the Taliban fighters were said to have arrived; it turned out that the girls had all gone home for Eid holidays a couple weeks ago, and not been back since. The intelligence source, intentionally or not, had misled our reporter. And now the Taliban were furious at us.

We held a meeting to decide what to do. "We have to apologize for the story," one worried producer said. Another argued that our story, which focused on the intelligence agency's investigation, was fundamentally correct, and important for the Afghan public to know. "We didn't say the rapes had happened," the producer said. "But it's still a story that the government is looking into it." We decided that on the 10:00 p.m. news, we would run a revision. It contained a Taliban denial, and an interview with the dean of Kunduz University, who categorically stated that there were no girls at the hostel when the Taliban arrived. Some on our news team thought that the update was not sufficient, and that, to be safe, we needed to air an apology. But senior management shot them down; any news agency anywhere in the world would see our clarification as sufficient, we thought. We had admitted fault, we had shown what we knew of the truth, and surely that would be enough.

Three days later, the Taliban released a statement calling the story a "clear shameless example of propaganda" by a "satanic network" and vowed to punish TOLO. Up to this time, the Taliban had a stated policy of not targeting journalists, and, although reporting in the far reaches of the conflict was inherently dangerous for all reporters, we didn't worry about our staffers being kidnapped or killed by Taliban because of their jobs. No longer. "Henceforth," they wrote, "no employee, anchor, office, news team or reporter of TOLO news channel holds any immunity." We were now a part of the war.

TOLO REPORTERS HAVE covered the war from all angles: the death and destruction whether meted out by American or Afghan forces, but also the reconstruction efforts that accompanied the occupation. We'd maintained close relationships with several American and NATO officials; Zalmay Khalilzad, the Afghan-American diplomat who grew up in Kabul, and was the ambassador to the United Nations under George W. Bush and later special representative for Afghanistan reconciliation under both Trump and Biden, regularly came to our studios for interviews, as did embassy officials and representatives from NATO and US forces. We had a duty to bridge the gap between their vision and the ordinary Afghan experiencing the outcome of that vision in many different ways in different parts of the country. Our connections and the stories we wrote spanned all aspects of the war, but our audience were Afghans.

Over the years, TOLO reported on countless drone strikes, night raids, and extrajudicial killings. When the US forces gutted villages with mass arrests of "military-age males," and many of those arrested were taken to detention facilities on US bases, we sent reporters to those villages, and when Afghans were released from Guantánamo, we interviewed them on TOLO. There was a naïveté among some of the Americans I met during these years, with so little understanding of, or interest in understanding, those they were fighting against. And every now and then the muscle of the US military was used to settle petty local disputes; there were stories of American soldiers raiding a village in search of terrorists, on the tip of a local who only wanted his cousin imprisoned because of a generations-old land dispute. If the people they arrested were combatants, they picked up arms a long time ago and in a different conflict that had nothing to do with America or the Taliban.

Over the years, as our credibility grew, Afghans from all over the country shared with our reporters stories of repression and injustices, whether because of the occupation or the local leaders or Afghan security forces. Government employees called our reporters to complain about misdeeds they witnessed at work. "We can't go to the courts," they would tell us, just as they had told Sima, Massood, and Humayoon during the early days of Arman FM. The judicial system was full of corruption, they'd say. "So, we are telling you."

In 2008, American planes dropped bombs on a wedding party in Nangarhar province. It was a bloodbath, mostly of women and children, on what should have been a day of celebration. We put all our resources into covering that strike. Also in 2008, an American air strike killed nearly one hundred civilians, most of them women and children, in a village in Herat province. We sent a reporter who was based in Herat city, figuring he would be able to get to the village quickly, because he was nearby and could move confidently through checkpoints. Roads were too dangerous and long to take all the way from Kabul, and flying there would have taken all day. We were one of the first news outlets at the scene, airing interviews with survivors who were screaming furiously against the United States.

Violence wasn't perpetrated by the Americans alone, of course. TOLO ran scores of stories on the Afghan National Security Defense Forces, the military and internal security forces who had been armed and trained by the Americans, and their mistreatment of Afghan civilians. But we also profiled their soldiers, highlighting those who had a good reputation and did good work. When they were killed in the line of duty, we reported on that, too; their work was dangerous and often their deaths meant their families were left without an income.

We covered countless acts of Taliban violence. In Kabul, as the years went by, Taliban attacks became so common that it could feel like we were reporting on them the way a local news agency in the US would report on traffic. "You're amplifying the message of the enemy," Karzai's ministers would rail at me. Because an increase in violence in Kabul was scaring away investors, aid workers, and so many of the Afghans who had returned after 2001, the officials were often furious with TOLO's work. The ministers did not want to come across as inept at protecting their own people. But Afghans deserved to know what was happening. "People have kids and wives and siblings, who might be out for school or work," I would reply. "They need to know where exactly the bomb went off. They need to know which roads are open, and which are closed. They need to know if their loved ones are safe, and how to reach them."

Over the years, we made a lot of enemies because of our journalism. The Americans tended to reflexively deny responsibility for the attacks or say they would investigate or call them "mistakes" and hint at something about collateral damage, since militants were also killed. While the Taliban felt villainized by us, the Afghan government was telling us we were Taliban sympathizers, and the ANDSF echoed the government's accusations that we were too soft on the Taliban. We were accused of being funded by Iran, or being too close to the Hazara community, of being anti-Muslim, pro-West, anti-Afghan. We were made to feel vulnerable to all kinds of raids, arrests, closures, threats. But, somehow, we had never been attacked. Then the rumor of rapes in Kunduz turned out to be false, and the Taliban made us a military target.

WHEN A SUICIDE bomber drove a car laden with explosives into our minibus, it was carrying thirty-three Moby employees, men and women heading home for the day. The oldest who died was a fifty-four-year-old transport technician; the youngest a twenty-one-year-old dubbing artist. They were editors and drivers, welders and carpenters, cameramen and producers. None of them worked for our news division or had any involvement with the Kunduz story. Seven of them were killed, and fifteen more seriously injured, losing their eyesight, or suffering third-degree burns. They all had families, of course. Many had children. Most of them were the sole breadwinners for parents and children, as well as aunts, uncles, and cousins, even friends. A Taliban spokesperson gloated that the "vehicle was destroyed and swallowed by fire with all its spies, and its corrupt passengers killed."

On *Cleaning Up the City*, the hosts wept. Shafic was among the Moby leadership who spent the night identifying bodies. It was wrenching work, bodies so burned they were almost unrecognizable. I took the first flight home from India through Dubai and went from hospital to hospital—the victims were taken to different ones throughout the city—talking to the injured. The day was a blur. There was the Kabul traffic to navigate between the hospitals, the bureaucracy to contend with, piles of paperwork. I was lucky; because of the sheer amount of work that needed to be done in the aftermath of the bombing, for me, those hours weren't characterized only by grief. My own children were outside of Afghanistan. I had promised their mothers long ago I would never pressure them to visit.

We went to see each of the families. Their homes were scattered throughout Kabul. Some had some money; others were living paycheck to paycheck. They had lost loved ones who were also sole providers, a kid who looked after their younger siblings in the absence of parents, a father figure, an actual father. Massood, who got on the first flight out of Dubai as soon as the news broke, wondered if some family members waiting outside of the hospital for news would, understandably in their grief, be angry with TOLO. You killed our brother, our son, our daughter, they could be thinking. But all I remember is the resignation on the parents' and siblings' faces, a tired look, as if now that their worst fears had come true, they had finally stopped trying to outrun the war.

With nothing to say or do that felt anywhere near sufficient, we paid for the funerals, for the food and tea they felt compelled to offer visitors, and for any other expenses we could think of. We instituted a policy of supporting the family long term, paying the victim's salary for ten years and hiring their relatives to come work at Moby.

The day after the attack, I asked our exhausted staff to gather outside in the backyard of one of our villas in the Moby compound for a meeting. In January, temperatures in Kabul can drop close to freezing. It's a dry cold, sucking moisture out of your skin, cracking your lips. Our homes are mostly unheated, and so you sleep next to a fire or a space heater, maybe wrapped around hot water bottles. Everyone had shown up to work that day, and everyone came to the meeting. They wanted to be near one another when the shock wore off.

If we crumbled each time we witnessed suffering, or each time we faced suffering, we wouldn't be able to continue living, and we certainly wouldn't be able to continue living in Afghanistan. That day, though, our staff members were overcome by grief. They wanted the people who had killed their friends to also be hurt, and who could blame them? We had clarified the story. We had done our job as ethical journalists. And still the explosion had been strong enough to shatter glass miles away.

"We have two options," I said. "And it's up to you. If everyone thinks we should shut down, I understand. I'm happy to do that. But if we remain open and working, we can't be angry, we can't call for vengeance. We can't work in fear or hostility. We can't become part of the violence."

"We have to push back," a producer said, and there was a murmur of agreement. Many among the staff felt that now we needed to take on the Taliban even more aggressively.

"But this media company belongs to the people of Afghanistan," another said. "We have to continue to show all sides; we can't be guided by our anger. We are accountable to those who remain."

At least, they said, we should adjust programming for the next few days out of respect for the dead. "How can we have shows with people singing, when our friends have been killed by terrorists?" they asked. "We may lose viewers," they said. "But if we keep airing our shows like nothing happened, people will think we have no respect for our colleagues." The idea of running the existing schedules, with reality show competitions, comedies, soap operas, ads for energy drinks, and news stories about anything but the loss of our colleagues seemed, to them, abhorrent.

I saw how deeply they had been wounded. But I thought of our responsibility to our millions of viewers. I worried that if we removed our usual programs, replacing them with nothing, even for a few days, we would be imposing our sorrow on those viewers, who likely had enough sorrow of their own. More practically, I thought that a temporary suspension of programming would set a dangerous precedent—I was older than most of them; I could not imagine that this would be the last time something bad would happen at Moby. Still, that day I felt that the company belonged to the young Afghans who worked there, many of whom had never left the country and couldn't leave if they wanted to. They had worked side by side with the dead, every day. They had said goodbye to them before they left work that day. They would decide the company's future. And so, for a few days, we suspended our music shows and soap operas, replacing their complicated plots, lavish costumes, and happy performances with the heavy silence of dead air.

Both President Ghani and former president Karzai showed up to the funeral. I worried it would be a target of more violence. When Ghani left and nearly all the security followed him, I joked to the person next to me, "If we see our fallen colleagues soon in the afterlife, it will be courtesy of the president." But nothing happened. We were united in our grief. Across the country, Afghans watched the funeral on TOLO and mourned with us.

PART IV

CHAPTER 19

SAFIA

KABUL, 2023

My mother, Safia, visits Kabul every few months, as often as she can make the trip from Melbourne, where she lives in an apartment in the same neighborhood where I spent my teenage years. As long as the planes are flying—flydubai most recently, Kam Air or Ariana prior—she will be on one of them. We all learned long ago that it was useless to ask her not to go. I worry about her, but I'm also envious. More than two years after the US withdrawal, I still haven't returned, not out of concern for my safety but because I worry a trip will be seen as de facto support for the Taliban regime's more hard-line policies, particularly regarding women's rights and girls' education.

The first time she went back after the US withdrawal and the fall of Kabul to the Taliban, she didn't tell me, Zaid, or Wajma. Instead, she sent a selfie from the Kabul airport, a faint smile on her lips, the dead of the airport in the background. At least she was with Jahid, who was still in charge of our Afghan operations. "He felt like he was escorting me," she says. "But really, I was looking after him."

My mother insists that she is not an optimist—"At least, not compared to Saad," she says—but she has often been the brave face of our family. My happy childhood and teenage years in Tokyo and Australia, where we felt quite welcomed, were in large part owing to how hard my mother worked to make sure that none of her and my father's anxiety over money, or their home-sickness, trickled down to the children. She baked a cake for us every day, extra on the many occasions we had friends over, and the house was always full of laughter. Their longing for Afghani-stan was transformed into our cultural education.

While it took my father some time to find work, my mother did so easily. "It was my curse," she jokes. First, she took a job as a teacher and when she had some money saved, she bought a small cafe and bakery. Her entrepreneurship was contagious. As a teen, I already had two jobs, sometimes three, and we all helped when we were needed, taking turns delivering the ingredients for the sandwiches and baked goods to the shop—our car always smelled pleasantly of carrot cake and chocolate cookies—and in my early twenties, when I moved to Sydney, Zaid took over even though he didn't yet have a valid driver's license. Our father had started working in Adelaide by then, about an hour by plane or more often an eight-hour, much cheaper, bus ride, visiting as often as he could. My mother would have done anything for her family. For her, my father, brothers, sister, and I were by far the most important thing in life, and what she is most proud of. But she also loved her homeland and, as we got older, her independence, and so it should have come as no surprise to us that in 2022 my mother, missing Afghanistan, insisted on returning to Kabul, no matter who controlled the government.

When my mother goes back, we do what we can from afar to keep her safe. We send a secure car with a driver and a guard to take her from the airport to the Moby guesthouse, a building within the complex that has been appointed with the furniture and textiles that were moved from our rented family home that we'd vacated after the Taliban took over. A carved wooden door, once the entrance to a grand Afghan house, serves as the coffee table, while a smaller version of the door hangs on the wall in the dining room. Intricately cut wooden chairs sit by the floor-to-

ceiling windows that look out to the front lawn. My mother's embroidered Afghan dresses—traditional garments she once wore at
diplomatic functions—hang in the closet waiting for her.

At the guesthouse, our stalwart Jan Agha makes my mother a
cup of green tea and tells her on-the-ground stories about how
the company has been coming to grips with Taliban rule—the
news presenter who recently left for Pakistan, the head of news
under pressure, the program postponed indefinitely. He relishes
giving her any good news, and there always is some. "There are
so many new reporters," he tells her. "A lot of women." He tells
her of the teams of stringers we are putting together in the provinces; the eighty-minute-long interview on TOLOnews with
the Taliban acting minister of defense, Mohammad Yaqoob, in
which our interviewer posed hard-hitting questions; the progress
made in putting together our educational programming; the way
staffers from across the company are becoming more adept at
dealing with the more moderate members of the Taliban, and
braver standing up to the more hard-line.

On these trips, my mother finds herself a confidante for many
staff members, as she has been ever since we founded the company. There is something about "Madar jan"—"dear Mother"
in Dari—both tough and approachable, that compels people to
share with her their worries and their achievements. In the early
days after we founded the company, they might have shared
things with her that they hoped would make their way back to
her children—missed promotions, scooped stories by foreign
journalists who were brimming with resources, bribes they had
been offered and declined, even bad food in the Moby cafeteria.
They would also tell her things that were more personal: the
host sparring with a cohost; competitiveness with foreign outlets, with all their resources, that sometimes bred resentment;
petty jealousy between colleagues—it all made it back to my
mother.

As the years went by, and Kabul again bore the brunt of terrorist attacks, staffers began to fret more about security. "IS-KP bombed the mosque just minutes before my father got there," a producer told her. "We can't get home to visit my uncle, and he's sick," another would say, when security forces were blocking entry to the neighborhood where they were conducting a sweep. After the 2016 attack that killed seven Moby employees, each time any of the staff left the compound—to report, to go home, to buy lunch—they would say goodbye to everyone they saw on the way out, "just in case I never see you again." In her stoic, comforting way, my mother absorbed their pain, and celebrated their resilience. "Every time they leave the compound to work, they really believe it's possible they will never see each other again," she told me. "But they still go." I may be more optimistic than my mother, but she is more empathetic.

Staffers sometimes vented to my mother about things she was also angered by—corruption in the government and the military; the ghost schools and ghost roads that existed only on paper or were cheap versions that fell apart shortly after they were built; tens of millions of dollars allocated for aid and reconstruction disappearing, and obscenely enriching only a certain few. In 2014, when Ashraf Ghani became president after an election widely suspected of fraud, some of the staffers groaned and threw up their hands. "Madar jan," they would say, "nothing we did, no story we covered, did anything to stop the corruption," they said. When the suicide bomber killed seven of our employees while they rode the bus home, my mother was in Melbourne. She mourned with the staff the moment she returned, and mourns with them still.

Now, after the return of the Taliban to power, even with many of our original staff gone, employees continue to seek her out when she's there. On her first visit back, most wanted to know if she could help them leave Afghanistan. "How can I get a visa?"

they asked her. "What happens when I get to the airport? Can I take my grandmother with me?"

"Once you have your papers, the airport is easy," she would answer. "It's not like it was before, though."

Many of their questions, she couldn't or didn't want to answer. "I think your family can go with you," she would say. "But I don't know."

A few of them professed their commitment to staying in Afghanistan, no matter what, but visited her in secret. "We don't want to leave," they would begin. "We can't just start over in a new country." But, they wondered, if they were to change their minds, could she help them get to Australia?

"If I could, I would get everyone out," she would tell us later. "I would rent a bus to the airport. I would charter an airplane." But she can't. All she can do is listen.

She listens to the news announcer who, when his visa application went through, ran off camera in the middle of a segment to the bathroom, "so he could cry alone," she says.

She listens to the female journalist who can't get anyone in the Taliban government to take her call. "They tell her, 'We don't have to talk to you,'" my mother says. "They tell her to put a man on the phone."

My mother listens to the security guard who now shares his post with a Taliban soldier. "The same people who want to kill us are now protecting us," he tells her. "It doesn't make any sense."

She listens to Qasim Ibrahimi, the beloved comedian, who once commanded a whole soccer stadium of fans and now breaks down in tears on the sofa of the guesthouse, scrambling to come up with ideas for shows the Taliban might allow him to star in. "What about a sketch show celebrating and satirizing Hamid Karzai?" he says, a bit unrealistic in his enthusiasm. "I know Karzai; he would love the idea!"

My mother sits with Shogofa, a host of *Ruksana*, a popular women's talk show on our Pashto channel, Lemar TV.

"Everything we do is controversial now," Shogofa says. "We ask our guests about their businesses, what they are doing now to make a little money, what their daughters do now that they cannot go to school." She felt pressure to stay on air, knowing how important the show was for the millions of Afghans, especially Afghan women, still watching.

Shogofa shares with my mother that she adjusts the severity of her appearance depending on who might be around, or the route her car takes home every day, through which checkpoint passing which ministry, or even, now, which Moby office she goes into, what time she decides to eat lunch in the shared cafeteria. She no longer trusts even her male colleagues not to judge her or chide her if she shows a little hair or skin. "Every man has a little bit of Taliban in him," my mother says.

"With the girls, it's the worst," she says to me later. "They tell me they feel worthless. They are angry, but there aren't a lot of places where they can express that anger. What can I tell them? That they cannot give in to despair because they have a family, and their family needs them?"

During one of her visits, Taliban officials were putting pressure on the producers of one of my mother's favorite programs on TOLO TV, *The Festival of the Pomegranate*, a fairly innocuous show in which young and old Afghans sat underneath an image of a pomegranate tree, drinking juice and eating rice flavored with the seeds, and talking. "First they said they had to do separate shows, one for women and one for men," my mother vented. "So they did. Then the girls had to wear masks to cover their faces. So they started wearing masks. Then the Taliban called and asked, 'Why are the women laughing so much? Why are the women talking so loudly?' So the girls started lowering their voices and stopping themselves from laughing. Eventually, they stopped talking altogether."

My work now demands that I find and talk to the people within any organization or government who can be convinced that Afghanistan is not a losing game. For many people, this kind of work might make them more pessimistic, but for me it has the opposite effect. I see opportunity in even the most notoriously hard-line government, and there are plenty of them in our world nowadays. There is always someone willing to listen and to change their views, and I am always willing to listen to theirs. And Moby remains open, despite the immense challenges, employing hundreds of people, its TV programs being broadcast by satellite as well as terrestrial and online, and still watched by tens of millions in Afghanistan and in the Afghan diaspora.

But my mother's relationship to Afghanistan is different from mine. She was in her thirties when the country that she had grown up in changed so abruptly and then changed so many times more that it must have felt like living through a series of earthquakes. She is a woman in a country that by conservative tradition or through government decree has so often tried to control women's lives and silence their voices. After she spends time with the women at Moby, she returns to Melbourne or Dubai a little depressed. "They say that the country and the government must think they are completely worthless," she says. "And what can I tell them? They are right."

WHEN THE TALIBAN took over Kabul in August 2021, its streets were immediately deserted. Shops closed, restaurants shuttered, silence settled where once there was the noise of a bustling metropolis. Those who knew they stood no chance at getting on a flight or a bus or car out of the country decided not to leave their houses until they were sure it was safe to do so. Memories, first- or secondhand, of the Taliban of the 1990s shaped the response to the Taliban of today. Once that initial shock faded, the silence was replaced with a desperate commotion on the roads around the airport, where thousands amassed, trying to get onto evacuation flights out of the country.

I watched those images in near disbelief. By then, social media was also flooded with videos of Taliban fighters, in their usual attire and carrying American M16s, manning security points around the city; Moby staff told me about how they checked mobile phones for incriminating photographs or text messages. During those weeks, protests, several by brave defiant women, erupted and were violently dispersed. And then, in the months to come, while there were still some scattered demonstrations, the city resumed its rhythm; the deadly violence that had characterized the American war years—having been, of course, perpetrated mainly by the group now in charge—faded. Petty crime was punished so harshly that even the truly desperate would think twice. With the economy in shambles, Afghanistan hurtled toward a humanitarian crisis. But there was an irony that characterized Taliban rule. Within that environ of restricted human rights and crippling poverty, there was a return to an eerie sense of personal safety.

On her first visit back in the spring of 2022, my mother shook with nerves when she and Jahid disembarked the plane, not because she was scared something might happen to her, but because she feared what she might see. The first two days, she didn't leave the Moby compound. She didn't want to explore the city and be confronted with all that had changed, had been lost. Her restraint, of course, came as a relief to us. At least at Moby we had safe rooms stocked with water and satellite telephones, armed guards at the gates, and contacts we could call for updates on her and Jahid's well-being.

But after two days, my mother felt restless and ready for the city. She first went to her tailor, and then to Chicken Street to browse the jewelry made by shopkeepers she had befriended over the years. They showed her a bright green stone, a beautiful shade she had never seen before, that they were using in some new pieces. She was amazed that life had gone on in that way; they were so proud of their new work. On return visits, she began retracing some of her own childhood in the city, visiting her father's family house, which has always offered rooms to relatives in need, eating the bolani her nieces, one of them pregnant, had been selling out of their garage, drawing crowds with a delicious stuffing made out of pumpkin and green onion. Across Kabul, women were finding ways to make a little money.

Our home with the wooden gate that our father had fought so hard to regain, and then sold, had been demolished to make room for a small apartment building, but children still played football in the street at the foot of the mountain. The plot of land my siblings and I had purchased near Qargha Reservoir, intending to build a home for family and friends, was empty except for the beginnings of a sizeable orchard full of fruit trees and flowers, thriving under the watch of a kind gardener who lived on the land with his young family.

One day during a recent visit back to Kabul, my mother had the driver take her to where her father's orchard had been, now a small community just on the outskirts of the city. It would be the first time she'd returned since the land was sold, many years before. She preferred to remember the orchard the way it had been before 1978, a place where she had been happiest as a child and where she'd brought her own children, picking walnuts with shells so soft you could open them with your hands, eating them in the shade of the giant tree that produced them. She wasn't sure, now, what she might see.

They drove by small farms, many of them still funded by international NGOs and some run by farmers who had relocated during the American occupation from the south after their poppy fields were destroyed in antinarcotic campaigns; past small stores selling kites and candy; and past the demolished walls surrounding what she swore used to be the king's farm, asking for directions—the new roads and buildings had made the neighborhood almost unrecognizable—until they reached a tall, black iron gate. After a little shouting, two old men opened it, and she went inside.

I have not returned to that orchard since I visited it in 2002, when I found it neglected, and heard that it'd been used as a front line during the civil war. I vowed to purge those images from my mind and remember only the orchard of my childhood. But that day in 2023, my mother left the orchard feeling lighter, happier. It was different—for one, the original orchard was now split into two separate properties—but doing well. The farm beyond the black iron gate was thick with fruit trees, some flowering in the early spring. The new owners were in the process of building a large family home where they planned to have gatherings of loved ones much like what my mother remembers from her childhood. She posed for photos with the head gardener in the lush greenhouse he had built, and beneath a new walnut tree that had been planted in the center of the property and ringed by a low bench. It was half the size of the old one, but it was thriving, the nuts ripening on the high branches.

Outside of Afghanistan, even though plenty of news reports after the initial withdrawal focus on the ways the city is carrying on, it can be easy to imagine Kabul as listless under Taliban rule; my mother had fallen into that trap on occasion herself, thousands of miles away in Melbourne. I had also let the thought cross my mind in those early days after the American withdrawal, when no one knew what would happen, that the city might die. But, of course, it did not, because it could not. Everywhere in

Kabul, even amid the poverty and the sadness, life continued. My mother goes back to Afghanistan again and again, looking for that life, and each time she finds more.

On her first return visit to Kabul, my mother barely looked out of the windows of the armored car as she was driven from the airport to the Moby compound. Baby steps led her to the tailor, Chicken Street, the orchard. But by April 2023, she was going out for ice cream after dinner—curls of sweet milk flavored with rose water and pistachio, hand stirred and crunchy with ice crystals—riding in the company car after dark with some friends.

The restaurant, though, a three-story place with long tables around which families and groups of friends could gather and decorated with Technicolor posters of scenes from Bamiyan, was practically empty. A few men huddled by the entrance and my mother looked at them warily as she passed, wondering, as she did about many men, if they were Taliban. My mother was accompanied by two men who worked at Moby and of course had been driven to the restaurant by a male driver. The men averted their eyes respectfully when my mother, an older woman, entered the restaurant. "They are friends, and I'm buying the ice cream," she felt like saying to the men, but she didn't say anything.

Seated with her companions on the third floor in the otherwise large, empty room—on a Friday, no less, when she recalled it used to be full of people—she suddenly noticed all the flaws in the restaurant she hadn't seen before. The Bamiyan posters were garish. And had the staff always looked at her so suspiciously? Were the men standing beside the entrance Taliban monitoring who went in and out? It was becoming harder and harder to tell who she could look at, and who she should avoid.

The lights were too bright, and the glass tabletop was a little dirty, she noticed; luckily, Haris, one of my mother's favorites at Moby and our head of sales, is notoriously tidy and had brought along his own disinfectant wipes. They paged through the gigantic, laminated menu; offering hamburgers and noodles and kebabs, the restaurant had catered to the international aid worker and journalist crowds, which were now mostly gone. Just like Chicken Street, long known for its colorful shops selling tchotchkes, antiques, rugs, and jewelry to foreigners and wealthy Afghans, or the hotels nearby, or even the airport, which now catered only to the two airlines flying into Afghanistan, the restaurant had begun to feel like a relic.

The ice cream, though, was the same as she remembered—sweet and cold. The spirals arrived at the table arranged vertically in shallow white bowls, a little cityscape. As usual, even the single portion was far too generous for one person. My mother happily watched half of it melt in her bowl, as she had scores of times before in another life that was now feeling less remote.

She was waiting to pay the bill and getting ready to leave when she heard voices coming up the stairs. Suddenly, the room started to fill up with women and girls—"Mothers and daughters, I think," my mother later told me. They were laughing, the younger ones holding on to the older ones' burkas. The waitstaff pushed tables together, brought out stacks of menus, opened their notepads to take down large orders of ice cream and other treats. My mother and her companions waited by the door for the crowd to pass.

Since their return to power, the Taliban leadership had issued decrees forbidding women from traveling between cities without a male relative, and with the closure of secondary schools and workplaces and universities and even parks to girls and women, they had largely disappeared from public venues; it was easier to stay at home than not follow the rules and risk being punished, often arbitrarily. *Are they with a male relative?* my mother wondered. *Or are they breaking the rules?* Across Kabul, she knew, women were fighting back as they could.

Then, in the rear of the group, appeared a man. He looked haggard, trailing just a distance behind the women and girls, glancing passively at his phone while they chatted and laughed; he was a necessary accessory, like a license plate on a car. When the group had all ordered, and the waitstaff had left, the man pulled up a chair at a nearby table, just beside the women whose voices filled the room, put his phone away, and closed his eyes. My mother and her friends waited until they were in the car to laugh at him. "Poor guy," they said. "The Taliban has made his life so difficult."

CHAPTER 20

AFGHAN STAR VERSUS HERAT

The Herat International Airport, like so many modern things in Afghanistan, has gone through several cycles of birth, destruction, and rebirth. Constructed in the 1960s by American engineers to facilitate air travel to western Afghanistan, it was used by the Soviet military during the '80s, captured by the Taliban in 1995, bombed by anti-Taliban forces the following year, then bombed again in 2001 by the Americans, who later patched up the landing strip and used the airport for logistics. The Italians funded its renovation in the early 2010s, and by August 2021, it had been seized again by the Taliban.

Heratis are known to be unwarlike but, still, fiercely independent. They had staged tragic but hard-fought uprisings against the Communist government and the Taliban, and Herat is one of Afghanistan's oldest and largest cities, with its identity built just as much around a love of poetry as a talent for trade with Iran. More than an independent spirit, which is perhaps a characteristic shared by all Afghans, is the Herati's reputation for being cultured that precedes them. The city itself—the alleyways in its historical quarters snaking between homes built around large gardens, ornate mosques, public baths, and even an ancient synagogue—is primarily populated by Tajiks living alongside people of Pashtun, Hazara, Uzbek, and Turkmen background. It has long been seen as a cosmopolitan oasis in a conservative region; during the early seasons of *Afghan Star*, more contestants per capita came from Herat than any other city in Afghanistan. And one afternoon in

2017, the Herat airport, the military workhorse that had been destroyed and rebuilt and passed between so many hands, became the last-minute audition site for season thirteen.

Wajma and Jahid, both viewers of *American Idol, The Voice,* and similar shows, proposed the idea for *Afghan Star* in the early days of Moby, when we all sat around the makeshift offices, throwing ideas against the wall to see what stuck. *Afghan Star* wasn't the only reality-based talent show they pitched, but it's the one that became a jewel in Moby's crown. Wajma and Jahid were firm in their belief, as obvious as it sounds in retrospect, that Afghans, like Americans, would tune in to cheer on the making of home-grown superstars. They drew up the rules around auditioning and voting and proposed a schedule and set design. They envisioned the studio, a small stage in front of a judge's booth with some seating for fans, all built locally on the cheap.

At first it seemed a bit out there—too Western, too frivolous—and we weren't sure we would be able to find enough talent in the country to sustain a singing competition week after week. Afghanistan is a nation of music lovers, but we had been at war for a long time, and music had been banned under the Taliban. Singers and musicians had had to practice in hiding, without the guidance of teachers; those who had grown up as refugees didn't always have the means to invest in their talent. We worried that *Afghan Star* would just be an elaborate way to prove that musical talent had withered in Afghanistan.

Afghan Star's viewership was massive from the first season in 2005, and it near instantly became our most iconic show, as tied to the Moby brand as the news itself. It produced new superstars of contemporary Afghan music and enraged its critics so that they nicknamed it "Satan's Star," with some calling on President Karzai to shut it down for spreading "immorality." The singing competition also became a barometer for democratic practice in the nation, more so than the presidential and parliamentary elections; unlike those elections, the voting, done via mobile phone, was seen as fair and transparent (even amid reports of voters buying multiple SIM cards so they could vote in bulk for their candidate, or communities campaigning for a winner based on ethnicity). In 2009, a British documentarian brought international attention to the show with her film *Afghan Star*. The film follows four contenders from the show's third season, including a female singer from Herat whose brief dancing onstage subjects her to intense harassment, including death threats, and a male Hazara singer, for whom his community launched an ultimately unsuccessful grassroots campaign for his victory. In later seasons, one of the show's judges consistently drew ire from conservatives for her unapologetic women's rights activism and formfitting attire. Every year, until the end, the audience grew bigger and more passionate.

In 2012, for season eight, we appointed Mustafa Azizyar, a DJ who had started at Arman in 2003 when he was just sixteen years old, as host. Azizyar had a kind, handsome face, and a warm charisma; even the shyest contestant found him easy to talk to on camera, and his humility was a welcome counterbalance to the egos of several of the contestants and the judges. Azizyar was almost painfully earnest in his belief in the power of music to change Afghanistan, particularly young Afghans like him, and for *Afghan Star* to unite Afghans across the country. In 2019, when Zahra Elham became the show's first ever female winner, Azizyar fought back tears on air. Holding the box containing the winner's name, "I prayed that Zahra's name was in there," he later told his family.

During the years that Azizyar hosted the show, fans would approach him on the street, some of them certain the show was fixed, and that the host knew the name of the winner in advance. In those interactions, Azizyar was the ideal ambassador for TOLO, trying his best to persuade skeptics of the show's inherent virtuousness, which he so fully believed in. "We are transparent," he told them. "I don't know who wins until the very last moment, when all the text messages have come in." He wanted Afghans to share his belief in the integrity of the show, and we loved him for his earnestness, which, on a good day, we all shared. Zahra Elham is Hazara, and in years prior, a few other Hazara singers had also won the contest, which looked to some as a gaming of the system, since Hazaras make up only 20 percent of the country's population. But Azizyar considered such results a victory for the country, for a unifying national spirit. "It shows that everyone knows they can vote," he said. "The rich, the poor, Hazara, no matter who you are, and the votes are counted equally." In the months after the 2014 presidential elections, he and other young staffers would go on social media and cheekily remind Afghans that while they may have lost faith in those elections to deliver fair results, they shouldn't delay voting in *Afghan Star* rounds. "People wrote that if you held the presidential election like *Afghan Star*, it would be much more transparent," he told us.

During the early years of the show, I practically lived at the Ministry of Information and Culture defending *Afghan Star*; Abdul Karim Khurram was appointed minister around the time the first season had its finale. No longer could I spend my days in the office, spitballing new programs with our staff or helping to build the studios. My talents, for better or worse, seemed to be best deployed in assuaging the worries of censorious officials.

Again and again, I would find myself sitting in dull offices, listening to whoever had called me in for a meeting or, worse, one of their deputies list their grievances against TOLO—phone calls from angry viewers, letters from furious mullahs, chewing out from other irate government officials—and fighting with them to try to ensure that TOLO could continue to operate in the way we wanted. It's no wonder that as the years went by, I got exhausted by the ritual and felt happier and more energized opening new offices in Asia and Africa, or meeting with officials in Washington, DC; we hired a team at Moby dedicated to communicating and smoothing out irritants with the Afghan government. "Why do you air these things?" the Afghan officials used to ask me. "People don't like it. They call in every day to tell us how much they hate seeing it on their television."

"They're still watching," I would reply. "Our viewership has only gone up." Generally, the more complaints arrived about a show, the more popular it was. As Kabul, and the rest of the country, seized up tighter because of the war—roads around the country became impassable, Kabul itself a maze of checkpoints— people were spending more time at home in the evenings, watching the television shows they loved. Afghans needed our entertainment programs never more so than during the worst points of the war. Ministers rarely had anything to say about that. Most of them, they admitted in private, watched too.

But no one seemed to understand why I would bother putting in the time to visit the ministry in person just to defend *Afghan Star.* "What's the big deal?" officials would ask, rolling their eyes. "It's just a silly music show," they would say. "Why do you spend so much time arguing for it?"

It was much easier to justify the worthiness of a political news show, a hard-hitting interview, or an exposé on corruption. Those things rankled officials, but they couldn't attack them directly lest they be accused of challenging free media writ large, which the government still ostensibly believed in and preferred to suppress mostly via private pressure. When it came to documentaries on social issues, minority rights, or programs delving into emotive subjects like the war on terror itself, I could walk into the president's office knowing we had the clear moral upper hand. It was more difficult to summon the same confidence over a pop singer showing some skin. I quickly learned that the issue wasn't convincing everyone to like a certain show, or to see value in the music or soap operas, but rather to see all of Moby as a package, and to defend the entire entity as vital for free media in Afghanistan. It worked, for the most part.

For sixteen years, *Afghan Star* never missed a season, until we canceled it in 2021, hearing from sources that one Taliban official, at least, had said that shutting down the show would be their first act in power. Before that, we had filmed spin-offs and Nowruz concerts, sent newly minted superstars to perform at soccer championships, and recorded music videos and tracks that we aired as clips between programs and played on the radio, which attracted lucrative deals with corporations like Pepsi, which sponsored an "unplugged" music show. In the end, hundreds of new stars came out of the audition process alone, as well as plenty of hilarious flops. *Afghan Star* revived traditional songs and nurtured new voices. Rather than showing that our national talent had been suffocated by censorship and war, like we had worried, it proved that the opposite was true. Afghanistan has always been, and will always be, a nation of music lovers, even if some of the more conservative among us would spend a great deal of time and energy pretending otherwise.

OUR TEAM LANDED at Herat airport a day before the scheduled auditions, hoping to outsmart local religious vigilantes who, led by a thirty-three-year-old cleric named Mujib Rahman Ansari, had vowed to protest in the streets and stop the event from happening. For years, Ansari had been steadily growing his profile in Herat city, delivering aggressive, antigovernment sermons to a growing audience of people, mostly young men, who were already dismayed by the corruption and ineptitude they saw in the city. The role that media was playing in changing social mores especially drew his ire, and in 2010, he'd railed against *Afghan Star* while giving a sermon to a crowd of hundreds: "Shame on that father, on that mother, on that brother, on that uncle that allows their daughter on the TV screen." The video of that sermon was watched thousands of times, and by October 2017, when season thirteen of *Afghan Star* was set to film, Ansari's following was so great and fervent that no one in Ghani's government, or the provincial government, even tried to challenge him. When we reached out to local security forces to let them know that our team had been threatened in the lead-up to the Herat auditions, they threw up their hands. *Afghan Star* was on its own.

Waiting to disembark onto the tarmac, Azizyar wrapped his head in the crisp white turban that was worn locally, which had been given to him by airport security, and encouraged the other men to do the same. "It will help you blend in," the security officer had said, looking worried. Supporters of Ansari, online and through word of mouth, had warned Azizyar and the team to stay in Kabul, and they were not naïve about the power the cleric had in the city. Our judges, Obaid Juenda, Saida Gul Maina, Qais Ulfat, and Shahla Zaland, all of them beloved singers, followed Azizyar's lead, as did the handful of producers, the women pulling their headscarves lower on their foreheads and tucking in any stray bits of hair. They hoped that by taking such precautions they wouldn't attract attention, although if anyone saw them up close—the women in heavy makeup, the men in track pants and designer sunglasses—their cover wouldn't last very long.

As they were driven through the city, Azizyar was taken in by the beauty, the blue-tiled mosque on the way to the market road, full of shoppers. Heratis were shopping for fruit and vegetables, eating together on blankets in the park. The city seemed normal, not full of angry protesters; no one noticed the car, no one tried to look in the windows. Still, it was only once they were checked in to their rooms at the hotel, a nondescript place in the middle of the city, Azizyar and the judges and crew finally felt like they could breathe. They took off their turbans and headscarves and started to prepare for the auditions; around fifteen contestants had been preselected to appear on air, and producers were already fielding calls from the more eager singers, asking where they should show up to audition. After a few hours at the hotel without incident, producers went downstairs into the restaurant where they planned to start the long process of setting up equipment and decorations in preparation for auditions the next day.

Azizyar and the rest of the team, however, soon started getting panicked calls from local government officials. Supporters of Ansari, seeing the producers setting up in the restaurant, had reported their movements to the cleric. "Leave Herat," Ansari's followers wrote on social media. "Or be prepared for anything to happen."

"He's directed protesters here," the government official said, arriving at the hotel. "We're not sure there's much we can do. It might be best for everyone if you go back to Kabul." There were already calls on social media for righteous protesters to surround the hotel and expel "Satan's Star" from the pious streets of Herat.

The hosts, judges, and producers went to sleep that night, worried they might have to cancel or face the consequences, whatever they might be. In the morning, Azizyar woke up to a commotion outside the hotel. Protesters filled the street outside, chanting, "Death to *Afghan Star*," and screaming for the Moby team to leave Herat. Moving quickly, security ushered everyone into the same hotel room. "We can't record here," one of them said, and it was agreed that the auditions would take place at another hotel, in another part of the city.

It was a beautiful autumn day, but sneaking out through the hotel's back entrance, even our can-do host began to feel overcome by anxiety. The protesters looked more furious than he had imagined. They seemed to think that *Afghan Star* represented the downfall of Afghanistan, that the singing competition was evidence of TOLO's collusion with the Americans. Their numbers might not have been huge, but there had been enough of them to block the street outside the hotel's main entrance. Azizyar, watching them from his hotel window, had to assume some in that crowd carried guns.

While they drove away from the hotel, producers feverishly called up the contestants, telling them the auditions had been moved and to not, under any circumstances, show up at the original venue. The hopefuls would be of all ages, dressed up for the occasion, many bringing their own music, along with paperwork full of personal information like family names and addresses. "They don't want to have to push through a group of protesters," a producer said, harried. "They all live here."

Azizyar still had faith that the Herat government would protect them and the contestants. He'd grown up in Kabul, and the years following the US invasion had been the most stable that he had experienced in his young life; even when violence was at its worst, and the streets became glutted with the Afghan and international security personnel, he took that as evidence of some kind of attention to safety. At the very least, he thought, Herat security would manage to control the protesters, to cordon off this new hotel and keep the screaming people away. Although he knew that Ansari had managed to shut down a concert the year prior, he hoped that this time, with a smaller gathering, the Herati police would be able to protect the *Afghan Star* team.

At the next hotel, his team rushed to set up in the dining hall. Shahla sat in a chair by the back, touching up her makeup. The men used their hands to flatten the wrinkles out of their slacks. Producers hung lights in the corners of the room, holding their breath until they stopped swaying. Participants began arriving before anyone was ready, but they were let in anyway, crowding just in front of the door, a dozen practicing voices clashing together.

After an hour, though, the singing was drowned out by the sounds of the protest, which had followed the team to the new hotel and which Herat security forces had failed to control. It wasn't a massive crowd, but they were furious, pounding on the front door to the hotel, demanding to be let in. "The protesters have found us," a security guard said to the hotel owner. "What should we do?"

Azizyar and the judges were rushed upstairs to an empty room. "We will pause the auditions," a producer said to the crowd of hopefuls. "Stay here; we'll let you know what to do." The prevailing emotion was disappointment, not fear.

From their room, the *Afghan Star* judges watched while the hotel owner and a man calling himself a representative from the protest spoke in the courtyard. If they were angry, it was hard to tell from a distance, and it was impossible to know for sure what they were saying. In another world, Azizyar thought, Herat would be a place for concerts, not protests against music. In that world, hotels like this would be full of happy travelers. Perhaps, Azizyar thought, watching from his window, it was the hope for that peaceful future that explained why the owner argued with the protester so passionately and for so long, risking becoming a target himself, out there in the lovely courtyard of his besieged hotel, before giving up.

PEOPLE ALWAYS ASK us what the impact of *Afghan Star* was. Journalists ask us this; people who might support us today during all the tumult ask as well. The officials at the culture ministry berating me over some complaint, some perceived violation, would ask me this in an exasperated tone. What *was* the point? We were at war. Troops withdrawn; troops surging. More people dead. Extremists getting a larger foothold, people staying at home out of fear, people fleeing. And in the middle of it all, the show never missed a season, the audience kept growing, the finals hosted at Moby studios overflowing into our gardens. "It gives people joy,"

I would tell them. That was really the best answer I had. Joy goes a long way.

But the joy itself isn't uncomplicated. It's not the rush that comes from eating a piece of candy, or the release of a cheap laugh. It's complex, multifaceted. *Afghan Star* was about singing along, about cheering for new superstars. It was sometimes about laughing at an ego being busted by an affable judge, someone getting cut to size, about creating heroes for a younger generation of Afghans. It was about seeing Afghans from all ethnic backgrounds on television, about a woman judge embracing a woman who had won, and that victory being at the hands of a country of voters who wanted that woman to win and who cheered when they hugged. *Afghan Star* was a pleasure, and a protest. Celebrating it today is a protest too.

That day in Herat, the hotel owner finally came to them with bad news. "You'll have to leave," he told the team. "They said if we let you record the show here, they will attack the hotel." He had to protect his property, and there were a lot of other guests there that day. "Please leave as soon as you can," he said politely.

At that point, the team was close to giving up. The head producer called Shafic, who got onto the next flight to Herat. He spent the rest of the day meeting with security and local officials. He was determined that the show would be filmed. But after a day, as protests grew and Ansari's followers continued posting threats online, even he wasn't able to see a way out of the situation. "I think you have no choice but to go home," he told the team. "The mayor himself told us it's not possible for anyone to control these protests."

Azizyar and the crew got into the van to leave. "You'll have to come to Kabul to audition," they said to the crowd, knowing that most of them wouldn't be able to because of the cost, security concerns, or any other of the million reasons so many Afghans couldn't easily travel across their own country.

"No, no," a singer said. "Don't leave us alone here. We will come wherever you want. Are you going to the airport? We can come to the airport."

They paused. It wasn't the craziest idea in the history of Moby. Herat airport had survived wars. There were international troops and a succession of checkpoints to pass through even before getting to the entrance. If anything went really wrong, at least there was security. "What are the acoustics like?" a judge asked.

At the airport, weary producers set up for a third time in a garden near the arrival hall. Our private security argued with the airport officials, who were reluctant to let the contestants in until they heard what it was for. It was the fastest setup Azizyar had ever seen. Soon he was lined up with the judges on the grass in front of a hedge, everyone smiling calmly while the first contestant sang, pausing every so often for a plane to make its way out of earshot.

CHAPTER 21

TRAUMA

As an entrepreneur in Tashkent in the mid- to late 1990s, I came across all kinds of people—diplomats and journalists, smugglers and exiles, former mujahideen turned regional power brokers, holding court at one of the many four- and five-star hotels that had cropped up in recent years. Some of the Afghans I encountered were rightly despised by other Afghans whose communities had suffered terribly at their hands during the civil war, but there is no denying that even they had interesting stories to tell, and that they liked to talk. I was a sponge for any information about Afghanistan; I listened more than I argued, although I argued quite a bit. Each anecdote helped to put together the puzzle of a country I had left when I was old enough to love it, but too young to really know what it was exactly that I loved.

One cold afternoon, I visited one of Tashkent's ubiquitous saunas—the city was full of both medieval hammams as well as newer offerings from the country's days as part of the Soviet Union—and found myself in conversation with the son of a regional strongman, also warming his body near the spitting coals. His father was a very rich man who had profited off the civil war, and the son, influential in his own right, was fat and self-satisfied by the time I met him, taken to lording his knowledge of Afghanistan over anyone he met, and especially other Afghan men. As he talked, every few seconds, his face twitched violently, as though shot through with an electrical current. It had twitched, according to mutual acquaintances, since he left Afghanistan, the result, perhaps, of some fight or malady, but the man seemed blissfully unaware that his body betrayed his arrogance and made him easier to poke fun at. I liked to dole out backhanded compliments that would make everyone but him howl with laughter. "How do you keep so fit?" I asked once, to which he replied, "Every day I walk down four flights of stairs."

But he was also perceptive, and could succumb to moments of philosophical thought, which I appreciated. Perhaps he was more aware of himself—who he was, where he came from, the irony that in spite of his power and wealth he couldn't control his own body—than he let on. "You know, half of all Afghans are traumatized," he told me, leaning against the wooden wall of the sauna. "We are a nation of people who suffer from anxiety and depression," he continued, his face twitching. "You and I are lucky that we've remained so normal."

It was a short exchange, but one I still think about periodically. If Afghanistan is a nation of traumatized people, why were we all so eager to return to the scene of the primal wound?

The day I ran from my middle school to the sound of gunfire echoing through the neighborhood, looking for my mother, I had been immensely lucky. My mother had been waiting at home, all three of my siblings and my father also made it back safely, and a few months later, while the city tightened under the pressure of political upheaval, we were extremely fortunate that my father was sent on a diplomatic mission to Japan, in spite of his open dissent against the Soviet-aligned governing party.

We were also lucky that after he resigned from the foreign ministry, my mother's job made it possible for us to stay on in Japan, and that my parents' connections eventually led us to Australia, where they found work and we went to school, made friends, enrolled in university, polished our already fluent English into English with Australian accents, qualified for citizenship, and got good, high-paying jobs. In my life I have rarely paused to think about what I've been exposed to as trauma, and I don't think I've ever worn it on my face like the strongman's son.

Many of the people I know from that time were not as blessed as we were. Classmates ran from the school that day just like I did. They were probably also looking for family. Over the coming years, some made it to Pakistan, and some went elsewhere. Some didn't. One of them I met again decades later. He and his family had stayed on in Kabul, and, after the US invasion, he took a job in the heady chaos of Kabul airport. We didn't run into each other until years after I'd first returned, but when we did, we spoke easily, as if no time had passed. Our circumstances were so different—I was passing through the airport to Dubai or Delhi or Melbourne, and he was struggling to support his family. I gave him some money when he was willing to accept it. I never asked him about his life during the civil war or under the Taliban, and he never volunteered any information. It would have been useless for us to talk about how different our lives had been since the coup, even though we had both started out at the same elite school, eaten the same school lunch in the same canteen, run from the same gunfire.

I have an Afghan American friend who talks so often about being nearly shot by Taliban fighters that when you hear him begin, it's hard not to roll your eyes at his story of near death. "I was staying at a guesthouse near Kabul," he says. "When the gunfire started, everyone started running everywhere. It was chaos."

By some miracle, my friend finds a ladder. Propping it up against a wall, he climbs up as quickly as he can, as three other panicked people, strangers who are going to scramble up the ladder after him, wait. For a moment, my friend feels like a genius, like an action hero in a movie. "I get over the wall," he says, "and I hear someone behind me scream." Just below him on the ladder, a man had been shot. "If it had been a second later," he says, "I'd be dead."

There are too many of these moments, these coincidences, these close calls. And there are far too many stories about people who aren't as lucky, the innocent kid who gets killed or loses an eye or a parent. The story of the guy running for the border who has his leg blown off by a land mine when he is just ten meters away from safety, or the family in the wrong place at the wrong time. Somewhere in Kabul, while my friend tells his story for the hundredth time, there is also the story of the man behind him, who didn't make it over the wall.

In 2016, two weeks after we lost seven Moby staffers in the Taliban attack, we brought in a therapist to the office, an Afghan American woman who had returned to Kabul and was doing her part to help fill the enormous gap in Afghanistan's mental health services. A lot of our staff couldn't or didn't want to talk to their colleagues about what had happened. Many admitted they hadn't even been able to talk about it with their families or friends. It was too difficult, and those closest to them might use the conversation as a chance to convince them to leave Moby; the job had always seemed dangerous, but now it seemed reckless.

After a while, though, during one of the group therapy sessions, some of them began to share how they'd experienced that day and how they'd been coping since. One of the men, a comedian, was coincidentally walking with his children close to the site of the explosion when it happened, and so he ran toward it, in case he could be of some help. Arriving at the scene, he carried two injured children toward the ambulances that had just arrived, one in each arm, trying to soothe them with words he could barely grasp, before remembering that, in his urgency to help strangers, he had left his own children where they stood at the edge of the chaos, shocked and weeping. It'd been two weeks, and he was still having dreams about being there, not able to find his own children after helping the others, about being caught up in the explosion himself.

A Moby driver shared that even before this attack he had worried that this kind of carnage was beginning to seem all too normal to him, that he might be getting desensitized. "We would hear about the explosions, if we didn't hear the blasts ourselves," he said. There were times when he himself had driven the company car to the scene to see if he could help—ordinary Afghans often had to step in when first responders failed to arrive in time. "Once I just put the wounded person in the back of my car and drove him to the hospital," he said. "I don't know if he survived or not."

Before I moved back to Afghanistan, I had in mind a stereotypical image of a war reporter—an adrenaline junkie reading about faraway wars at his or her childhood breakfast table in Berkeley or New York, those news stories like comic books in which they imagined themselves appearing someday as a character. For these reporters, war is a thrill, and the stories within the war to be collected like treasures; whoever gets there first gets the most jewels. Many of these men and women are my friends now, and of course most of them have more complicated origin stories than the one I imagined, and they do great work, but they would have to admit that for them the story of the war in Afghanistan is very different than it is for an Afghan reporter. Most Western reporters would spend a month or so in Kabul at a hotel with the best security. They had the luxury of beginning to analyze an attack as soon as it happened, for they didn't need to pause to digest it emotionally; not like a local reporter would have to, anyhow. Most importantly, they could always leave Afghanistan and go home.

The reporters at TOLO were quite different from these international war reporters. Most weren't even journalists before applying for a job at Moby. They were poets, writers, academics, intellectuals. They joined TOLO because they were multilingual and spoke passionately and articulately about any number of topics. One of our most beloved journalists, Mujahid Kakar, was first recruited by my father to create programming about Sufism, one of my father's many interests. One day I asked Kakar to read the news in Pashto, which was his mother tongue, and over time I watched as this poet and philosopher transformed into a hard-hitting presenter, eventually covering some of TOLO's most controversial stories and being appointed the first head of TOLOnews. Until his death in 2020 at age fifty-one from cancer, he was one of the most courageous journalists we had, but he would never have thought about seeking out war in order to report on it. War was not a professional calling for him, or something he could theorize. He reported on the war because he lived inside a war.

After the bus attack, some of our reporters admitted they were fearful of going to investigate Taliban violence. When they did, it was sometimes difficult for them to maintain a necessary distance from the families of the victims. "We can't get too emotionally involved," I would caution them. "Think of it like a character you're playing. That character is rational and objective, he doesn't get angry, he doesn't get emotional."

Knowing the Afghan government could not guarantee our safety, and that we couldn't send reporters out to work if the Taliban considered them military targets, we did what we could to further protect ourselves. We reinforced our safe rooms, which were rudimentary spaces with a toilet, some bottled water, and a satellite phone, protected by a heavy door locked with a combination code. We paid the salaries of our deceased employees to their families and employed their siblings if they needed a job. We began offering life insurance, which was basically unheard-of in private Afghan companies at the time. And we asked Sapai, our deputy director at TOLOnews at the time, because he is a Pashtun who had lived his entire life in the country, to find a way to negotiate with the Taliban, while we made calls to our contacts within the group.

We had of course been trying to speak with the Taliban ever since they issued the October 2015 statement that labeled us a "military" target. After the January 2016 attack, Sapai and I continued our outreach, trying to find the right person, someone who had the authority to speak on behalf of the group and who was also amenable to talking, and persuadable. Finally, Sapai reached a Taliban spokesperson in Doha who was willing to open the door. "It all must be in writing," we said. "We can't leave any room for misinterpretation." The Taliban indicated that they were receptive to a letter.

Sapai labored for ten days over his draft, thinking about the colleagues we'd lost and the future of the company. "It must be very measured," he discussed with us. "It cannot give the impression that we are admitting fault." But how is it possible to maintain a professional tone with the men responsible for the murders of seven of your colleagues? How can you possibly approach them as equal partners in a negotiation? Was what we were naïvely calling a negotiation really a capitulation?

"I'm writing to a spokesperson," Sapai told himself. "The Taliban person who is most akin to a media worker, whose job is to interact with journalists. So I'll talk to him like one media person to another." In the letter Sapai wrote, he emphasized that all Afghans lived under the freedoms and constraints of the Afghan constitution, and that laws pertaining to the media were inscribed into that constitution. "Let's talk about why you made Moby a military target. Is that a reasonable decision?" he wrote. "Our job," he reminded the Taliban official, "is to inform the public. We are not a political party. We are journalists." Finally, after close to a dozen drafts and revisions, we sent the letter to Doha.

After a while, we were told that, although they did not officially reverse their death warrant, we didn't need to worry; the

Taliban no longer considered us a military target. Still, what had happened had happened. People had died. We all had to accept that working for Moby still entailed a risk. Anytime there was an attack anywhere in the city, we sent staff members to check the hospital morgues; if Zaid, Jahid, or I were in town, we would go ourselves. Although it was thankfully rare after that point that a Moby staffer was killed in an attack, it did happen. When it did, we often informed the families even before the authorities. Occasionally, we helped families with the procedural paperwork so that they could retrieve the body from the morgue more quickly. In that gruesome, bureaucratic way, also, we tried to heal.

THE FIRST ATTACK that Parwiz Shamal covered while at TOLO was by a suicide bomber near the US embassy in September 2006. Shamal had joined TOLO some months prior but had not been among reporters who had rushed to file stories from the sites of prior attacks. This time, Parwiz wanted to witness the aftermath for himself. Although he had lived in Kabul his entire life, he had been somewhat insulated by what was happening in the city by a doting, protective mother who, since her husband's untimely death, had raised her two children by herself, earning an income, including during the Taliban era, by managing to always find some kind of administrative job. Even when the Taliban shut down his sister's school and he had to wait hours in a line to buy bread, Parwiz felt content within his happy home life. It wasn't until he was much older that he even realized how difficult life had been for his mother after his father's death, and once at Kabul University, wanting to emerge out of that cocoon, gravitated toward broadcast journalism as his major, feeling that only through professional journalism could the reality of life in Afghanistan be truly exposed. By the time he became a producer at TOLO, he was resolved not to bring a shred of naïveté into his work. "No one at TOLO," he said, "should cover their eyes."

That morning, the suicide bomber had rammed his explosives-laden vehicle into an American military convoy, managing to kill two US soldiers. But the other fourteen who died were ordinary Afghans, most of them old men hired by the municipality for pennies to collect trash off the street or to sweep the sidewalks. It was a Friday, and they were working a few hours before going to the mosque, then home to be with their families. Hours after the attack, there was still flesh and pieces of clothing hanging from the trees. Parwiz followed TOLO reporters to the hospital where they interviewed survivors, and to the homes where mourning families now had no relative and perhaps no income.

Parwiz left that day with a visceral understanding of who bore the brunt of these gruesome Taliban attacks. Even if the Taliban succeeded in causing some harm to their enemy—the American occupying forces, or the Afghan government, which they considered a puppet regime—the attacks invariably killed and hurt many more Afghan civilians, poor and working-class Afghans like the men outside the embassy, all wearing the same dusty orange uniform, who were sweeping the road in front of the fortified walls. Those days when insurgent attacks were on the rise in Kabul felt to many like the days of the civil war, when small rockets would land indiscriminately on residential buildings, hitting the wrong side of a house and going into a bedroom, killing randomly, and plunging the whole city into fear. One of my cousins was killed during the civil war years in this absurd way, when a bomb landed in his garden and a piece of shrapnel pierced his heart.

That understanding stayed in Parwiz's mind during his time at TOLO, where he gritted his teeth through reporting, which required sitting straight-spined in a suit while listening to a parliamentarian give a press conference, and where he most enjoyed producing segments on minority communities in far-flung regions of Afghanistan. One of his earlier stories was from Bamiyan, then one of the calmest parts of Afghanistan, about pregnant women who, without access to a local clinic, had to travel for five hours for prenatal care. One woman featured in the story had been forced to give birth in a barn without the help of a midwife. "For women in Afghanistan, the Taliban are not the sole oppressors," Parwiz would say while pitching such stories. He'd also say, "The international press only cares about the cities. I want to report from places I've never been to before. In remote areas, women have nothing."

Parwiz was in charge at TOLOnews that evening in September 2018 when reports arrived of a suicide bomber detonating himself at a wrestling match. He sent two of his best staffers, a reporter and a cameraman, to the site. The reporter, Samim Faramarz, was live, describing the scene of young men carrying the bodies of the wounded, the smell of the blood in the air, when there was a second explosion.

When Parwiz saw the screen go dark in the middle of Samim's report, he immediately blamed himself. Both staffers had become like family to him. Ramiz Ahmadi, twenty-three years old, was the kind of cameraman that every reporter wanted to be accompanied by to a story. He was brave, smart, and agile with his camera on even the most demanding reporting trips. Samim, twenty-eight years old, was as much of a philosopher as he was a journalist. Parwiz would sometimes tease him that if he didn't stop thinking so deeply about things, he would become depressed. "In an era of passivity, fake reality and meaningless violence, what is it really we should look up to?" Samim had wondered on Facebook, in his last post a week before he was killed. "The corrupt leaders who are dragging us into more conflicts while filling their pockets? The disputed god who is watching the whole world being destroyed in vain? Or the highly overrated democratic system which is already falling apart? . . . We need universal thinking. We need to reach out and communicate. We need to imagine how others different from us are struggling and even just for once put ourselves in their shoes."

When we went to visit Samim's family, I brought my mother along, thinking she might be a comfort to his mother. Their house was very small, and full of people. My mother greeted the women while I spoke to the men, shaking the father's hand, saying what I could in condolences that I knew meant very little. The aunts and cousins offered my mother tea, accepted a word of sympathy, exchanged a short embrace. But his mother couldn't talk. She couldn't look up from the carpet on which she sat.

After that day, it seemed like nothing could lift Parwiz out of his depression. He was wracked with guilt that he had sent these young men to their deaths, no matter the risks of being a journalist in Afghanistan, and no matter that by any logical measure the blame for their deaths was on IS-KP, who had sent the suicide bomber that had lured them there and planted the second bomb that had killed them, not on the producer who had assigned them to the story. Parwiz felt the weight of their deaths fully on his shoulders. Sending him to the Afghan American therapist felt like asking someone in cardiac arrest to go to the dentist.

"You need a break," I told him after a few weeks had passed and he was still unable to talk about anything else. "Go to the Netherlands," I suggested. "There's a journalism workshop happening there; it might be good for you."

He had another idea. "I want to live like a monk for a couple of weeks," Parwiz said. "I want to be somewhere with no electricity, no technology." He suggested Pamir, an extremely remote, mountainous area in the northernmost tip of Afghanistan, nestled between Pakistan and Tajikistan, where our reporters had once tried to reach previously and returned after bouts of altitude sickness. "I read about it when I was a teenager," he said. "I'll take some pictures."

OVER TWENTY YEARS, I believe Afghans changed, sometimes because of what they saw and absorbed through media, but more often as a result of a million other things with the media primarily playing the role of cataloguing and reflecting those changes. We've tried to represent all of Afghanistan; from the beginning, our mission was inclusion, of language, ethnicity, class, gender, and religion. Afghans saw women and minorities on their television screens, until their presence was no longer a matter of tolerance but an expectation, even a desire.

Other aspects of being a media company in Afghanistan, though, were made more difficult by the fact of the war. Traveling through the country was full of challenges—checkpoints, security issues, terrible, impassable roads. Our travel show *On the Road* was one of our most enduringly popular programs because it took Afghans out of the villages or cities, where they felt trapped by war, into the rest of their country. And Afghanistan was, and is, a magnificent country.

But there were certain places that were simply too far, too remote, or too tucked into the mountains, which were near impossible to reach by car and too dangerous for the novice trekker to reach by foot. We convinced ourselves that there wasn't much happening in these places out of reach of war; there was so much to cover on TOLOnews, and so many guesthouses and restaurants and mosques to talk about on *On the Road*, that it was easy enough to forget about those parts of Afghanistan that were so distant that most people in Afghanistan's major cities thought of them as different countries altogether. That's where Parwiz, in his grief, wanted to go.

First, he traveled to Tajikistan, where most of the Pamir mountain range lies, to get a sense of the land. There, he met two French journalists who were trying to get visas to enter Afghanistan. They had plans for a documentary similar to the one Parwiz planned on making, about these Afghan Kyrgyz living in the mountains. "Would you help us get a permit to film there?" they asked Parwiz, and, ever the producer, he agreed.

Although they wanted an Afghan to help them navigate the region, when they saw that Parwiz had a camera with him, the French journalists didn't seem thrilled. "When we take photos, you can't take the same frame," they told him, beginning to lay out some ground rules. "You can't use any of our equipment, and we won't provide any electricity to charge your camera batteries." Although he was annoyed by the way they talked to him, Parwiz consented to these rules. It would be easier to travel with professionals, and he was interested to see how they worked. "I'm just going because I want to see the place," he insisted. "I want to meet Afghans I've never met before." He wondered, though, how it had come to be that he, an Afghan, was being made to seem like he was tagging along with the foreigners he was helping.

Parwiz was polite and never let on that he was angry. When, at the last minute, the Tajik authorities denied the journalists entry via the border crossing, Parwiz tried to hide his relief. "Please send us what you film," the two journalists asked, suddenly nice again. "Sure," Parwiz said, though he now felt protective about the project. He didn't trust the journalists to honestly represent whatever it was he saw or to show the Afghans they met the respect they deserved, since they had shown Parwiz so little.

Parwiz crossed into northeast Afghanistan by himself, a six-day journey on foot and horseback to get to the valley that lies below the Pamir mountain ranges. He found it more difficult to walk in the mountains than he had anticipated. The cliff sides were a crumbly gravel, made slippery with new snow, and he struggled to keep up with the locals—men with leathery brown faces and sure footing, herding flocks of Afghan sheep and goats across the valleys, hauling goods on slow-moving horses. He had heard about the difficulties the people living in Pamir faced. Still, he wept, seeing it for himself. Most of them had never seen a doctor. Their encampments had never been visited, they told him, by the international aid organizations that had been present in the country for nearly two decades. "You go up one mountain, you go down that mountain, and another comes. After that, there is another mountain. You go up, then you go down. After that, there is another mountain. You go up, then you go down," Parwiz said into his camera.

It felt like a forgotten land. Instead of the war we knew, Parwiz saw a quieter fight, in some ways much tougher, for daily survival in an otherworldly landscape, at such high altitude, where nothing grows. The people barter for bread and rice, surviving mainly on the meat and milk from their livestock, and use cow dung for fires in place of wood. "The bliss of this generosity will be gone if I ask the guests to give money," an old man told him, describing the tradition of hospitality among his people. They had solar power panels, though, and they let Parwiz charge his batteries as often as he needed. And, to his surprise—although he later felt guilty thinking he had underestimated their curiosity simply because of their poverty and isolation—they knew what was happening in the rest of the country. They knew about the new cities, the new schools and hospitals and their ghost counterparts, the war and carnage. They used their solar power to watch TOLO and had registered that none of our reporters had traveled to meet them. "We're forgotten," they told Parwiz. They hoped his film would lead to a health clinic, at least.

Parwiz had only one camera, but he collected so much footage that it took him quite a while to finish his documentary *What I*

Saw on the Roof of the World. After that trip, although he stopped often in front of the small memorial that we put together in our offices for the two journalists who had died and could never again bring himself to personally dispatch another reporter to investigate attacks, he stopped blaming himself. "There is so much suffering, everywhere," he told me. "I compared my guilt to the lives of these people in Pamir, and I thought, I can live with this pain in my heart."

CHAPTER 22

AFGHAN STORIES

As a teenager, Roya Sadat had decided she would make films about Afghan women in Taliban's Afghanistan, at a time when girls were forbidden from going to school and she and her sister had to be educated secretly at home by their mother, and when her love of the local theater was marred by her irritation over the fact that all roles were played by male actors. After 2001, when she enrolled in university, and began the process of producing her first feature film, *Three Dots*, she knew she wanted to produce the film in the villages surrounding her hometown, Herat, where it would be many years before women experienced any freedom, if at all, where the stress of ongoing war and extremism would end up erasing the optimism about girls' education, and where patriarchy was entrenched and the harsh conservatism that the Taliban had enforced never really went away.

"Why does Roya have to make movies in this dangerous place?" Roya's father asked her mother in their small family home, loud enough so that his daughter could hear. He knew that it was still unsafe on the outskirts of Herat, where Roya planned to film the story of Gul Afrooz, a young widow with three children who is forced to marry an aging former commander, and when he goes missing in a drug-smuggling trip, she herself is forced by a local warlord to smuggle drugs across the border into Iran. For several months, Roya had been going door to door in a very conservative village, trying to cast a woman who could capture Gul's mixture of vulnerability and strength and, most importantly, would agree to act in front of the cameras that her neighbors distrusted. Finally, she met a woman who worked in a carpet-weaving factory who was open to the idea and, importantly, had male relatives who, while they imposed restrictions—editing her name out of the end credits, prohibiting her from engaging in long dialogues with men on-screen, and making sure she was constantly shadowed by her husband—at least allowed her to be filmed. By then, Roya's father, who was generally very supportive and understanding of his ambitious daughter, had reached his limit. She had been casting the film for close to a year, and complaints and conjecture swirled around the area. "Young women were not allowed to do much then," Roya remembers. "And I was a woman making a movie about women."

Her father's worrying kept her up at night, not because she thought he would prevent her from doing her work but because she loved him and didn't want him to envision her being killed or kidnapped whenever she left the house to work on the movie. She stopped sleeping, and when they walked together, rather than telling him her plans, what she calls her love and her madness for her work, she stayed quiet. Early one morning, after his prayers, Roya heard her father shout up from the garden to her mother, who was on the balcony. "I prayed for her dream to come back to her," he said. He and her younger sister accompanied her that day, not only because her father wanted to see for himself whether his fears were justified, but also because he was curious to see his daughter in action, directing her first film. After that, he let her do basically what she wanted.

Roya says that *Three Dots* was made out of a pure passion that had been burbling for years. At Herat University, she studied law and political science, and though she'd done some theater as a young girl in school, her only knowledge of the practical side of things in filmmaking came via an uncle in Iran who sent her DVDs and books on cinema and script writing. She secured

$2,000 from a French NGO to rent some basic equipment and to pay the production crew and amateur actors who appeared in her film. Her subjects were taboo, and her characters were barely fictionalized versions of themselves or their neighbors. There were a lot of plotlines living quietly in those Herat villages. Looking at that film now, which was released in 2003, she sees how unpolished it was, and loves it even more for that reason.

In 2006, *Three Dots* was screened at a film festival in Kabul, winning awards in all categories. The following year, when we had a little more money and confidence in our audience—polls told us that close to 80 percent of Afghans with access to television were watching our Indian soaps—we commissioned Roya to direct the very first Afghan soap opera, which was created and developed by the renowned French-Afghan filmmaker and novelist Atiq Rahimi.

Atiq and I wrote the treatment for the first episode over tea in less than half an hour. Plotlines came quickly to us. By the time Roya came in, she had inherited a daunting project, and not just because an audience of hopeful Afghans and skeptical officials would be poised to pick apart the country's first original programming in this realm. Practically, we had a lot to overcome too. Even our most expensive reality shows, like *Afghan Star*, were manageable compared to the work it would take to make an Afghan drama serialized. We would have to hire more producers, writers, and technicians, local actors fluent in both Dari and Pashto, negotiate access to locations around the city, and possibly cope with officials complaining about plots and characters without having the option of mollifying them by blurring out a Hindu deity or dubbing over a Hindu chant.

Roya, at the time, had just completed a new documentary, and was trying to figure out how to fund her next feature film. She had never considered working in television before and wondered if it was a superficial medium compared to cinema. But she also saw that, with cinemas destroyed by war, television had become a powerful storytelling medium, and when Atiq reached out to her, she didn't hesitate to say yes. This would be the first time that Afghans would see their own stories being dramatized on television, and that was compelling. As was the money. Although she had traveled to South Korea and taken *Three Dots* around the world, the move to Kabul, a city she thought of as living in contrasts, beautiful and turbulent, felt a bit daunting. Her father, younger brother, and mother helped her, the first girl of the family to move alone to a city for work, settle in.

The Secrets of This House was a melodrama about a large, chaotic Afghan household, a metaphor, Roya and Atiq thought, for the country itself. For the first time, Roya was able to work with good equipment—track trolleys, expensive lenses, boom mics, and reflectors—and professional, or semiprofessional, actors.

Most of the actors who came to work for Roya did so not because they had always dreamed of the profession but because the job liberated them from their own lives, more tragic than fiction, and because they needed the money. One of the actresses had been married off, at thirteen, to an opium addict thirty years older than her; she had seven children with him and, after years of abuse, had attempted suicide. Another actress, playing the main love interest, a young woman just back from studying film and theater in America, came from a conservative Pashtun family and had been disowned by her father; when an uncle found out she had become an actress, he tried to kill her. For several of the actors in *The Secrets of This House*, there was a thin line between the drama of their real lives and the stories they acted out in front of the camera.

It was a risk for them to film, but important that it happen. We are hypocrites, I thought at the time, if we say we want to watch women on television but what we mean is *other* women—Indian and Turkish and American women—but not our own. Our own women we would like to keep at home, seen only by our own eyes.

The Secrets of This House dramatized a post-2001 Afghanistan that our Afghan audience was intimately familiar with, one full of returnees who carried with them a wealth of different experiences and desires, in which different generations of Afghans clash while living under one roof. A woman comes back from America and wonders if she must sacrifice all her freedom in order to be in her homeland. A man comes back from twenty years away to reclaim his Kabul house from a crooked former mujahid—a plotline my family was very familiar with. There was corruption on the screen, crime, drugs, depression, allusions to the war and occupation, thwarted love, and frequent moments of comic relief, usually delivered by a young male character who fumbled at social interactions—many of the ingredients, some happy and some toxic, that made up Afghanistan.

We trusted Roya to make the shows she wanted. But while she told one story about Afghanistan, people in the White House and the Arg were busy telling their own.

OVER TWENTY YEARS and through four US administrations, I've met with anyone who was willing to talk about Afghanistan. In the Bush administration, it was folks at the US embassy and USAID. Under President Obama, it was Richard Holbrooke, special representative for Afghanistan and Pakistan, and Lieutenant General Doug Lute, who was the lead coordinator at the White House for Afghanistan, Pakistan, and India. The Trump White House was a mixed bag on the subject, and I approached it with some wishful thinking; the only time I met Rex Tillerson, his first secretary of state, he mistook me for a Saudi visitor and then left the room in a hurry when I corrected him, I assume out of embarrassment.

H. R. McMaster, who served as Trump's second national security advisor, on the other hand, exemplified a more interventionist American attitude toward Afghanistan. McMaster, I think, cared deeply about Afghanistan—almost too much; he seemed emotionally attached and often told me he had sleepless nights over the future of the country. McMaster had a very black-and-white idea of people and institutions—he used that favored American term "good guy" a lot—and thought that a sustained commitment to Afghanistan was in everyone's interest, but the strategy he proposed was profoundly flawed. He advocated for an indefinite presence of US troops in Afghanistan, irrespective of ineptitude and corruption in local government, and even though there was no appetite among Americans—the public or the political class—for a "forever" war. Jared Kushner, another contact I had in Trump's White House, was always cordial but, by his own assessment, felt he had bigger fish to fry, something I understood, although never liked hearing.

I cared less about who was in the White House than what their plans were for Afghanistan. Steve Bannon, Trump's "chief strategist" during the first year of his presidency, was blunt and undiplomatic, but smart. He shaped and believed in the populist Trump agenda, as wrongheaded as it might have been, and he liked to argue with me about domestic issues. We met only a few times in person, in the White House Mess or in his office in the West Wing, and after he was fired by Trump, at the town house he called the Breitbart Embassy, where Bannon would delight in mocking Don Jr. for a few minutes or tell me ribald tales from life on the political road, much of which I assumed was just good storytelling.

Bannon wanted Trump to get out. "Afghanistan is just not a priority," he would tell me. Still, we would talk for a long time, about what had gone wrong, how personalities on both sides had tainted the project, the hundreds of billions spent and the tragic loss of life—both American and Afghan—and the ways, however difficult, that the US could withdraw smoothly, leaving the country to Afghan security and governance. "It's just a question of time before we leave," he would say, and when I heard that directly from Bannon, I knew there was no alternate path on the table.

By summer 2018, when Trump authorized peace talks with the Taliban in Doha, Qatar, Bannon and McMaster were gone. Tillerson, whom I hadn't had contact with since that disastrous first meeting, had also been cut loose. Trump had tasked his new secretary of state, Mike Pompeo, with getting the US out of Afghanistan. Pompeo brought Zalmay Khalilzad, whom I had consistently advocated for with Bannon and Kushner to play a role in the administration's approach to Afghanistan, to lead the project of reconciling the Afghan government with the Taliban. By the time Trump was voted out of office by the American public, there was an agreement in place that Khalilzad had signed with the Taliban leadership. It contained a timetable for the remaining American troops to leave Afghanistan.

It felt like I was always talking to someone or the other about the impending withdrawal. But looking back, a few phone calls and meetings from those final years stand out. Some were foreboding, others frankly head-spinning. Some I remember simply because they were final, the last conversation of their kind, tied to an era—twenty long years characterized by both progress and disaster—that was so close to being upended. On May 26, 2020, three months after the peace deal was signed in Doha, I had a one-hour phone call with Jake Sullivan, who'd been Vice President Biden's national security advisor, and who was part of Biden's presidential campaign. I had first met Sullivan when we were both serving on the board of the International Crisis Group. Sullivan was smart and knowledgeable about Afghanistan in a way that surpassed many of those in the Trump White House, and I had always liked him.

The call was not encouraging. Sullivan made it clear that then-candidate Biden did not intend to reverse the agreement on troop withdrawal. The war, Biden felt, was unpopular and unwinnable—troop surges under both Obama and Trump had been failures—and his campaign intended to avoid the topic as much as possible during the election season. A vague plan for ending American presence in Afghanistan included leaving a small contingent of American troops for counterterrorism purposes, and only if the situation on the ground allowed for it, a gesture, I thought, but toward what, I wasn't sure. Particularly in the context of the inevitable withdrawal, I preferred the possibility of a Biden administration. Biden, at least, seemed like a grown-up. Trump's White House shed staff too quickly. Those who cared about Afghanistan, like McMaster, were long gone, and by 2020 it could feel like every conversation was part of an attempt to hold up the scaffolding around the country in anticipation of a sudden, catastrophic collapse. We did not imagine the same thing happening under Biden. Still, when I hung up the phone that day in the summer of 2020 after talking to Sullivan, who'd be appointed Biden's national security advisor in 2021, I did not feel encouraged. The number of troops they suggested leaving in the country didn't even amount to scaffolding.

Back in Kabul, I visited the Arg. Although our relationship had repaired itself after Ghani's initial fury over TOLO's coverage of the election fraud, meeting with the president over the years was, without fail, disappointing. I rarely went out of my way to see him, and Ghani didn't seem all too eager to meet me either. He had only grown more arrogant since his election and then reelection, also disputed, in 2019, convinced that he knew the US political system better than any other Afghan. That said, our president also seemed so desperate for attention in Washington that Afghans used to joke that Ghani would throw himself in front of Trump on his way to the bathroom just so they could have a two-minute chat. In fact, he had needed me, the head of a media company, to arrange his first phone call with president-elect Trump, which I did through Kushner.

Later that same year, one of Ghani's senior advisors asked me to visit the president to give him the lay of the land, as I saw it, for the Trump presidency. That meeting, a few years and one president removed from the actual withdrawal, is one that has always stayed with me for illustrating, over the course of two days, Ghani's profound unwillingness to listen, even in the face of his better instincts.

In his office in the Arg, Ghani was as disconnected from ordinary Afghans as he would be if he lived in Washington, DC. He showed no real interest in what was happening in the country he'd been leading for the past three years, and his habit of lecturing rather than listening had become almost pathological. Knowing I was in touch with Bannon, he began summarizing a book on American history that had apparently shaped Bannon's worldview while I sat dumbfounded, waiting for the speech to end.

Forty minutes into what I had been told would be a thirty-minute meeting, I summoned the nerve to interrupt him. "Mr. President," I said. "Do you want to hear what the Americans are thinking?"

Suddenly, Ghani was in a hurry. "I've got five minutes," he said. He was late to give a speech, his staff told me. "Come back tomorrow," Ghani said. The following day, I returned to the Arg, and, in fairness to the president, this time he listened. Nothing changed, of course, over the coming years, but that day, Ghani was quiet, introspective, and seemed open to opinions. I tried to explain how vulnerable we were. I knew I was only restating what the president already knew, but it seemed worth emphasizing.

In September 2020, a few months after my phone call with Jake Sullivan, I called upon Ghani, rather reluctantly, to share with him what presidential candidate Biden was thinking about

American presence in Afghanistan. Ghani said that he had more well-informed contacts than Sullivan on Biden's team; he was convinced that Biden would not abandon Afghanistan if he became president. A month or so later, I saw Ghani again at a meeting, and repeated what I knew. But Ghani was again dismissive and convinced that he knew better.

When Biden became president in January 2021, he had inherited Trump's agreement with the Taliban that contained the withdrawal deadline of May 1 for the remaining 2,500 American troops in Afghanistan. The agreement also encouraged talks between the Afghan government and the Taliban; those had started after a long delay but had since stalled. The Biden administration began pushing for some form of power-sharing via a "transitional peace government," but Ghani was resistant, and in March, TOLO published a leaked copy of Secretary of State Antony Blinken's letter to Ghani expressing the administration's impatience with his stance on the peace talks. In mid-April, Biden announced that "it is time to end America's longest war" and that all US troops would leave Afghanistan before September 11.

Almost immediately, the impact of years of poor planning, corruption, and being treated as second-class within the American-trained Afghan security forces—Afghan soldiers received dreadfully low wages and were given subpar medical care compared to their international counterparts—began to show, and things started to fall apart. Under constant attack, feeling outnumbered by the Taliban, and struggling to cope with ammunition shortages and low morale, Afghan soldiers abandoned their posts. The Biden administration, in its haste to leave, never planned the transition from US to Afghan forces, including logistics like servicing equipment and aircraft, and those in the Afghan security forces who stayed oversaw a crumbling system in the face of a determined enemy. Contractors tasked with maintenance of hardware for the Afghan military were among the first to leave. By June, some of the Afghan military armored vehicles, bombers, and helicopters were already in disrepair. Desperate Afghan officers reached out to the contractors, now in Abu Dhabi and elsewhere, working on different projects, to try to learn how to fix their trucks via Zoom, but without the contracting system in place, even the vehicles that worked couldn't be refueled.

In July 2021, a couple of weeks after the Americans vacated Bagram, their last military base in the country, I went to DC, where, over the course of a few days, I met with the head of USAID, Samantha Power, Sullivan, and others. "The way this is going," I said, "the Afghan government will collapse completely by November."

"That's not possible," Power said. "You're being alarmist."

"We are willing to do what we can," Sullivan told me, "we just don't have any good partners in Afghanistan." He had spoken to General Mark Milley, chairman of the Joint Chiefs of Staff, who had expressed his frustration with his counterpart in the Afghan military. In recent years, Ghani had frequently shuffled and promoted loyalists within the military, irrespective of their competence and experience. The new chief of staff of the Afghan armed forces was completely hopeless. The corps commanders were terrible. Ghani held the incompetent and flattering advisors who surrounded him in the Arg closest, but it's also true that he had never stood a chance. Trump had announced in February 2020 that American troops would leave Afghanistan by the following year. The Taliban just had to wait it out; they had no incentive to work with the Ghani administration toward an inclusive government.

Two days later, on July 23, 2021, feeling like I was banging my head between two countries, I once again found myself on my way to the Arg. It was Friday afternoon, and with the weekend quiet and not much traffic, it took only ten minutes from Moby to get there, like the old days. I found Ghani sitting outside in the shade, looking fragile and defeated, his characteristic anger, and the explosive bursts of energy that came with it, totally absent. An ottoman was placed on the ground in front of his chair, and, shortly after we started speaking, he lifted his feet onto it, his soles facing outward toward me, which most Afghans would find offensive. It was clear that the president made the gesture not out of disrespect, but pure exhaustion, which I found even more alarming.

Carefully, I summarized my meetings in Washington. "The Americans are losing confidence in you," I said. "You have to accept that your government cannot survive on its own, and you have to find ways to keep the Americans engaged. You have to appoint a new national security advisor. Your entire inner circle needs to be changed." He watched me while I spoke. The withdrawal would be complete in a matter of weeks, I reminded him. There were accounts that his national security advisor, Hamdullah Mohib, was running his own command center to fight the Taliban out of the national security council building in the Arg compound, parallel to the Ministry of Defense, with Mohib playing at general. Rumors about who made the calls to bomb and where to fight painted a picture of a fully fractured Afghan military, with the chaos leading back to the palace.

"You need American support after the withdrawal, if you want to stay in power," I told him. I knew that even if he did all of these things, it was probably too late to get the Taliban to agree to a peaceful transition. But I didn't want to imagine what would happen if he didn't at least try. "You have to make some changes."

Ghani shook his head. As shriveled as he was, he was still prideful beyond sanity. "Biden is calling later," he said. I could tell he was bracing for something difficult. But he wouldn't concede any points.

"Mr. President," I repeated myself, "with all due respect, you need to get rid of all the incompetent people around you." Rationally speaking, it was clear that the best Ghani's government could do was secure major cities; it was lunacy to believe they could control the entire country. The plan couldn't be to defeat the Taliban, but to come up with workable ideas for something resembling a smooth transition to an interim government based on talks between all Afghan actors, with support of the international community. "You need to understand that your government cannot stay the way it is, if you want it to survive," I told him. He looked defeated. I knew he had heard it all before.

Ashraf Ghani told himself his own stories. He had met Trump a few times: in 2017 at the Arab Islamic American Summit in Riyadh, where McMaster had to prod the American president to engage with Ghani; a few months later at the United Nations General Assembly in New York; and two years later, when Trump paid a surprise visit to American troops stationed at Bagram Air Base over Thanksgiving. While Ghani addressed Congress during Obama's administration, and met Biden at the White House during his, he never met Trump at the White House.

Ghani was openly in conflict with the US government over their peace talks with the Taliban in Doha, which excluded his government. Yet his behavior reflected the government's dependency on the American president. Ghani would often brag to people about his close relationship with Trump, a fiction. "He acts like he is an employee of the US," Parwiz told us, showing us footage of Ghani greeting Trump at Bagram; Ghani, who had been told just a few hours prior of the visit, had accepted an invitation to meet Trump there. That footage, in which he seemed so deferential to an American president who gave him only glancing attention, was the real face of Ashraf Ghani, Parwiz said.

In the last two years of Ghani's presidency, Parwiz had been putting together a documentary on the president for TOLO. Our producer found it dispiriting work. "He wants to be an icon," he told me. "But he doesn't want to hear any bad news. He doesn't listen to the people in the provinces."

Ghani didn't seem to want to listen to anyone. I didn't get the sense that he cared very much at that point about civilian casualties or any of the abuses Afghans faced during the occupation, and it seemed that he registered the US withdrawal only in the context of his own claim to power. He was intent on undermining and outmaneuvering Khalilzad, and was certain the Americans would never abandon him. In the oasis of the Arg, he was oblivious to the pain and suffering of ordinary Afghans, what they faced on a daily basis, circumstances created or perpetuated by his own government's corruption and ineptitude, and their inability to deliver on any promises. He disparaged those who fled in anticipation of the collapse to come. Blinken's letter had been leaked to us not by an American diplomat or a foreign journalist, but by someone who was ostensibly a supporter of the Ghani administration, an Afghan, worried about his country and furious at his president.

Reporting out of Afghanistan had become resoundingly dire in its tone and content; long gone were the starry-eyed narratives of women's beauty parlors and schools being built in the provinces, and in their place were accounts of district after district falling under Taliban control, the disarray among the Afghan security forces. But Ghani told me that he still never watched the news, preferring to read only the summaries presented to him by his staff.

"Those summaries don't show you emotion," I had told him. "You don't hear a mother screaming because her son has died, or someone weeping because their family doesn't have enough food, or their village has been destroyed."

"I know what's going on," he had insisted.

The next day, July 24, 2021, I went to the Arg for the last time to meet with Ghani and his vice president, Amrullah Saleh.

Ghani had asked me to return, and I had hope that the call with Biden had knocked some sense into him.

This time, I found the president full of energy, practically thumping his chest. Fifteen hours earlier he had been forlorn, defeated. Now he was convinced he could stay in power and resist the Taliban, even without the Americans. I found out later that Biden, during a fifteen-minute call, had pushed Ghani to project an image of unity by holding a press conference with rival politicians, and to make public his government's military strategy if the Americans were to agree to conducting air strikes on Taliban positions. Neither he nor Biden seemed to predict that Ghani's government was on the brink of collapse. Khalilzad, under pressure to make the deal and with a recalcitrant Ghani, had to negotiate with the Taliban before he could turn to an intra-Afghan negotiation, perhaps the death warrant for the Afghan government. At the time, however, it seemed to me that whatever was said during the call had only put Ghani more in denial about his doomed fate; he had been given the impression of stronger American support, perhaps, but in truth no one would have believed what was about to happen. Sitting beside his vice president, he said to me, "We will prevail. Afghanistan will prevail."

I said goodbye and drove home. On Saturday there was a bit more traffic, a bit more life in the streets of Kabul. My driver honked a few times trying to get me back in time to pack for my trip later that day to Dubai, then Greece, where I would meet Tom for a few days. No one had any idea what was about to happen, or how quickly. Still, preparing for my trip, I told my assistant to hide some of our valuables and family photos, just in case.

THE SECRETS OF *This House* did quite well. It caught the attention of the *New York Times Magazine*, which did a feature on the show, and also the complicated, obstacles-ridden path to Afghan female empowerment and liberation. Roya preferred the subsequent shows she directed for TOLO, including a drama serial that she felt was even more truthful about the lives of Afghan women and that she told us "can't be about politics at all." To Roya, the story of Afghan women transcended who was in the Arg, or the White House.

The women in the show *Silent Heaven* spanned generations, with each in her own way pushing for some kind of societal change. On-screen, they confronted the men in their lives—the fathers, sons, brothers, husbands, male cousins, and nephews, all those men who came in and out of the house, making demands, asking questions, judging—to change and support the women around them. Roya's women were activists and students, they ran a newspaper, they studied political science and music, they complained about how difficult it was as a woman to help support her family when independence was greeted with suspicion and wages were so low.

Within the family conflicts and marital concerns, the new Afghanistan showed up on-screen, one in which the real societal shift came from the heart of the country, not from the outside. Change, in Roya's work, wasn't external, the fruit of interventions by the Americans. It wasn't the result of desperation, like the pull toward religious extremism. It didn't happen because of war or the threat of violence. It didn't come about because men felt they had no choice but to listen to women. In Roya's work, change came from within each Afghan character. It was organic and good and welcome. It had always been here and just needed to be nurtured. "It was a story about a new Afghan generation," she said. "About how it is slowly but surely changing."

Roya took her work to international festivals, where she would meet young Afghans who had been raised far from the country, in Europe or America or Australia. They spoke Dari poorly and many of them had never been to Kabul. What they knew of the country was being told to them through stories in Western media, and the speeches of Western politicians. They thought Afghanistan meant war and had grown up a little bit embarrassed by their country's reputation, something they would never admit to their parents but were eager to unload onto Roya. When they watched the few Afghan movies that were being produced, they told Roya, for the first time they felt proud to be Afghan. "This is the magic of art," Roya would say.

In Kabul and Herat, Roya suddenly found she was something like a celebrity herself. People recognized her on the street, which made her uncomfortable until she realized the attention was almost always positive. The villagers who might once have looked askance at a young woman coming to their streets with a camera were now in cities, and approached her, glowing with pride or curiosity. The women hugged her, and the men asked her sincere questions about her work. They wanted to know who the characters were based on—they had a cousin just like this girl; their neighbor had the same temper as that one—and would she be filming a show based on their village? "You are Roya Sadat," they would say, smiling broadly. "You made that television show about the Afghan girls. We love that show."

CHAPTER 23

FALL OF KABUL

A decade before the United States withdrew the last of its troops and the Taliban, once again, took control over Afghanistan, my family and I bought a piece of land in Qargha, an area on the western outskirts of Kabul known for a massive reservoir of the same name where families gathered to swim, picnic, and fly kites. It was a small piece of land, behind a rickety metal gate along a dirt road, which was barely passable in the best weather and became, after it rained, treacherous, full of potholes as deep as wells that would catch the tires of even the most efficient four-wheel vehicles.

We intended for the land to be the Mohseni family home in Afghanistan, something we hadn't claimed to have in a long time. Even after my father had won back our childhood house, no one had wanted to live there. It was far from the Moby office, surrounded by featureless apartments, and not in the most secure area; perhaps it was also a little haunted by our past, our memories of the coup, or the figure of the thug who had fought so hard to keep it, or by the corruption that my father battled to get it back. In any case, we had sold it many years ago, and it was no longer ours.

By October 2010, when we bought the Qargha land, we were all living outside of Afghanistan at least half of the time—my father for health reasons, my mother to be with my father, and the rest of us for work and family—and we wanted a place that would entice us back to Kabul together, not separately and only when the duties of Moby called or when we had a meeting with officials. My children might eventually go spend some time there as well, I thought, if in years to come there was some relief from the hassle and danger of Kabul; they would soon be old enough to decide if they were interested in seeing the country for themselves, and the same was true of my nieces and nephew.

In no hurry, we first hauled a small white trailer onto the property and hired a gardener to begin planting flowers and fruit trees, a tiny version of my grandfather's orchard, which we also no longer owned. The gardener soon moved into the trailer with his wife and young son, and expertly tamed the rutted yard into three rows of even terraces onto which he planted roses and cherry blossoms, apples and peaches. Just above the highest row he laid a flat patio of stones and covered it with carpets, inexpensive versions of the hand-knotted wool rugs we had bought for our rented homes, placing a small grill on the edge. "You can have dinner here," he told us proudly. We considered how to build a house on the awkward plot, leaving enough room for the fruit trees we hoped would transform the property into an orchard like my grandfather's. The house would have to be somewhat oddly shaped and built against the back wall that surrounded the property, to account for the slope of the land, but big enough for all of us and anyone who wanted to visit.

Near the property, at the bottom of the hill, Qargha Reservoir, all twelve thousand acres of it, lapped up the concrete walls of the dam that had been holding back the Paghman River since the 1930s. From our makeshift patio you could see teenagers launching small paddleboats onto the water, their parents sitting with smaller children on blankets by the bank, eating lunch. There is a fish hatchery stocked with rainbow trout, and a small golf course nearby, as well as several restaurants. In 2011, a bad year for the American war, the US Army Corps of Engineers published a study about the potential for developing hydropower around the dam, an improbable idea given the history of drought, but exciting nonetheless.

People say that during the first Taliban regime in the 1990s, when Kabul was a fraction of its size and no one visited the reservoir out of fear, the water in Qargha receded until there was almost nothing but a dry pit surrounded by sand and concrete. They say this as though the water left in protest—perhaps across the border into Pakistan or Iran, following hundreds of thousands of Afghan refugees—and with such conviction that no sane or kind person would try to argue with them. Anyone who lived through those years in Afghanistan has a right to their own folklore.

IN JULY 2021, it felt as though the air was being sucked out of the city. Driving to the airport, I had a vague sense of dread that was similar to what I'd felt as a twelve-year-old leaving Kabul for Tokyo. Both times I could tell that something was wrong, although neither time had I had any idea that I was leaving the city for good.

I made it to the airport, only a ten- or fifteen-minute drive from Moby, thinking about Ghani's reckless delusion that he could keep the cities from being taken over by the Taliban. On the plane I received messages from TOLO reporters telling me that Kandahar was nearly completely besieged by the Taliban, and shared stories with me about Afghan forces in the provinces who were seen taking off their uniforms and fleeing the Taliban.

In recent weeks, Abdullah Abdullah and Hamid Karzai had been making a last-ditch effort to persuade the Taliban that an Afghan government that included representatives from the current and previous administrations would give them a chance of avoiding sanctions and isolation, and to persuade Ghani that holding on to cities including Kabul, without American support, was impossible. Abdullah met with Taliban representatives in Doha and Karzai met with Ghani in Kabul. "Ghani is being stubborn," Karzai told me over the phone. The president didn't like being told he would have to give up power to the Taliban. Still, Karzai carried that message to the Arg again and again until finally it seemed to get through to Ghani. On August 6, the first provincial capital fell to the Taliban, and by the fourteenth, many more had toppled, including Kandahar and Herat. "He's accepted that he must resign," Karzai told me on the phone that day. The Taliban were just a day away from the city.

On August 15, Karzai and Abdullah, with Ghani's blessing, were scheduled to fly together to Doha to reach an agreement with the Taliban on an orderly transition. I was in London. At around 11:00 a.m., 3:30 in the afternoon, Kabul time, I got a call from a friend, a Western official, telling me that Ghani had fled the country on a helicopter bound for Uzbekistan. "He said he was going for lunch then slipped out the back with two advisors," he said.

"It's true," Abdullah told me when I reached him. "But please don't let this get out." Not even Ghani's chief of staff, Matin Bek, still waiting in the palace, knew the president had left. "It's ridiculous," he told me when I reached him. "The rumors are false. We have control of the city."

"How long can we wait?" I asked Lotfullah Najafizada, the head of TOLOnews at the time, who was working around the clock in our Kabul office.

"Let's run it on the six o'clock news," he said. We were being generous, we thought, giving people at the palace two hours or so to figure out how to spin the news of the president fleeing the country.

The story ran on the six o'clock newscast as our lead headline. President Ashraf Ghani had left Afghanistan. That evening, soon after the news broke, the Taliban were inside Kabul, and the city fell apart.

BETWEEN AUGUST 15 and August 30, nearly one hundred thousand Afghans were airlifted out of Kabul, mostly to Doha and a US Air Force base in Germany, which had the capacity to become processing hubs for fleeing Afghans. Among the first to be evacuated were well-known members of civil society and politicians who worried their visibility would make them targets of the Taliban, as well as many American citizens and green card holders.

Details of those horrible weeks are, by now, well documented. Terrified families rushing into the utter chaos outside of Kabul airport. Desperate men clinging to the wheels of military planes as they take off from the runway. An IS-KP suicide bomber killing nearly two hundred people at one of the airport gates while the new Taliban government urges people to stay calm and stay in the country, and vows to capture the group's leader.

Everything felt grotesquely improvised. Some of the thousands of people who had worked with the Americans, translators for the army mainly, for whom their former bosses were pleading safe passage back in the US, were put on evacuee lists, corralled through the maze of security, and packed into airplanes, although of course too many of those who had worked with international organizations were still left behind. Humanitarian and media organizations chartered planes to get their staff out. Private citizens in New York and London, telling me they felt guilty watching Afghanistan fall apart so quickly, worked behind the scenes to rescue whom they knew and whom they could.

Profiteers entered the scene too, some notorious and some plain old grifters willing to turn the desperate exodus into a moneymaking opportunity for themselves. Finding someone with money and a conscience, they present them with a list of evacuees and a list of needs: twenty-eight female judges, say, who will be targets and twelve special forces guys plus a plane from Albania to get them out, in addition to their fee. Suddenly, guys like this are hiding in all corners of the city, still in khaki pants and military boots with five days of beard growth and scarves around their necks, hoping to make a dollar off the desperation of Afghans left behind. You could probably have picked them out in a blurry satellite image and known exactly what they were up to; one of them, it was rumored, posted his credentials online, bragging about a stint with the CIA, which meant that either he was lying or he had been a terrible spy.

Working for the media certainly made you a target, and in the first few weeks we lost the majority of our on-air staff. I was on autopilot, fielding interview requests and phone calls from friends and Moby staff looking for help getting out. I did what I could, which, in the scheme of things, was not much. Zalmay Khalilzad connected me to a staffer at Qatar's embassy in Kabul, who was arranging buses to the airport. A friend working at George Soros's Open Society Foundation paid for planes, and another friend of a friend on the French special forces escorted some particularly high-risk Moby employees into the terminal. If someone found a safer route to get to the airport from the office, or a good spot to scale the airport wall, or got through to an embassy offering seats on airplanes, we passed along that information to those seeking to leave. Jahid and I updated that growing list of people, which included their children and spouses and parents, hundreds of people, each of whom had every reason to believe that if they didn't leave Kabul immediately, they would be killed.

Roya was in the US at the time, working on an adaptation of Khaled Hosseini's *A Thousand Splendid Suns* for the Seattle Opera. Over the coming months, during the day, she tried to focus on the opera and a new film project, and at night, when the sun was just coming up in Kabul, she coordinated with an international women's rights group and other Afghan artists and writers to evacuate the female stars of her TV shows and movies.

Our Moby employees went to Dubai, Pakistan, and any country in Europe that would take them. Mustafa Azizyar, the *Afghan*

Star host, settled in Uzbekistan. Shafic Gawhari watched from afar in Germany, where he was visiting family. Parwiz Shamal had moved to Istanbul in February 2021, when he discovered that he was on a list of Taliban targets. Unable to return to Kabul, even to visit his mother's grave, he was easing his guilt by making a documentary about Afghan migrants in Turkey, but stopped production because of increasing pressure on Afghans by the Turkish authorities. In August 2023, after months of futile waiting for an American visa, he appealed to Canada instead and settled in Toronto.

Despite the chaos and the fear, TOLO staffers worked to make sure that the screens did not go dark. Najafizada left through Uzbekistan before making his way to Istanbul and eventually to Canada, but not before interviewing Blinken. TOLO was the first TV channel to break the news of Ghani's departure, and the first to broadcast images from the airport tarmac. When Taliban officials visited our offices in those early days, some curious and others angry, Sapai suggested that Beheshta Arghand, twenty-four years old and who'd been at her job for just a month, interview their spokesperson. Arghand did a formidable job, and she received so much attention for that interview that within two weeks she felt it was too risky for her and her family to remain in Afghanistan. She is now in Canada.

For the twenty years it was broadcast on Arman FM, *Cleaning Up the City* was as popular as any of our TOLO television shows. With the Taliban in the city, our hosts and producer knew they needed to get out. Humayoon Danishyar watched footage on television of the Taliban releasing hundreds of prisoners from the main Kabul jail. Several of them he had helped convict through a popular Moby crime reality show he had produced and hosted. A television spin-off of *Cleaning Up the City*, it asked viewers to call in with complaints and tips, and with the justice system made useless with corruption, Afghans came to rely on the show to deliver a little bit of justice. Now, with so many of those prisoners freed, Humayoon was certain he would be subject to their vengeance. Packing what he could into a few small bags, my cousin took his family to a hotel, and then to the airport, where they waited for three days to be evacuated by US soldiers to Albania, eventually making it to Canada, where he's living, once again, as a refugee.

Massood Sanjer wrapped a scarf around his face and boarded a bus at the Pakistani embassy bound for the airport. Worried about security and about his children's education, he had moved his family to Istanbul a couple of years before, but they had been visiting in the weeks before the collapse. His younger son cried when they got to the airport, out of fear, and didn't stop crying until their airplane was flying over the mountains.

On Saturday, August 21, at two in the morning, not knowing what else to do, Sima Safa texted Massood, who'd arrived safely in Istanbul. "I don't have a passport," she told him. "I don't have any money." She'd married a man who had fallen in love with her voice on *Cleaning Up the City*, but over time he had become abusive and controlling. He didn't want her to work and didn't want her to study English, thinking it would make her drift even further from his ideal of a docile housewife. Still, she knew that if she had any hope of leaving the country with their son, she would have to use her Moby contacts to get everyone out. "Just get to the airport," Massood told her. "Then call me."

Sima, her husband, and their son, as well as her husband's first wife and their son, took a taxi to the airport, where they waited in the disarray. She wasn't sure what the next steps might be or who, exactly, was going to help them. There were thousands of people there, American soldiers pushing them back with tear gas, Taliban guards beating them. Sima and her family spent the night on the street next to the airport wall, she told me later. Nearby, a pregnant woman sat weeping and screaming for her daughter, whom she had lost in the crowd.

The next day, a woman called Sima on WhatsApp. She spoke Dari with an Iranian accent but didn't identify herself beyond telling Sima that Massood had mentioned she needed help getting out of Kabul. "Go to this location," she told Sima. "They'll be able to help you."

Sima and her family pushed slowly against the tide of people toward the address. She was disappointed to find it was just another curb outside the airport, no quieter than the first but at least farther away from the soldiers firing tear gas. Nine other people who had been given similar instructions were also there waiting. Eventually, they were approached by an American guard, who checked their documents and began helping push people over a locked gate. First, they let in the American citizens. Sima watched as they struggled to get over the wall, heaving their bags before them. Next, the guard asked for those who had served in the military to come forward, and when they had disappeared over the wall, two French citizens were given the signal to follow. Finally, the guard gestured at Sima and the other Afghans. "You can come now."

On the other side of the wall a military truck waited to take them to the plane. Everyone was first patted down, a little roughly, although Sima, at that point, barely noticed. As long as they put her on an airplane, they could handcuff her for all she cared. Next thing she knew, she'd been separated from her family and seated on an airplane bound for Abu Dhabi. At the Abu Dhabi airport, she waited for three hours until they joined her, and then they all boarded a military plane for France. It was the first time in a long time she'd been alone. Months after arriving in France, she took her son and left her husband, and started taking French classes.

Khpolwak Sapai had been promoted to director of TOLOnews when Najafizada fled to Canada at the end of September. Sapai took his new heftier responsibilities in stride; he had already experienced so much during his six decades in Kabul. In February 2022, six months after the withdrawal, Sapai interviewed Hamid Karzai on TOLO. Sitting in a room lined with bookshelves, the former president answered Sapai's questions about the collapse of Ghani's government on August 15, and the future of Afghanistan. Both men were dressed neatly, Karzai in his trademark green and blue chapan, but anyone who knew them could see that neither had been sleeping well.

During an exchange about the Doha meeting between the Taliban and the Ghani-approved delegation including him and Abdullah that did not take place, Karzai stumbled. "We were supposed to travel in the afternoon or evening, but . . ." He trailed off.

"And, by then, everything came to an end," Sapai said.

A few minutes later, Sapai uncharacteristically turned the focus onto himself, his eyes pained behind his brown-rimmed glasses. "The pain of starvation," he says. "I am sixty-four years old and turning to sixty-five. I have never migrated from Afghanistan. . . . This is the first time I'm experiencing such famine and such a high level of unemployment. I have never seen it before in the four decades of chaos in Afghanistan."

It wasn't something Sapai wanted to acknowledge to his staff, but after Najafizada left and the responsibilities fell on Sapai's shoulders, he often felt anxious about the future of the country and of TOLO. Almost every day, he would call me saying, "I don't think we can survive tomorrow," and every day I tried to pick him up just enough without pressuring him to stay on. It was indeed remarkable that Sapai had never left Afghanistan. He had stayed through the Communists, the civil war, and the first Taliban regime. He stayed through the worst years of the American occupation, hearing stories of unimaginable, unpredictable violence in some parts of the country, and when the relative safety of Kabul was so often shattered by suicide bombings. Sapai not only lived through these eras; he decided to become a journalist and report on them.

"I have been here all the time," Sapai told the former president.

"Well done," Karzai replied. "You did the right thing."

Eight months later, in October 2022, utterly drained and feeling that the work he loves had become impossible, Sapai filled out his paperwork and moved with his family to the Netherlands.

PEOPLE STAYED, OF course. Some couldn't leave, and others didn't want to. They weren't sure what their lives would be outside of Afghanistan, and they liked the work. Jan Agha stayed, tending to the offices and the guesthouse. The idea of leaving Kabul was ludicrous to him. Even if his family had a small amount of money, where would they go? Naim Sarwari stayed, as did Esmatullah Niazee, one of our higher-ups since the withdrawal, who says he will only leave if, when his daughters are old enough, schools are still closed to them. Nafay Khaleeq, our head of legal, continues his work in the city he still loves. Countless others stay and keep Afghans informed and entertained as best they can.

Our gardener in Qargha, like Jan Agha, doesn't have the means or connections to leave, and says he wouldn't even if he did. The piece of land near Qargha is his project, and his home too. Although our plans for a house never came together, the garden, he tells us, is flourishing. In the summer, roses climb the trellises, and the flowers on the trees, higher every day, give way to fruit. His son, now old enough to help, is already flattening out other parts of the yard to expand into a small orchard.

All is well, he tells us. When my mother visits, he shows her around like a museum docent. Life is more or less unchanged for him. Although he avoids a new neighbor, the son of a Taliban official who has taken over one of the vacated houses, and he locks the gate at night just in case. A curious thing is happening to the reservoir, he tells us. He's never seen the water this low, even lower than during the first Taliban government, almost disappearing into the dirt. Visitors, men and boys mostly, of course, have to walk for ten minutes from their cars to dip their feet in, and the water is hot like bathwater. Global warming, he says. He saw a story about it on the news.

ACKNOWLEDGMENTS

Over the years at Moby, we were lucky to have so many allies and collaborators who helped and continue to support us in any way that they can. Said Najib Tahmas, Ahmed Rashid, David Miles, Andrew Kaszubski, Ashley Schwall-Kearney, Domenic Carosa, Timmy Byrne, Bob Wilson, Dominic Medley, Tariq Said, Pavlin Rahnev, Sayed Makhdoom Rahin, Parwin Towfique, and Marvin Weinbaum were instrumental in those early, uncertain days, while later on Atiq Rahimi, Siddiq Barmak, Latif Ahmadi, Pari Mahmroum, Abdul Hamid Mubarez, Fatima Gailani, Rahnaward Zaryab, and Mujahid Kakar helped us develop our programming and navigate the complicated Afghan political, religious, and cultural landscape.

Thanks also to Tom Freston; James, Lachlan, and Rupert Murdoch; Santo Cilauro; Chris McDonald; Matthew Anderson; and Joe Ravitch, who stepped in to support us in expanding and refining our programming.

Matthew M. Johnson, Jeff Shell, Rod Solaimani, Aryana Sayeed, Hasib Sayed, Marc-Antoine d'Halluin, and Omar Waraich were staunch defenders of our work and lent their support when we needed it the most.

Thank you to Amanda Urban, who pushed me to tell the story of Moby; Sameen Gauhar, for lending her meticulous eye to the manuscript; Noah Eaker and the staff at HarperCollins for seeing the book through; and Jenna Krajeski for telling our story as an insider.

Most of all, thank you to our staff, past and present, who are steadfast in their commitment to Moby; Alexandra Meyer, for her patience through all of it; my maternal aunts, whose dark humor, wit, strength, and intelligence did so much to shape the characters of their niece and nephews; and especially my siblings, who made Moby what it is. Without them, this story wouldn't exist.

ABOUT THE AUTHOR

SAAD MOHSENI was born in London to Afghan parents in 1966 and lived in Kabul, Japan, Australia, Uzbekistan, and Pakistan before returning to Kabul in 2002 after the US invasion. He is the cofounder, chairman, and executive officer of Moby Group, Afghanistan's largest media company, and has brought top-tier news and media content to emerging markets for the past two decades. He was named an Asia Game Changer by the Asia Society and in 2011 was one of *Time* magazine's "100 Most Influential People in the World." Mohseni serves on the board of the International Crisis Group and is a member of the International Advisory Council for the Middle East Institute. He lives in London and Dubai.

ABOUT THE COAUTHOR

JENNA KRAJESKI is the coauthor, with Nadia Murad, of *The Last Girl* and, with Mondiant Dogon, of *Those We Throw Away Are Diamonds*. Her reporting and essays have been published in the *New Yorker*, the *New York Times*, and the *Nation*, among many other publications. She was a 2015 Knight-Wallace fellow in journalism at the University of Michigan.